GUTS 'N GUNSHIPS
What it was Really Like to Fly Combat Helicopters in Vietnam

A True Story

Mark Garrison

Acknowledgments

Since I returned from Vietnam, I've had a burning desire to ensure that my story did not die with me. Perhaps, I thought, that people would understand the day to day, nuts and bolts of the war a little better when seen through the eyes of a combat helicopter pilot. Added to this, was my family's insistence through the years that I write my memoirs before they are lost to time.

Most importantly, I would like to thank my son, Andrew Garrison, for his priceless help and advice that allowed me to successfully navigate the e-book world. Without his assistance this book would probably not exist.

A couple of other people were also involved with the technicalities. First of all, I would like to thank Mr. Ronald Gawthorp. Being a published author himself of, *"Richer Than the Rockefellers,"* and *"Glimpses of Glory,"* he was invaluable in helping me develop and edit a manuscript.

Several other people have encouraged me through the years to write this book, but one in particular deserves special mention. The late Mr. James Donnelly, a dear friend and avid reader, formerly of Davenport, Iowa, tried to light a fire under me to write this memoir for decades. Well, Jim, may you rest in peace, you finally succeeded. I sincerely thank you for your perseverance that finally trumped my incredible procrastination.

One other thing was at play here. That is that I felt I had to write this book as a kind of cathartic exercise to clear the combat cobwebs from my mind. It has seemed to help some. Time will tell just how much.

Contents

Foreword

In 1967, hundreds of young men were lured into the U.S. Army's Warrant Officer Rotary Wing Aviator Course. Mark Garrison and I were two of these young men. We could not know the reality that would face us a year later. Being a helicopter pilot in Viet Nam was serious business. Mark and I were helicopter gunship pilots, both in the 119th Assault Helicopter Company stationed at Pleiku in the Central Highlands. Mark has captured the essence of what it meant to perform that duty in *Guts N' Gunships*. I have read the book and I can say without question that Mark has told a true, honest and brutal account. We fought for each other and most importantly for the men on the ground. And in that fight we were wounded in physical and mental ways that would only manifest many years later in our lives. This true story is a must read for anyone who is interested in knowing about the lives of the young men who wore the coveted U.S. Army Aviator Badge in Vietnam combat flight.

LTC Richard L. Gill
Master Army Aviator
U.S. Army Retired
(Croc 4, sometimes known as Waldo)

Introduction

This book has been rolling around in my head for a long time. First of all, it started with the concept that there was no way in hell that I even had the capability of writing a book, especially one like this one.

Then I went through a phase where I made the astute observation that there were a lot of books sitting around in bookstores, so there must have been people writing them. There was also a constant howl in my ears from family members and others, that this book should be written, if for no other reason, than posterity's sake. A strong desire began to develop in my mind to at least try to tell people what it was like to be a helicopter pilot during the heaviest fighting of the Vietnam War. It was a surrealistic experience to say the least and one that has been extremely difficult for me to simply transpose to paper. It is almost impossibly difficult to describe war, especially to those who haven't experienced it firsthand. There are really no words in the English language that can adequately describe the brutality, incredible violence and outright terror that war entails.

So, from these humble truths, the story began to take shape.

This is my story, and I have written it as I remember it. Many of the names have been changed to protect people's anonymity, but the encounters and episodes that I have described here are true and correct to the best of my recollection.

There was a television series in the 1960's called *The Naked City*. It was about New York City, and its population at the time was approximately eight million people. The program always ended with a voice saying, "There are more than eight million stories in The Naked City. This has been one of them."

In the same vein, I am only one of many helicopter pilots who served in Vietnam with their own stories. This is one of them.

PART ONE:
HOW DID ALL THIS HAPPEN

The Wake Up Call

We were on mid final approach in a UH-1H (Huey) helicopter. I was in the copilot's seat and could clearly see the bright, streaking tracers from AK-47's coming at us. The landing zone, or the LZ as we called it, was in sight and there were mortar rounds impacting all around it. I glanced to my left, expecting to see Cowboy, the Aircraft Commander (AC), adding power to abort and make a go around. But he wasn't, we were apparently going from the frying pan to the fire. You could now hear the AK's and the mortars, as if some sadistic director of a morbid film had ordered more reality.

I started to say, "Cowboy, are we still going in? It's awfully damned hot down there." But the words wouldn't leave my mouth. I felt like I had just learned how to put on boxing gloves, and had then been thrown into the ring to fight for the heavyweight championship.

Cowboy adeptly dropped the aircraft into the LZ. It was a frenzied chaos on the ground, with American troops running everywhere, as North Vietnamese enemy troops attempted to breach the perimeter. Just then, what sounded like several rounds impacted the aircraft, making a slapping "ping" sound as they ripped through it.

It was a surreal world, with far too much sensory input for my brain to process. I couldn't wait to get the hell out of there, but the clock had virtually stopped and everything seemed as if it were happening in slow motion. My ears started to buzz and all the violent sounds merged into one. I saw the AK round hit the plexiglass right in front of my face, but then again I didn't. My brain had divorced itself from all of this and it was like I was watching it in third person. I mean, come on now, it couldn't be this violent, this crazy, this fucking insane. Could it?

Then a few thuds, and the ship shook as troops boarded. There were four of them; one who had been carried and all appeared to be wounded.

A mortar round exploded close enough to hurt my ears and dirt and shrapnel hit the ship. At that, Cowboy added power and began our ascent out of the hell hole. I heard several more pings as we made our way out. Apparently the North Vietnamese troops decided they didn't want us to leave the party just yet.

My eyes continually scanned the instruments. Gas producer (N1), (N2) RPM, exhaust gas temperature (EGT), transmission oil temperature, transmission oil pressure, engine oil pressure and the entire master caution panel. Fortunately, everything remained in the green, normal zone.

We continued our ascent and headed straight for the medical pad at Camp Holloway in Pleiku, Vietnam. We had leveled off at about 2,500 feet above the ground but the elevation there was 2,500 feet also, so the aircraft thought it was flying at 5,000 feet, or about a mile up. As copilot, it was my job to handle the radios. There were three of them, the UHF, for talking to the other troop deployment helicopters (slicks), the VHF, for talking to the gunships giving fire support, and the FM (FoxMike), for talking to the guys on the ground. They actually expected you to listen to three conversations at once. Being new to it all, the only thing I heard was an unintelligible swirl of bullshit.

In my dazed and confused state, I somehow managed to dial in a radio frequency to tell them we were coming with wounded. Just then, something softly touched the left side of my neck a couple of times. I had flight gloves on and I reached up to feel it and when I brought my hand back, it was covered with blood. Then something touched me again and I got another hand full of blood. I thought I may have been shot. I had never been shot, and thought it possible that maybe you didn't feel anything sometimes. This time I glanced over my left shoulder and saw a wounded soldier lying in the middle of the cargo bay. His booted left foot was up around his head, because his left leg had been virtually blown off, mid-thigh, and was only held on by a few strands of twisted muscle, tendon, and skin. His femoral artery was severed and it jerked back and forth with each heartbeat and squirted streams of blood, sometimes hitting me in the neck and shoulder. He appeared to be no more than 18 years old. I was 21. In my mind, I imagined him running through a lawn sprinkler with other children back home in the States just a few short years before. Now, if he lived, he wouldn't be running anywhere.

With the whine of the jet and the beating of the rotor blades, you couldn't hear what he was saying. But the expression on his face was easy to read. The poor kid was terrified. As I screamed at a crew member to tourniquet the leg, I read the kid's lips as he stared blankly forward, with vacant eyes and a bluish cast to his face.

He was saying, "Mom, Mom.........Mom."

In my heart, I was calling for my mother also.

I know the boy was alive when we got him back to the medical pad with the others, but I wasn't in a position to learn his identity so I don't know if he made it or not. It haunted me then and still haunts me today. That ghost, even after all these years, has never died.

We, however, were just beginning. Cowboy, the crew and I, had to go back to that damned LZ again. Three more times we went back and each time members of the NVA tried their best to kill us.

When we finally, miraculously I thought, made it back to Camp Holloway in Pleiku, Vietnam, and shut the aircraft down, my mind was a blur. I had just experienced massive sensory overload. I glanced at Cowboy, who was about my age, had dark brown hair and eyes, a well-trimmed mustache, and was about five feet ten-inches tall and weighed around 160 pounds. We both held the rank of Warrant Officer grade one, or WO1, but he had more time in grade. He calmly unbuckled his seatbelt and shoulder harness. His fatigues were a light washed out green from the many launderings they had received. His jungle boots, with leather bottoms and an artificial canvas material up the sides to make them cooler in the tropical heat, were worn and tattered, but nicely shined. During this entire episode, Cowboy had stayed calm and in control, at least on the outside. He had been hardboiled and I had been somewhere between scrambled and poached. He acted as if he were used to this sort of thing, and I was having trouble believing that any human could ever get used *to this sort of thing.* Cowboy threw open the door and said, "Let's go get a beer, Garrison. How'd you like your first mission?" He had been there almost a year, and was still acting as if nothing unusual had just happened. I, on the other hand, who had just got to Vietnam, in my brand new dark green fatigues and unblemished boots was thinking that *a whole shitload of unusual crap had just happened!*

This had been my very first mission in country after my proficiency check ride, and I remember distinctly what I thought at the time.

How in the hell do they expect anyone to live through a whole year of this incredibly insane violence?

02.

I Was Just A College Student

How in the hell did I get into this mess anyway? I had been a student at Southern Illinois University in Carbondale, Illinois, a year and a half before. I had just finished my second year on my way to a bachelor's degree.

I had applied for a student loan through the Illinois Student Loan Program and was working at a factory that manufactured oil, air, and gas filters for automobiles, in the summer of 1967. I had planned to save all the money I could, and borrow the rest to fill the gap.

I still well remember, the nice, warm, sunny day that I got the letter from the Illinois State Student Loan Program, approving *only half* of what I had applied for, which left me running out of money in the middle of a term. I felt I had no choice but to drop out for a while and work in the private sector and save money as quickly as I could.

This was before the draft lottery was implemented in 1969, and you had to report to the draft board any change in your student status right away. This was required by law, and if you failed to do so, you could wind up in a pile of deep shit with no shovel. I reported my change in status and quickly went to category 1A. This meant that you were near the top of the list to be called by the military. I thought that if I played my cards right, I could get back in school before I was drafted. After all, Vietnam was flaring and no one in their right mind *wanted* to go over there.

Well, the way it worked out, I was quick but the local draft board was quicker, and I was ordered to report for duty in just a few short weeks.

Damn it! This never happens to rich kids does it?

Even then I knew war to be a rich and powerful man's game fought by sons of the poor.

I was trapped in a circumstance that few envied, to say the least. Then I started to control my own future as much as possible. I visited a local army recruiter and asked him what my options were. My brother, who was a couple years older than me, had learned to fly and I had an interest in aviation, so I asked the recruiter about military flight school.

The recruiter said, "You know, you would be a good candidate to go to helicopter flight school in the army."

I said, "How do I do that?"

He said, "I can set it up for you. You will have to go to St. Louis, Missouri, to take a first class physical, and there is some aptitude testing involved that you must pass."

"Set it up. At least I want to learn something worthwhile in the army," I replied.

Now, please understand that I didn't want to do any of this crap. None of these choices were mine. Like kids across the nation I was caught in circumstances beyond my control, and I felt that my choices were bad, worse, and worst. I was just a twenty-year-old kid from a small town in southern Illinois. Just a few years before, I had been playing Pony League baseball. My biggest problem was that I couldn't afford to buy a decent baseball glove. Needless to say, my problems had now escalated by about six orders of magnitude.

I went to St. Louis and took the flight physical and passed. The next step was an aptitude test called the "Flight Aptitude Standard Testing" examination known as the FAST test.

I was told that a person could only take this test one time, and if he failed it, he was rejected at that point and the process ceased. The test was pass/fail.

Tests had always come easy for me and I didn't have any trouble with this one.

The next step was to sign a form of contract with the U.S. Army, guaranteeing flight school entrance for me, as long as I continued to meet the standards and requirements of the program.

I signed the contract.

For some obscure and mystifying reason, I had not considered that I was, indeed, mortal, and that flying helicopters in combat may not have been such a great idea from a personal safety standpoint. As Mark Twain once remarked, *"It's too bad youth is wasted on the young."*

I left St. Louis by train headed for Fort Polk, Louisiana, on August 23, 1967, to report for basic training. Later I would learn all the Warrant Officer Candidates (WOCS) were sent to Fort Polk for basic, and a WOC is what I had suddenly become.

When I signed up for flight school, I had done so under the Warrant Officer Candidate Program, as most guys did. When you completed flight school, you received your wings and were appointed a Warrant. You outranked all the enlisted men and noncommissioned officers (NCOs), such as the privates, corporals, specialists, and sergeants. At the same time, you were technically under the commissioned officers from lieutenants to generals. You were basically off in a separate branch by yourself. Most of us didn't care about the rank anyway. We just wanted to learn to fly.

But first, I had to get through Basic Training, and I had heard plenty of horror stories from my friends about the nature of this particular beast.

03.

Basic Training

I was at the ripe old age of 20 when I arrived in Shreveport, Louisiana. I disembarked the train and got on a waiting bus for the rest of the trip to Leesville, an army town that hosted Fort Polk. Fort Polk was the major civilian employer and an economic shot in the arm of the entire area.

As soon as the bus went through the gates saying, "FORT POLK," I noticed how neat and clean everything was. The grass was manicured, the buildings well kept, and there was not as much as a cigarette butt lying around on the ground. Every few yards, it seemed, we would pass a group of soldiers combing the grounds for litter and debris, called *policing the area* in the military. At least that explained why everything was spotless.

And my god, was it hot! Temperatures edged above 100 degrees amid lung-baking humidity. You knew because the sweat just ran off you and drenched your clothes and just *would not* evaporate. In other words it was miserable, and I was becoming more apprehensive by the second. This *was not* going to be a pleasant experience.

Basic training is just what the name implies. It is training to convert a civilian to a soldier. The course in the U.S. Army was, at the time, eight weeks long. It consisted mainly of arduous physical conditioning and of the unforgettable instilling of military protocol. A large percentage of the green troops in my platoon didn't know the difference between a private first class and a four star general. In other words, many of us didn't even know what a salute was; let alone who you were supposed to salute.

The bus pulled up and stopped in front of a large building with a sign out front that said, "Registration." The bus was filled with several new recruits, and we all were *asked* to form a line and wait to be processed. That was the last time I was *asked* to do something for the next eight weeks. From then on I was *told*, in no uncertain terms what I *could, would and should* do, and the commands were usually punctuated not with exclamation marks, but with pushups.

We all went through various processing stations at this registration depot and then were *told* to re-board the bus to be taken to the Quartermaster, known as supply in the civilian world. Here we would be issued our military gear, such as clothing and other items necessary to complete basic training. All this gear was stuffed into a duffle bag by each of us and we were told to re-board the bus to be taken to our assigned unit.

When we arrived at our destination, several sergeants swarmed the bus and started screaming at us to get off and stand on one of the numbers that were painted onto a large black asphalt parking lot. Soon we all *assembled by the number* on the parking lot, in August, in Louisiana, with our duffle bags in the 100-degree heat and 100- percent humidity. Next, a first lieutenant started screaming at us from a makeshift podium. From his tone it was obvious he thought one of us had just burned his wife at the stake and kidnapped his children.

He screamed: "You are all nothing but green recruits, and there's nothing lower on God's earth than a goddamned, fucking green recruit." After that poignant summation, he "really" started cussing us. This is where I began to learn profanity was a necessary part of military communication.

Well hello, U.S. Army!

We were next herded like cattle into a torture pasture and the games began. We were *ordered* (not asked and not told) to strip off our civvies and dress in the newly issued military garb. We were given five minutes to figure out how to dress, take it out of the stuffed duffle bag, put it on, and get everything else that we were not actually wearing back in the bag.

The drill sergeants then lined us up at our civilian facsimile of attention. There were three drill sergeants, men who had been in the army several years in most cases, and they all held the rank of E6 or above. The army has a ranking system that goes from Private E1 to Sergeant Major E9. Those from E1 through E4 are known as enlisted men. From E5 through E9 are the Non Commissioned

Officers, (NCOs). To give you a breakdown of all their titles, I offer the following clarification table from lowest to highest rank.

The E system denotes pay grade next to the rank. Everyone in the "E" pay grade group had the same base salary. Specialists were generally not considered to be in the general chain of command.

E1 - Private
E2 - Private
E3 - Private First Class (PFC)
E4 - Corporal / Specialist 4
E5 - Buck Sergeant / Specialist 5
E6 - Staff Sergeant
E7 - Sergeant First Class
E8 - Master Sergeant
E8 - First Sergeant
E9 - Sergeant Major

The drill sergeants (aka "Yes Drill Sergeant!") were trained in the specialty of taking perfectly normal civilians off the street, breaking them down to the lowest human denominator and reassembling them into homicidal maniacs. On this occasion they started with the closest guy who was attempting the position of attention. They got in his face and screamed at him with all the volume they could muster. Apparently, they considered him an idiot for not knowing how to dress himself in military gear. They verbally berated the poor guy until he was a pile of trembling flesh, then they proceeded with the next guy.

I remember thinking that these guys must be complete idiots if they couldn't even put their pants on right. But, at attention you must look straight ahead at all times with your eyes fixed on an imaginary point and not move a muscle. That much instruction had been given. All too soon, these yelling, screaming life forms found me. I learned then and there that I was apparently even a bigger idiot than those who had already been critiqued by the welcoming committee. In fact I was a total dunce when it came to donning military garb. They ripped me up one side and slashed me down the other until leaving me in a smoldering heap of would-be military trash before they moved on. I was convinced after my first encounter with these aliens that their training had included several courses in sadism and its related application and implementation. *In short they were nasty bastards!*

After convincing us that we were all imbecilic morons, one of the drill sergeants suddenly appeared in front of us, properly dressed, and taught us how to dress just like him. I remember thinking at the time that they had the order of things reversed.

Basic training painfully drug on with all of its nuances for what seemed like forever. We would march a mile in step, and then jog a mile in formation until you were absolutely ready to drop in the Louisiana heat and humidity, and many did, only to be converged upon by the screaming sadists to be further derided.

Once, we were trudging around a seemingly endless track that circled a wooded area. I was thinking about stopping and catching my breath, when two covert drill sergeants from the woods, converged on a collapsed soldier who was vomiting all over himself, and started kicking and cursing him for stopping. That incident was motivation enough to keep me moving.

During small arms training, if one of us were foolish enough to call our rifle a gun instead of our weapon, he would be made to stand in front of the whole platoon and announce the following over and over:

> *"This is my weapon (holding up his rifle)*
> *and this is my gun (grabbing his crotch)*
> *My weapon's for killing*
> *My gun is for fun."*

I'm well aware that this little incantation was made famous by the movie, "Full Metal Jacket," but believe me, it was alive and well at Fort Polk, Louisiana well before the movie was made. We all screwed up sooner or later and wound up in front of the platoon reciting that little poem.

In the army, when you learn to march, you must be in-step and in-formation whether you are walking or jogging. This is done with the drill sergeant marching alongside you singing a cadence song, such as "The Fort Polk Boogie." This song gives the platoon rhythm and makes staying in step much easier. I am sure you know the rhythm refrain from army movies:

> *Sound off!*
> *Sound off!*
> *Sound off one, two*
> *Three four!*

There are a thousand different obscene ditties made up to go with this little refrain, but frankly I do not feel the need to recite them here.

In all truthfulness, I was pretty out of shape when I got to basic training. I wasn't overweight, but I was soft and out of condition. I had dark brown hair and brown eyes, was five feet ten inches tall and weighed one hundred and fifty pounds. By the time I finished basic in eight grueling weeks, there wasn't a soft spot on me. I was as Bob Seger says, in the song, *Like A Rock*. Every ounce of fat had been left with the tough old Fort Polk drill sergeants.

To graduate from basic, soldiers were required to pass a rather difficult physical test of strength and stamina, known as a PT Test. During the giving of this test in the last week, I got very ill with a virus and high fever and went to "Sick Call." This is what you did if you were sick in the military. I was immediately placed in Fort Polk's hospital for a couple of days. I feared that I would be held back to repeat part of basic, so as soon as my fever broke, I told the doctor I felt fine to get on with it, even though I felt horrible. I really had to push myself with that PT test, but I did. I passed. Thank God for that. I didn't want to go through any of that again.

I was now done with Fort Polk and its boogie and off for a few days leave at home before heading for flight school. *One goal achieved! So far, so good!*

Flight School Preflight

After basic training I got a much needed leave. While I was with my family in Illinois, I watched the news every night which was always riddled with coverage of Vietnam. One night, while watching, a journalist on the ground captured live footage of a firefight between an American platoon and several North Vietnamese troops. I saw several American dead and wounded, being evacuated by helicopters. One of the helicopters, on final approach into the area was shot down, crashed and burned, killing the whole crew. This left a rather unsettling image in my mind, to say the least about it. They were calling it the Vietnam Conflict, since the United States had never officially declared war. Well, it sure as hell looked like a war to me.

After a few days of leave at home in Illinois with my family, I shipped out by train from St. Louis to Dallas, Texas, on the way to Fort Wolters in Mineral Wells, Texas. Fort Wolters was the primary flight training center for rotary wing aircraft for the Warrant Officer Candidate Program in aviation for the U.S. Army.

After a *short* wait, which is an unusual event for the army, I was transported by bus the eighty or so miles west to Fort Wolters. Like cheese, I was once again *processed* and put up in a barracks reserved for beginning flight students in the preflight program. This was basically a program that taught more military protocol and began to orient the candidates (WOCs) about aviation. That's what they said, anyway. We soon found out that it was a severe harassment period where they did everything they could think of, short of outright killing you, to see if you could take the pressure. Some guys did break down and quit at this point, having decided that they had had enough before even setting foot in a helicopter. They were usually then assigned to Advanced Individual Training (AIT) in the infantry. *(Gee guys thanks for trying.)* That's one thing that kept me going and putting up with their bullshit. I definitely did not want to wind up as a ground pounder in Vietnam, also commonly known as a grunt. I intend no disrespect with my use of the term "grunt," either. I grew to understand and respect these men immensely a few months later in Nam. They suffered horrible conditions and often fought for their very lives. They fought with valor and bravery second to no soldier before them. This harassment lasted for about four weeks before I was then assigned to a beginning flight school class in November of 1967.

I then *processed* to a barracks on "The Hill," a slight rise in elevation where housing had been built to accommodate flight students. We lived in two-man cubicles, so each of us had a roommate. My roommate was a fellow by the name of Al Gafton. We got along fine.

The cubicles were not big, but adequate and a big improvement over the open barracks of Basic Training. They were enclosed on three sides by solid walls, and the absence of a fourth wall created an opening to a spacious hallway, where one could see clearly into the cubicle across from it. They were equipped with bunk beds on one side, and a dresser-like piece of furniture on the other side in which we kept personal belongings and things for routine inspections. On the third wall was a small table and two chairs under a window that gave you a view of the outside road and buildings directly across the street.

The barracks were two-story, and the bunks were filled with flight school candidates. The number would dwindle somewhat, however, as flight school progressed because of the constant pressure and harassment.

We arrived at the barracks on a weekend and classes started first thing Monday morning. One week your flight would have classes in the morning and fly in the afternoon. The next week the order was reversed. Academic studies in class included subjects such as meteorology, avionics, and the aerodynamics of flight, etc. Flight time, of course, meant actual time in the aircraft with an instructor pilot. Most of these instructors at the beginning student level were civilians who had contracted with the army. Later, more and more military instructors were employed, especially ones who had returned from Vietnam after flying combat.

Primary Flight School

The very first time I climbed in a helicopter, I didn't know jack diddly damn about one. I quickly learned, however that a helicopter is much different than a fixed wing airplane. I knew a little about flying small airplanes from flying with my brother, the pilot. I had hogged and wallowed one around a few times and at least landed without crashing or even damaging it. But this thing didn't even have wings that were fixed in one place. Instead it had two rotor blades that were slung around in an arc at about three hundred plus RPM. This whole affair was attached to the aircraft by one nut, commonly called the *Jesus Nut* for obvious reasons.

It didn't have control surfaces like an airplane's ailerons, elevators, rudders or flaps either. The stick coming up between a helicopter pilot's legs was called the *cyclic*. This cyclic controls pitch and roll by affecting push pull tubes that alter the arc of the main rotor system. Push the cyclic forward, and the nose drops, pull it back, and the nose comes up or flares. Move it to the left or right depending on what direction you would like the aircraft to go. It didn't have rudder pedals either, but anti-torque pedals, which controlled the small tail rotor in the back to counteract the torque of the main rotor system. Even the pedal you pushed during flight was generally the opposite of an airplane. These pedals counteract the torque of the aircraft and are used to keep the nose straight forward during normal flight. In a fixed wing you apply right pedal in gasoline-powered aircraft when you add power, on takeoff, for instance. In a helicopter, you apply left pedal when adding power for takeoff in normal wind conditions to control the direction of the nose or yaw.

And, there is the collective pitch control in a chopper. This is a stick that is to the left of the pilot with a throttle control on the end of it, much like a motorcycle throttle on the handlebar. The pilot raises this collective when he wants to takeoff while at the same time he rolls the throttle on to add power and keep his RPM up.

To better illustrate: Think of a fan you have running in the summer blowing cool air across you. The fan does this by having a preformed angle of attack to the air around it, giving it the capability of pushing the air. If you would flatten the blades so that they would have no angle of attack, or pitch, the fan wouldn't be able to move air. The fan would just sit there and rapidly spin. The same thing happens in a helicopter. As the pilot raises the collective, he increases the angle of attack that the blades have in relation to the surrounding air mass. In so doing, the blades create a high pressure area under them and a very low pressure over them which creates lift. This is exactly what an airplane's wings do by the virtue of forward airspeed. It is also the reason that a helicopter can fly with no forward airspeed of the aircraft itself, and a fixed wing airplane cannot. This is because the chopper's blades, or airfoils, are moving through the air in an arc, powered by an engine and therefore, can create its own lift.

◆ ◆ ◆

My first flight instructor was a civilian named Bela Toth. He was a Hungarian American who had been a U.S. Army chopper pilot and had served a tour in Vietnam. I, at the time, was twenty years old, and had worked at various jobs since my father died when I was thirteen. I worked to help my mother keep a roof over our heads. These jobs included driving farm tractors, working in a filling station, helping rebuild and overhaul automobile engines, etc.

Apparently Toth was unimpressed with my mechanical knowledge, because on about my third or fourth hour in the air, he made the comment, in heavy Hungarian brogue, "Garrison (Gad-i-son), you've never been around machinery, have you? I can tell because you seem to have no concept of RPM."

"Well, yes, Sir, I have operated a lot of machinery, but nothing like this beast."

With a wave of his hand, Toth rejoined, "You should have stuck with cars and tractors! You're trying to kill us in this thing!"

If Toth was trying to humble me, he succeeded.

Let me explain something about a helicopter in those days. You have an RPM gauge in a chopper that shows both rotor system and engine RPM. These needles should be joined and in the green (normal range) at all times as long as the engine is running. In the Hiller OH23D helicopter that I was attempting to learn to fly, there was virtually no dependable automatic throttle governor to control RPM for you. You had to do it yourself by constantly making manual adjustments to the throttle to keep it in the green range. It's extremely difficult to do at first; ask anyone who has ever flown a Hiller.

The OH-23D Helicopter in flight.

Toth, of course, knew this and was just fucking with me. I do admit that, at first, the only time the RPM needles were in the normal green zone was when I was passing through it. I either throttled too much or not enough.

After finally learning the basic controls and how to use them, it was an intensive endeavor to put it all to practical use and actually fly the aircraft. After you had been taught how to make various standard rate turns, fly straight and level, climb and descend, and to do an autorotation in the event of an engine failure, it was time to hover the beast. And was it ever a beast in the beginning!

I swear that the first time I tried to hover the Hiller, they must have thought I was going AWOL (absent without leave), and taking the instructor pilot with me as he was fighting for the controls, after I had him securely gagged and bound. I couldn't keep the damned thing in a 40- acre field. I was up, down, over and out and all over the place. Toth had to take it away from me several times just before I put it in the ground in a flaming heap with us in it.

A helicopter such as a Hiller, like this OH23D, that I was attempting to stabilize at a hover, has what is known as a control lag. This means that when a pilot moves the cyclic stick between his legs to move fore, aft, left or right, there is a fraction of a second where the aircraft hesitates (does nothing) before it responds by moving the arc of the main rotor system. To the inexperienced student pilot this usually results in over corrections on the controls. In other words, when I moved the cyclic forward and it did nothing for a moment, I moved the cyclic further forward. Then when it decided to respond, it lurched forward, keeping instructor Toth on his toes. Likewise, when it lurched forward and I pulled the cyclic back, it went through the same lag time so I pulled it too far back. When the aircraft again responded to my control input, the nose would pitch up and she would rapidly come back, to be followed by another exaggerated control movement on my part. In just a few seconds, we were galloping through the air like a wounded horse and virtually out of control. As a matter of fact, that's basically the admonition he gave me the first time I tried to hover.

He said, "Candidate Garrison (Gad-i-son), I've got it, you're losing control of the aircraft!"

Whereas I sat there put in my place once again. There would be several of those kinds of moments in flight school. I know of no helicopter pilot, then or now, who was not humbled when they first attempted a hover.

Day by day we went to class for half a day, and then flew with our instructors for the other half. One week we would fly in the morning and do the academics in the afternoon. The next week we would have academics in the morning and fly in the afternoon. There was never really a free moment during a weekday in flight school. You were gotten out of bed at 5:30 in the morning, when you showered, shaved and dressed in your uniform. We wore starched fatigues that were pressed with precision, and changed daily. Our combat boots were expected to be spit shined to the point of a mirror polish. Our hair was cropped very short. The fatigue shirt that you wore had a U.S. Army insignia above one pocket and your last name above the other.

After dressing in the morning, everyone would fall out into a platoon formation at attention in a parking lot just outside the barracks. Then one of us, when our rotation came, would call cadence and march us to the mess hall, which is military lingo for cafeteria. We would stand in line and enter single file, pick up a tray, and it would be filled by other enlisted personnel who worked in the mess hall.

You were expected to eat quickly and regroup, to march to class in formation unless it was your week to fly in the morning. During those weeks you were bussed by a military vehicle from the mess hall to the flightline.

When reporting to the flightline, and may God help you if you forgot, was your helmet carefully stowed in a helmet bag and your pre and post flight checklist for the kind of helicopter you flew. The preflight of a Hiller was exhaustive and you were expected to do it, by the book, every time just before you flew.

Many times in civilian and military life, experienced pilots get complacent about preflight checks and don't do them. Maybe it's because they just flew the aircraft and they assume everything is still alright. Or, maybe they just get in a hurry. Almost all of them will tell you, however, that a good preflight check is not a good thing to skip, and has caused a lot of pilots and passengers to be seriously injured or killed by some malfunction or damage that would have been found and corrected had a preflight check been done.

Consequently great emphasis was placed on a proper preflight check, and I have been grateful through the years for the military beating that concept into my head.

In the evenings, after flying and class all day, you again marched to the mess hall and were fed. Everyone learned quickly to eat what was offered, even if you couldn't identify it as plant or animal. If you didn't eat you went hungry. Simple as that. And with the stress of military flight school you needed the nutrition, believe me. A lot of moms have rules like that but at least you could identify what was on the menu.

After eating in the mess hall you returned to your barracks and had some time to study in the evening and prepare your uniform for the next day. The time had to be used wisely, because it was lights out at 10:00PM and you were expected to be in your bunk promptly at that time.

It was also a time for socializing with your comrades in the adjacent cubicles who found themselves in the same predicament as you. Many Hiller horror stories were exchanged. You could also write to your family. I recall after an exasperating day of trying to fly a helicopter I wrote a letter home to my brothers which said,

"If you see a helicopter fly over, don't believe it. No one can actually fly one. It's a figment of your imagination."

I was single at the time, and had not left a steady girlfriend or fiancé at home so I didn't have to write as often as the married guys did. I was quite pleased with the fact that I was single. At least I didn't have a wife at home constantly worrying about me and my welfare. I considered that a plus.

06

The Solo

When instructor Toth had valiantly given me eleven and one half hours of dual time (instructor pilot and student), he deemed me ready to make my first solo flight. This is a rather huge deal in the life of any student pilot. It's the first time that you take the aircraft up all by yourself.

As I said, Toth had gauged me ready to go. I wasn't so damned sure about it as he stepped out of the chopper while the engine was running and told me to fly three touch and goes around the patch. He waved goodbye as he said, "You'll do fine Gad-ison, just remember what I've taught you."

He then nonchalantly turned and walked away, ducking, of course, under the slinging rotor blades as he left.

All of a sudden, I realized that I was terribly and incredibly alone.

This momentous event happened at a *stage field*, as it was called, a small airport in the Texas countryside. It was one among many where flight instruction was given to military students. My instructions were to fly three right hand patterns, taking off and landing each time. A pattern consisted of a takeoff leg into the wind if possible, followed with a right climbing 90-degree turn called the crosswind. Next came another 90-degree turn to the right, leveling off at 500 feet above the ground (called the *downwind*). When you reached the end of the runway—that you keep in sight to your right—you made yet another 90 degree descending turn on base leg. Lastly, you pulled another 90 degree turn to line the aircraft up with the runway on final approach. In other words, you had just flown a large rectangular pattern.

I was to repeat this pattern three times to complete my solo and proceed with flight school.

I wrapped power on, with the motorcycle-like throttle on the collective, with my left hand to bring the aircraft out of flight idle and up to engine and rotor system RPM. The Hiller OH23D, with a 275 horsepower Lycoming power plant sitting right behind you and roaring like a grizzly, operated at a hover at 3200 RPM. You have to manually keep it at that level, or very close to it, while you fly the aircraft. Too much RPM and you can blow an engine or sling a rotor blade, which is generally not good for pilot or machine. Too little RPM and you lose the centrifugal force needed to keep the blades in a proper arc, and they can cone upward and lose all lift as you go down to terra firma like a homesick brick. That's not very good for your health either.

But, at that moment, I was too preoccupied with how I was going to control my beast to worry about such trivia as that.

When I got to 3200 RPM, I slowly added collective pitch to put lift in the system and pushed left pedal as needed to counter the torque of the main rotor system and keep the nose straight. The old girl came right up and behaved nicely.

I made a left turn from a three-foot hover and proceeded out to the taxiway, made another left turn and slowly hovered forward to the end of the taxiway, made a 360 degree traffic clearing turn and called the control tower for permission to takeoff. When the tower gave me clearance for takeoff, I nosed the cyclic forward and the aircraft crept down the runway. It hit *translational lift* and the aircraft shuddered and then gained altitude and picked up speed.

Translational lift is a phenomenon of rotary wing aircraft that provides greater lift as you start to gain speed close to the ground, because of forward airspeed and ground effect combined. The aircraft will shudder, dip in altitude momentarily, and then gain altitude and speed suddenly.

I glanced at my airspeed indicator, altimeter and engine RPM and everything appeared to be right on the money. The RPM was, miraculously I thought, still at 3200. I gained about 300 feet on takeoff leg and turned 90 degrees to the right on crosswind, where I gained another 200 feet and turned right onto downwind leg. There I leveled the chopper off at 500 feet above the ground until I turned base leg at the end of the runway and descended. When I turned right on final approach, I was at the proper 300 feet of altitude.

The only thing I hadn't done by the book so far, was that you are supposed to roll the RPM back in a Hiller at altitude to 3100 RPM. I didn't do that. I thought that everything seemed fine at 3200 and if it wasn't broke, I sure as hell wasn't going to fix it. Besides, I remember thinking, if I leave it at 3200 RPM, it's just one less adjustment to make when I return to a hover.

I descended on final and brought the aircraft to a three foot hover, made another 360-degree clearing turn for traffic, and took off again. I did this without incident three times and was feeling quite smug and sure of myself as I taxied the aircraft to the ramp to set it down.

Then, right out of the blue, the wind shifted 180 degrees, and what had been a headwind for me became a nasty tailwind.

In fixed wing and rotary wing aircraft you always take off and do close to the ground flying with the wind coming right at your nose whenever and wherever you possibly can. You always land into the wind whenever possible as well. A helicopter tends to get very unstable if the wind is at your tail. It's difficult to control, even for experienced pilots, and the engine and rotor RPM tend to bleed off and you run out of left pedal control. Even a small reduction of rotor RPM is visible to the trained eye.

Just as I had wallowed and hogged the Hiller back to a parking spot, after looking at the windsock only to see that there was a strong wind now at my tail, my RPM started to bleed off.

I thought, *"Shit a brick! What's the chances of that happening?"* No matter what I thought, the helicopter ghouls had struck again.

Since, by now, I was directly over my parking spot, instead of slightly lowering the collective pitch and adding more power to get my RPM back, I saw that the aircraft was settling in toward the ground, so I just let it settle and hoped that I wouldn't run completely out of left pedal and lose my directional control. As I settled in, the engine groaned and the RPM continued to bleed as I pulled more and more pitch to cushion the touchdown. The blades were obviously slowing and arcing somewhat upward. I ran out of left pedal just as I touched the aircraft down. Thank God for that. I was back on the ground safe and sound.

As I rolled the power off to shut her down, I glanced to my right and saw a foreboding pair of the aforementioned *trained eyes* glowing in immense disapproval. As these eyes, which happened to belong to Toth, grew ever larger as they rapidly approached my aircraft, I saw they were encased in a head that was shaking back and forth negatively so briskly I could almost hear his perfectly hardened brain rattle. In this, my zenith flying triumph, the trained eyes beheld only mortal sin. *"God damn it! What dirty luck! Son of a bitch!"*

When he got to me, I had my flight helmet off and the engine was winding down,

"Gad-i-son! Why didn't you add power? You got your tail into the wind, you idiot!

I sat there castigated, feeling like a moron. The Hiller OH23D had yet again humbled me and exposed me as an earthbound wretch when I had but sought to escape the surly bonds of earth.

I would understand later Toth realized I'd really done an excellent job in not piling the chopper up in a fiery ball when the wind shifted to my tail. This was the *Army Way* for flight instructors. Keep maximum stress and psychological pressure on the candidates. If they couldn't handle the stress now, they sure as hell wouldn't be able to endure the incredible strain of a hot mission in Vietnam. They knew. They had been there and done that.

"If you are going to break," they thought, "break right here, right now."

<<

07

The Seniors and Super Seniors

Once a student soloed, he wore a rectangular bright orange felt, tab on his shirt. Army fatigue shirts had two front pockets with a U.S. Army insignia tag sewn on above one and your last name sewn on above the other. They had flaps that buttoned down and closed the pocket. This is where you proudly put the orange tab that had a button hole sewn into it.

This was a coveted tab and worn proudly by the student. It meant that he had survived basic training, the harassment of preflight, and the grueling first few hours of instruction and ground school, and actually soloed an aircraft. It was no big deal to those ahead of you in flight school, but those who were behind you held it with awe and respect.

Remembering those ahead of me in flight school brings to mind the seniors and super seniors. The seniors were in the last few weeks of instruction at primary training at Fort Wolters, and the *super seniors* were finished at Wolters and awaiting transfer to either Fort Rucker, Alabama, where most of us went, or to Hunter Army Airfield/ Fort Stewart in Georgia, for instrument flight training and jet transition into the Bell UH1 Huey.

The seniors wore a black vertical stripe in the middle of the orange tab and the super seniors had two vertical black stripes. These candidates were to be treated by junior flight students as if they were already military officers and were to be saluted by their juniors.

It seems they were encouraged to harass us at every opportunity to increase the stress level further. *As if there wasn't enough pressure already.*

When marching in formation these sadists would descend upon the platoon in a swarm and proceed to hurl insults at their underclassmen, finding fault anywhere they could.

If nothing was wrong, and there usually wasn't, they would manufacture some supposed wrongdoing on the spot.

We candidates had to stand there and take their bullshit while saluting them and treating them as exalted superiors. You didn't dare question them or try to defend yourself if you wanted the encounter to pass quickly. *That was the Army way.*

All but a few hotheads learned this rapidly.

I deeply resented the way many of them let this newly found power go to their heads. Some too quickly forgot their own former misery and enjoyed being the harasser way too much.

Once we were marching in formation and were stopped by one of these super seniors, who proceeded to verbally berate everyone in the platoon. It seemed at the time he saved his best derision for me.

He methodically went down every line of our platoon as we were all at attention, stopping and finding nonexistent fault and verbally taking each candidate to task. When he reached me, he started screaming in my face, so close that I could smell what he had just eaten and feel the spittle hit my face.

Apparently my boots were not shined to his standards.

"Sir, Candidate Garrison," I finally said, 'may I look down and see what is so wrong with my boots that you're so upset about."

You always had to say, candidate and state your last name when you were addressing a superior, if you didn't want further trouble.

He said, "You damn right you can look at 'em, candidate!"

I looked down but could see nothing wrong. He started screaming again as he rubbed the sole of his own boot over the toe of mine, scuffing and ruining my spit shine.

He screamed, "Can't you see that scuff candidate, are you blind?" This really pissed me off and I was on the verge of decking the prick but I checked my emotion one more time.

"Yes Sir! How foolish of me to have missed it. I promise to spend more time on my boots and I'm very thankful that you have pointed out the errors of my ways."

He could barely hold back his laughter, but somehow did, and launched himself into another tirade with the next guy.

I realized even at the time that this harassment was designed to help weed out those that were weak. So I didn't really hold most of those guys in contempt. Notice that I said most of them. This prick I did. He was one of those who obviously relished the opportunity to pull rank for no reason other than to unload their newly found power on someone.

Everyone got to know those who fit this category quickly, and they were avoided whenever possible. Sometimes they laid in ambush and you couldn't avoid them. And like I said before, you just had to stand there and take it while they made personal insults about you and your family.

Things like: "There were a lot better examples of manhood that ran down your momma's legs when your daddy nailed her. How in the hell did you ever get born in the first place you motherfuckin' weak-assed excuse for a man? What have you got to say for yourself, candidate son of a bitch?"

And if you wanted to salvage your past accomplishments, you could only say something like: "You're absolutely correct, Sir. I will try my best to improve myself. My goal is to be as strong and wise as you are, Sir."

He would reply with something to this effect: "You'll never be as strong and wise as I am, candidate son of a bitch, but since you're trying I'll let you go this once. But there had better be one hell of a lot of improvement by the next time I run into you or there will be hell to pay."

"Yes, Sir, thank you for your attention to my shortcomings so I can know how to improve, Sir."

So much for the seniors and super seniors—especially the senior and super senior pricks.

08.

The Out of Uniform Bust

When someone soloed they often let us celebrate with a keg of beer for everyone in a small wooded area on a Saturday. All the guys who soloed were honored by the whole flight platoon.

When I had my solo party the beer flowed and lot of it hit me in the mouth. It was warm for a mid-December day in Texas, so many of us had taken our fatigue shirts off and just had on the underlying T shirt.

Mike Bliss, friend and fellow classmate, was married and had gotten a pass to deliver something to his wife. He asked me to go with him so I did.

In the military at the time it was against regulations to leave the post and go into the town of Mineral Wells in fatigues if you were a flight student. You had to wear civilian clothes (civvies) or be dressed in Class A military clothes like khakis or dress greens. Also, you were *never-ever-ever* to mix civilian clothes with military clothes. You were not only considered out of uniform but a cast out leper. In the eyes of the military it was a *No! No! No!*

I was soon to discover how seriously the army took these unbendable rules. It was one time in this long process that I foolishly put my candidacy in peril.

I got in Bliss' car, with both of us half looped on the keg of beer. Mike had a pass to get off post but I didn't, but I planned to stay in the car while he delivered the package to his wife at a nearby military building that was off the main compound.

So to get through the gates and the guards, I slipped on a civilian shirt that he had in the car. I now looked like I was dressed in civvies. The guards looked at his pass and let us through. I just stayed in the civilian shirt and fatigue pants because I was going to stay in the car anyway. Right? When we arrived, he got out of the car and said he would be back in just a few minutes.

Well, as I sat there for about an hour, the beer continued to be processed through my kidneys and sent to my bladder for disposal. My bladder must have doubled. I held it as long as I could, until it felt like it was going to explode. I got out of the car with no one around and emptied it on the asphalt behind the car.

Just then, as luck would have it, a CW2 drove slowly by and saw I was out of uniform off-post. He stopped his car and got out and approached me and said,

"Come with me, candidate."

I went with him since I didn't have a choice.

He took me in the building to a captain's office and dumped me there, thinking that he was very important, and acted as if he had just foiled a terrorist plot on the White House. He then went his merry way and I'm certain that he is an example of what super senior pricks become later in life.

Good for him. May the longtime sun shine upon him.

To be fair, let me say now that most warrant officers are not like this guy. They usually thought that a lot of the army regulations were just as ridiculous as I did. They wouldn't have given me a passing thought, let alone taken me to the brass to be humiliated and punished. It's too bad I didn't encounter one of them.

The Captain acted as if I had just abandoned my post on the front lines of combat, allowing my comrades in arms to be slaughtered by the enemy.

The captain berated me to the nth degree. My explanation was worthless. The world was black and white to this guy and I was a maggot dressed in half green. A lot of officers in the army who plan to stay in and make it a career are *gung ho* sons of bitches. They think they have to be. Captains are especially vulnerable. If they don't get promoted to major within a few years, they are asked to leave the military. The world is clearly delineated to this breed of cat. There is no middle ground for them and they don't negotiate grey areas when they present themselves.

The captain indicated he would court martial me and dishonorably discharge me if he could, but through some technicality that he gave me about this being a lack of judgment on my part, you can't court martial a soldier for a simple lack of judgment.

Well he had me there. *I was guilty* of lack of judgment and my ass was in a sling because of it. It was all not that big of a deal but right then and there I felt the sword of Damocles dangling from a horse hair above my future. I was still sweating but not from the beer.

The captain also knew that the offense wasn't nearly serious enough for a court martial. Finally, he opted to give me an Article 15. This is a form of non-judicial punishment in the military, much like a misdemeanor in the civilian world.

I signed the paper saying I accepted the penalty and admitted to the heinous crime of having on a civilian shirt and military fatigue pants. My penalty was a month's pay reduction at E5 rates and no off post passes for six weeks. You see such transgressions almost any day on the streets around a military base.

At least, I thought, it wouldn't get me kicked out of flight school. That's what CW2 Adams, our tactical officer for the platoon, told me when I came back to the barracks to get yet another royal ass chewing. I still remember it like it was yesterday.

"What the fuck's the matter with you Garrison. You can't do that shit around here. A lot of these guys are fuckin' *lifers*! That's how we who weren't planning a military career derided those who did.

"I know the son of a bitch that turned you in," he said referring to the chief warrant officer who took me to the captain. "He'll do anything to get a few brownie points." He paused as if debating whether to tell me more. Finally he did.

"I knew him in Vietnam. He would come up with the most lame, chicken-shit excuses to keep from flying that you've ever heard."

CW2 Adams was a cool guy and I really liked him. He was a Vietnam veteran who had flown choppers himself and was now our Tactical Officer (TO). Every platoon had one and he served as a kind of advisor to our flight platoon. He had been a flight instructor on the flightline when he first came back, but apparently some sort of medical condition had grounded him and he wound up with us.

I'll say one thing for myself. *I never ever went off post in a mixed uniform again.*

09

The Piss Poor Excuse for a Display

Just because I resolved to do better, didn't mean I avoided further ass chewings for undeserved reasons. No, the salvoes continued to fly, but in one I actually came out ahead of the game.

Each Saturday morning we stood inspection by the company commander, Captain Bolt. He was another former Vietnam helicopter pilot who had been assigned a flight platoon when he returned to the States. Sometimes these inspections were white glove, where he would put one on and feel about everywhere to see if he could come up with any dirt or dust anywhere. *God forbid if the white glove should ever be soiled on your station.*

Well, of course, he always could soil the glove. It's virtually impossible to get every speck of dust out of your cubicle no matter how hard you try.

They used these inspections as an excuse to make flight school an even bigger pain in the ass than it already was. Somehow the U.S. Army equated specks of dust with moral decadence.

During these inspections we displayed our personal toiletry items, extra belt buckle meticulously shined, carefully folded socks and boxers, etc., for the inspector to admire.

The razor, toothbrush, etc. was supposed to be the one you used every day, but everybody, even the inspectors, knew that it wasn't. But, they couldn't prove it, because you had hidden your regular worn day to day stuff outside the cubicle.

These items were displayed in an open drawer on a pristine white towel and were expected to be immaculate.

On one of these inspections my cubicle mate and some other guys in the platoon decided to play a little joke on me at my expense.

Before the inspection a sentry was usually posted by the door to give everyone a heads up when the captain was coming. I happened to be the sentry this time and was away from my cubicle. I had just placed my items for inspection on the white towel and they were as impeccable as required.

While I was watching for the captain, these guys ran out the side door and retrieved a handful of mud and grass and brought it back in and rubbed it on my display. It was spread over the white towel, toothbrush, belt buckle, everything.

They knew it was time to stand by the door and greet the captain military style and I would not be able to return to my room before he came in.

Finally came the captain and I greeted him at the door with all due respect.

"Sir, Candidate Garrison, good morning Sir." Then I followed him into the room, not looking down at my display. Why should I? I knew it was perfect because I'd checked it several times that morning.

Then came the barrage. The captain flew into a blinding rage and administered an ass-chewing worthy of a drill sergeant. I was flabbergasted, not knowing I had been sabotaged.

Once again, I was torn to pieces and left in a smoldering heap.

When he regained his composure—probably out of breath— I started to ask permission to speak. But I wasn't quick enough. He launched another verbal assault that would have put Bobby Knight into shock.

When he started hyperventilating and couldn't speak for a moment, I used the opportunity to get a word in edgewise.

Once again he regained partial composure and said.

"You had better goddamned well have a damned good explanation, candidate, or your ass is a field of weeds and I'm a fucking bush hog."

"Sir, Candidate Garrison, may I look down and see what you are so upset about, Sir?"

He gave his permission.

I looked down and saw the incredible mess.

Realizing that I had to think quickly on my feet, I said,

"Sir, do you think I would be fool enough to have done this? I'm not crazy and I'm not a masochist. If I were you, Sir, I would suggest you check my bunkmate and the other guys in the cubicle just across the hall and see if they have any traces of mud on their hands."

These guys were not being successful at keeping a straight face anyway.

At that, the captain, letting common sense prevail, checked their hands and did indeed find evidence that they had been the perpetrators.

Then the captain gave them a verbal lashing that made mine look like a Sunday school lesson. I thought he was going to have a stroke. My bunkmate and the other guys didn't look much better.

The captain grounded them to the post for six weeks.

He then turned to me, and since my Article 15 punishment had been completed, said,

"You've been through enough Candidate Garrison. Just living with lowlife criminals like these has been punishment enough for you already. You get a pass for the entire weekend. Have a good time and drink one for me."

When the captain left the building he screamed at my joke-happy friends and led them into a small parking lot. As I left the post for a much needed break an hour later, they were still low crawling through the asphalt parking lot on their hands and knees.

The captain was calling cadence for them. Between verbal assaults, that is.

◆ ◆ ◆

Relating this story made me think of another guy in our flight. His name was Peter Lisko. He was from Hoboken, New Jersey, just across the river from the *Big Apple,* and I really liked the guy. He was super street smart and knew all the angles. All that said, Pete was more than a little gullible.

We had talked several times about where we were headed, and Lisko didn't like it one bit. He didn't think much of the idea of being a live moving target for at least a year in Vietnam.

I can't honestly say I blamed him.

One night we were talking in the barracks after another day of solo work in the aircraft, and I mentioned that I was from southern Illinois about a hundred miles east of St. Louis.

All of a sudden his eyes got big and he said,

"East St. Louis! I saw a film just before I came to the army and it said that East St. Louis was the roughest town in the country."

This uttered, remember, by a boy from New Jersey which had its own reputation. "They talked about a Shelton Gang that virtually controlled the whole state outside of Chicago, back during prohibition when Capone was there. They said even Al Capone was afraid to screw with the Sheltons and as long as they didn't move into Chicago, they could have the rest of the state. So they reached a sort of gentlemen's agreement."

"I believe that's pretty accurate, Pete," I said. "And, by the way, my great grandfather was a Shelton so don't fuck with me or I'll plug ya just like those crazy fuckers would've." The only part of that which is true is that I was indeed a Shelton descendant.

"Are you serious, Garrison? You're related to the Shelton Gang?"

"Yep, I sure am."

Immediately, Lisko's eyes widened and his face took on an expression of deep awe and respect. He was talking face-to-face with a descendant of violent, murderous criminals.

"Goddamn, Garrison, those bastards were crazier than hell. They had a scene in the movie where they were going a hundred miles an hour down the road side-by-side, shootin' it out with tommy guns. Is that right? Did they really do that?"

"Yes, apparently that happened. They had a war going with a rival group called The Birger Gang. Earl Shelton hired, maybe even forced, a pilot to fly an old biplane over their headquarters while he sat in the back throwing out homemade bombs trying to blow them up. I believe it was the first documented time that an aircraft was used as an air assault vehicle in the United States." That was also true.

"Garrison is all your family just as crazy as they were? What about you, are you that crazy Garrison?"

It was here I paused to take a deep re-evaluation of Lisko. Was he putting me on or was he actually serious. If he was street smart, he was history poor. The damned Mafioso had practically grown up in his own backyard. But, he seemed to be genuinely fascinated with southern Illinois crime? I decided to take him for a ride.

I replied looking very serious, "I don't know much about my family because most of them are in jail for murder, drug-running, bookie operations, or all three."

Pete's awe seemed to grow by the second. He obviously had a deep respect for those who played outside the sandbox.

He then said, "Yea, but you know 'em. What are they like to just talk to?"

"Pete, I never ever said much. Family wasn't even off limits if you said the wrong thing. And if you got that look from one of them, you knew right then and there that you wouldn't hear the rooster crow in the morning."

At this point, Lisko was enamored with the fact that he was not only talking to a descendant of criminals, but a man who had lived his life dodging their wrath. He then was curious about my stability.

"What about you, Garrison, do you go nuts if somebody crosses you?"

Still kidding but acting serious, I said, "You know it must be in the blood or something. I usually carried one or both of a pair of top breakdown 32 caliber revolvers strapped to my lower legs at about sock level, especially during high stakes poker games. These revolvers were passed down to me from none other than my Great Grandfather Shelton."

"Damn, Garrison, did you ever use 'em?" he said.

I said, now acting very serious, "A couple of times, but people learned damn quick that they sure as hell better not cheat if I was at the high stakes poker table."

He said, "Did you shoot a couple guys?"

I said, "I'll let you be the judge of that. I'll just ask you, what do you think those deep strip mining pits that are full of water up there are used for? There are skeletons galore in the bottom of those things that the fish have picked clean years ago. The cops can't prove anything even if they would happen to find the body.

I said, "We play hardball up by East St. Louis, Pete."

He said, "I can't believe I'm talking to a guy related to the Sheltons. I can't wait to tell the guys back home."

It was close to 10:00 PM and lights out at this point, so he left then, acting as if he believed everything I had said. I think he did because from then on he treated me like a king and confidant.

A few days later, Lisko came into my cubicle while I was spit shining my combat boots and said,

"I don't think I want to go through with this flight program, Mark. I think a guy's nuts to go to Vietnam voluntarily to get shot at for a year." He then said, "I think I know a way to get out of this, Mark."

Lisko was slumped with his back against the wall while sitting on my lower bunk bed. He had left his boots at the cubicle's entrance and had his socked right foot cocked up on the bed, and his left leg was sprawled out to his side. There was seriousness about him I had not often sensed before.

"How's that, Pete?" I asked. I was not sure I had heard him correctly.

"You'll find out soon enough" he said resolutely, "and I know I can count on you not to say anything."

He then left, and I wondered what Pete had up his sleeve. The visit and his remarks were somewhat unsettling but, what the hell, I had boots to spitshine.

10

Advanced Primary Flight Training at Fort Wolters

After a student finished the basic flight instruction at Ft. Wolters, he had to pass a checkride, given by another special group of instructors who were usually ex-military pilots turned civilian. This checkride was mandatory and a student had to pass it or be *washed out* of flight school. I had reached another critical junction on my journey. This was a flight where the instructor would tell the student what maneuvers to perform with the aircraft and the student would do his very best to accomplish the task correctly.

You could be asked to perform any flight maneuver on which you had previously received instruction. Things like straight and level flight, hovering, standard rate 180-degree turns, 180-degree climbing and descending turns, settling with power, and autorotations might be requested.

Let me back up and explain what an autorotation in a helicopter is. In simplest terms, an autorotation is bringing the aircraft safely to the ground after engine failure. At our present stage we already trained for mechanical failure. In military warfare the failure was often mechanical failure as a result of enemy fire. The U.S. Army mandated daily training for such an event. Simulation included engine shutdown to a complete, safe stop on the runway. Success was not a foregone conclusion. There was always danger of pilot error, weather complications, etc. Our life was literally in our own hands in practice.

The instructor first rolls the power off to flight idle. The first thing that you must do quickly in a helicopter to keep up main rotor RPM is to bottom the collective pitch control with your left hand. This removes the pitch, or angle of attack of the rotor blades (remember the fan blades example) relative to the surrounding air mass passing through the blades. Now, with the pitch at zero, the blades will spin on at normal RPM indefinitely. If you don't do that, the blades will slow so much that you will lose all lift and fall out of the sky to your death. That's a pretty good incentive to get the collective down in a hurry. Once you do that, you start to rapidly descend to the runway that you have chosen for touchdown. The pilot then stabilizes the airspeed at around 60 knots in a Hiller, during the descent. Then at approximately 30 to 40 feet above the runway, the pilot brings the cyclic back to flare and bleed off airspeed. This flare slows both the aircraft's forward speed and its rate of descent. Then as the aircraft continues downward, the pilot starts to put pitch back in the blades by partially raising the collective pitch control. *If done properly,* the chopper will slow its descent further and as it approaches the ground the pilot slowly raises the collective to maximum.

Expertly done, in an autorotation one can dispel all forward airspeed and runout of flying RPM of the blades just as the aircraft touches the ground. This is why, as a pilot of both fixed wing and helicopters, I would much rather have an engine failure in a helicopter than in an airplane, especially if over water or trees. Simply stated, because of autorotation *you can stop* all your forward momentum, and you sure as hell can't do that in a fixed wing where momentum just hurtles you forward, into anything in its path. Usually if you *correctly* autorotate a chopper you're going to collide with the water or trees without momentum.

Every candidate is nervous about a checkride. You know how to do the maneuvers, but you must *prove* that to the instructor. Some of the things you are expected to perform at this stage require enormous precision.

Some candidates clutch and bomb on these checkrides. Usually they were given a pink slip. We had reached a new plateau in our training. The system was no longer designed to chase you away but to salvage you and improve your skills. The instructor was told your areas of weakness, and he worked with you for a few days and then another checkride was given. The problem was that the candidates that flunked the first test, tended to get more and more nervous about the next checkride and would bomb it too, and collect another pink slip. Three tries and three pink slips and you were out of the system.

The U.S. Army had a lot of money invested in a student at this point and didn't want to see anyone fail. It was *a lose-lose* situation. Yet they realized that if a student failed three checkrides in a row, he probably wasn't cut out to be a combat pilot, or any other kind of pilot for that matter. So the candidate was *washed out* and usually assigned to the infantry or some other exciting branch.

At the end of my checkride, the instructor said, "I've got the aircraft, candidate. You can relax now and I'll take her in." When he asked for the controls my heart sank. I felt certain that I had bombed the ride and would be getting a pink slip. Surprise awaited me back on the ground.

"Congratulations Candidate Garrison. You delivered the best performance on a checkride that I've seen in a long time. You should be proud of yourself. I'm sure instructor Toth is very proud of you."

I thought, *Jesus Christ, is this actually happening? Toth acts like I'm going to kill us both every damned time we go up.* I sure as hell wasn't going to argue with the man. I was glad to get it over with. I'm sure that the aircraft I flew that day had my hand prints permanently embedded into the controls, I was holding on so tight. *I passed!* It was on to advanced primary flight at Fort Wolters.

In Advanced Primary Flight School at Fort Wolters, you were taught to land in what was called white, yellow, or red tire areas located in the Texas countryside, usually on the bluffs. These target areas had painted automobile tires in them that could be seen easily from the air.

The white tire areas were fairly large and spacious and comparatively easy to fly in and out of. The yellow tire areas were smaller and more difficult to negotiate, and a student had to be with an instructor or be cleared by an instructor to fly into them solo. The red tire areas were small, and it took a lot of precision to get in and out of them. A student had to be accompanied by an instructor to fly into them.

Working on more advanced maneuvers and flying in and out of these tire areas was the bulk of the rest of the training, along with continued study in ground school courses. When a student would fly solo into one of these areas, he would land and follow a precise procedure for safety's sake.

He would first land the aircraft and roll the throttle back to the reduced RPM of flight idle. He would next unbuckle his seat belt and shoulder harness and exit the aircraft, always careful to duck under the whirling rotor blades. Once on the ground, he would perform what was called a ground reconnaissance. He looked for obstructions to his upcoming takeoff and counted paces back to mark the area with a stick or similar object that could easily be seen from the cockpit, to tell him how far he could hover backwards before getting his tail rotor into trees or other obstacles. He would then climb back into the aircraft, buckle up, hover backwards to give himself clearance and take off into the wind.

Once I saw what appeared to be a large diamondback rattlesnake in one of the tire areas and I stayed as far away from it as I could and got out of there as fast as I could. A classmate and friend who made the same discovery dealt with it differently. It's a story worth telling.

Candidate Kevin Nielson was a real frontiersman, hailing from the mountains of northwest Montana, and came to flight school looking for adventure. He had hunted grizzly bears with a bow and arrow in his native mountains and lived through many other crazy-assed adventures. He claimed to be a practicing Mormon, but if, indeed he was, he was the least observant Mormon I ever met. He smoked like a chimney and drank like a fish.

Everyone liked adventurous, unconventional Kevin.

One day I had spent the afternoon flying in and out of the tire areas, almost to the point of tedium. Finished for the day, I brought my aircraft back to the main heliport and was shutting it down when I noticed another Hiller OH23D coming in on final approach.

It looked like it was being flown by someone who had no idea what the purpose of the controls were, let alone how to use them. The aircraft came to a wobbly hover and proceeded to a parking spot on the concrete ramp and was clumsily set down.

As I watched in amazement, the aircraft continued to run at full RPM for an inordinate amount of time before the power was rolled off to flight idle. It was then shut down but no one got out of the aircraft. I decided something was wrong with the pilot and approached it cautiously.

When I got to the Hiller, I saw the pilot sitting stiffly. Then I saw a huge diamondback rattlesnake coiled around the cyclic stick and one of the anti-torque pedals. The rattler looked as if it did not enjoy its first unsolicited helicopter ride. As a matter of fact, it looked downright pissed off.

The pilot sat motionless. The rattlesnake found the door, dropped to the ground and slithered away. The pilot then took off his flight helmet, revealing his identity. It was Kevin Nielson, and sweat was streaming down his face and his eyes were as big as dinner plates.

"Jesus Christ, Kevin," I yelled. "How did that snake get in there with you? I thought whoever was flying this bird was having a stroke!"

Nielson explained later that evening at the NCO Club over a few beers that he had seen the snake in a tire area and went back to the aircraft and got his helmet bag.

He then found a forked stick to pin the rattler on the ground just behind its head and had captured it and put it in the helmet bag and zipped it up. His plan had been to bring the snake to the barracks and let it loose just to see what the rest of us would do. "Just to have a little fun with you," he said. "Of course," he added, "I would have milked it of its venom, first." Like that would make us feel better.

The snake had other plans, however, and worked the bag open in flight and crawled all over him and the cockpit while he was attempting to fly the aircraft back at, 2,000 feet. That certainly explained the spastic approach I had witnessed.

"Goddamn! That's the last time I'll ever do that!" Nielson said.

As I said, everybody liked Nielson. I'm not so certain he would have retained his title as most popular if he had let the rattler loose in our barracks, milked or not. At least he left us an amazing and unforgettable story for the telling and we will always fondly remember the *crazy Montana mountain man*.

A few days after that incident, I was again doing solo work in the Hiller and heard a call come across the radio that one of our aircraft was down and right in my vicinity. Just a minute or two afterwards I saw a medical evacuation chopper hovering over some small trees not far from me. It looked as if they had the pilot out and there was no fire. I had no idea who the pilot was. When I got back to the company area, I was told that it was Peter Lisko, my pal from Hoboken who went down.

"Is Pete alright?" I asked the candidate who had shared the news.

The other flight student then said, "Yeah, pretty much alright, but he's complaining about his back hurting."

I thought right then and there that Lisko had finally executed his well thought out plan to get out of this mess called Vietnam. I couldn't totally blame him either. I smiled. If he wasn't detouring around Vietnam, maybe he was trying to get away from me, before I gave him one of those mean *Shelton looks*.

I never got to talk to Peter again, but I understand he was discharged medically for a service connected back injury. I thought to myself: *Lisko, you sly fox you. My best wishes to you.* He had indeed found a back way out. If that was indeed his plan, it was well thought out and masterfully executed.

The day to day grind continued as I prepared for my final check-ride at Wolters. One day seemed to merge with the next as everything blurred. Vietnam was on all of our minds because everybody knew without a doubt, that's where we were going.

The final check ride eventually came. I passed the check and all the academic requirements and then it was so long Fort Wolters and hello Fort Rucker, Alabama. The U.S. Army program was working its magic. At Rucker we would receive instrument flight training and jet transition to the UH 1 Huey helicopter, the original workhorse of the new war.

Fort Wolters will always have a special place in my heart, I thought, nearly tearing up. The guys I went to flight school with were the finest bunch of guys that I'd ever known to that point in my military career. I still regard them all with fondness, and will for the rest of my days, but little did I know there were new and brighter bonds to forge.

11

Instrument Flight Training at Rucker

The most difficult part of flight school (for me at least) was the instrument flight instruction given when you first arrived and settled in at Fort Rucker, Alabama. Fort Rucker was, and still is, a large army post nestled between the towns of Ozark and Enterprise, Alabama. This is southern Alabama. The fort is only an hour drive from Florida. Army towns in the U.S. were rather small and highly economically dependent on the nearby post. They are even yet today. The post provided jobs, commerce and cash flow into those communities.

Instrument flight knowledge is needed when you find yourself in Instrument Flight Rules (IFR) weather conditions. In other words, when you can't see a damned thing outside the cockpit, and have to keep it from auguring into terra firma by looking at your instruments, because you were crazy enough to fly through the crap in the first place.

Joking aside, a pilot sometimes gets caught in nasty weather unexpectedly, through no fault of his own. Therefore, it's necessary to know how to fly instruments or you're pretty much screwed, blued and tattooed. Civilian pilots who are not instrument rated tend to watch the weather closely, and only fly in Visual Flight Rules (VFR) conditions; or at least they should.

We were scheduled to fly the fully instrument equipped Bell 13 helicopter.

The Bell 13 instrument trainer.

Once in the aircraft, you put on a pair of special *goggles*. There was an orange film covering the entire plexiglass bubble in front of you. The goggles plus the orange film allowed you to see only black. In other words it simulated zero visibility conditions and you were forced to fly by instruments.

These critical instruments needed to fly in low visibility conditions were an airspeed indicator, an altimeter, a turn and bank, an artificial horizon, and an RMI (radio magnetic indicator) that had both VOR needles (omni), and ADF (automatic direction finder needle). You also needed your communication radios. It was an absolute necessity for the pilot to understand and correlate what these instruments were telling him at all times to keep the aircraft on course and behaving properly.

On my first flight, my instructor, CW2 Perkins, who was a Vietnam combat veteran, taught me one of the most valuable lessons that I would ever learn. That lesson was to never fly by the seat of your pants. In other words, do not believe what your ass is telling you about what position or attitude the aircraft is in, because your ass is probably lying. Instead, keep a constant vigil on what the instruments are telling you and believe them.

We studied the instruments in instrument ground school for a few days before our first flight. Nevertheless, I was nervous as I strapped in for the first instrument orientation flight.

We took off from the heliport and the instructor asked me to don the goggles, and immediately I couldn't see a damn thing outside. He then gave me the aircraft controls and told me to hold the altitude and heading and fly straight and level by reading the instruments. After a short while, he said:

"OK, I have the aircraft; take your goggles off now." I took them off.

Now I could see the orange world outside and the aircraft was in a steep right hand, climbing turn. In other words, I would have shortly crashed if I had been alone in real instrument conditions. I had been subconsciously listening to what the seat of my pants was telling me, and it was telling me I had been in a steep left hand descending turn, and I was subconsciously correcting for it, instead of interpreting what the instruments were saying.

I've never forgotten that lesson, and I'm extremely grateful to him for demonstrating it on the very first day. This helped me immensely from the outset of instrument flight training.

We received instruction for about a month as I recall. There was a checkride given in mid instrument training and one at the end. You were expected to pass both to move on to jet transition in the Huey. My first checkride was given by an army major. I can't remember his name, only his rank. I thought I had bombed the ride and was preparing myself for the worst when he said,

"OK, candidate, I have the aircraft, you can relax now." He then added,

"You did a fantastic job, candidate. You've obviously done your homework."

"But I'm going to give you a B. I don't believe in giving A's. It tends to inflate egos too much."

I couldn't believe what I was hearing. I thought I had bombed it. But alternatively, I thought why didn't you give me an A if I did a fantastic job, you prick? I was more than a little ambivalent about the ride. But I was just glad to get it over with and move on. Flight school was becoming more and more of a grind every day.

So on and on it went, through the military's complicated figure eight holding patterns, to complex maneuvers with nothing but the instruments to guide you, to the final instrument checkride. I was fairly comfortable with instrument flight at this point and passed the checkride.

Some guys didn't and were washed out and reassigned. I felt sorry for those guys. *So damned much work* to get this far and to be washed out seemed harsh to me, but the military was firm about it. There was no negotiation.

For those of us who made it, it was on to jet transition into the Huey. I couldn't wait. This was the last phase of flight school and I was ready to finish. My whole being screamed for release—even if it landed me in Vietnam.

Jet transition into the Huey is what we had all been waiting for, and we weren't let down. This last section of flight school was actually quite fun to me. Of course, we had to learn the nuances of flying a jet powered aircraft. Things like the importance of EGT (exhaust gas temperature), N1 (gas producer) and N2 (RPM). The degree to which a gasoline powered reciprocating engine was working was measured by the inches of manifold pressure that it produced. In a jet, there's no manifold, and how hard it is working is indicated by N1, or gas producer, and is expressed as a percent. This reading could go all the way to 101.5 percent.

The Bell UH-1 (Huey).
The workhorse of the Vietnam War.

The engine RPM is controlled for you by a throttle governor in the Huey and it keeps the RPM at 6600 for the engine and the rotor RPM at about 324. This little perk made the aircraft easier to fly than the Hiller, because the RPM was controlled for you as you raised and lowered the collective pitch control.

During this phase, after basic instruction in flying the Huey, we would fly mission simulations and insert and extract imaginary troops in and out of landing zones in farmer's fields around Fort Rucker.

The bullshit harassment had let up, and there were no super seniors on your case. The brass knew, and we students knew, we would soon have wings pinned upon our chests, barring a big time fuck up or a miraculous end of the war. The army had too much invested in each of us at this point for them to frivolously kick us out. It was never said but we knew it to be true.

However there was one thing we had not done. Something all of us had to complete before we could leave. They called it *escape and evasion training*. I, for one, dreaded it like the plague. Finally the day came.

One morning our entire flight platoon was called into formation, given a compass and one canteen of water, along with a map of a heavily forested area in southern Alabama. A coordinate position marked on the map indicated a friendly location we were supposed to reach to retain our freedom. In the forest, lurked several American infantry troops with red bands on their arms designating them the enemy. These troops were numerous and roved on the roads in military vehicles and scattered and skulked among the trees. They carried real weapons which were loaded with blank ammunition, and if you were captured, you were taken to a makeshift prison camp, located somewhere in the bowels of the woods. If you didn't want to participate in an extremely unpleasant prisoner experience, these red-banded guys were to be avoided at all costs. The enemy was legion and ubiquitous, just like in Vietnam. This was not real nor was it *Candyland,* the kids' game. If the red-band soldiers caught you they would torture you to the letter of the military law and possibly a step or two beyond. We had heard too many stories by graduates of the school of horrors.

After collecting our map, canteens and compass we were separated into pairs, and dropped off at starting points that were several miles from your destination and given, as I recall, twenty four hours to make the journey without getting caught by the bad guys.

A guy named Bob and I were dropped off, and we started through the woods, using the map and compass as a guide. It was miserably hot and humid, and the woods were pregnant with obnoxious insects. It must have been standing room only for them.

Nevertheless, we were able to travel several miles toward safety unseen. When we got to a small trail within about an eighth of a mile of the designated safe home, we became complacent and decided to walk the trail instead of fighting the bush and bugs.

Mistake! The red-arm-banded enemy pounced upon us and took us by truck to the infamous prison camp.

It was now nightfall and the first thing our captors did was strip us to our boxer shorts, dog tags, and unlaced combat boots. They then put a tightly fitting, burlap bag on our heads, making it extremely difficult to see anything. Then the harassment began. The only thing you were obligated to tell them, by Geneva Convention standards and the Military Code of Justice, was your name, rank, and serial number. But believe me, all that was thrown out the window as they asked everything they could think of—in as many ways as they could think of— to extract information from you. All the while they were subjecting you to all kinds of harassment.

Bob and I held out, so they placed us upside down, back- to-back in a fifty-five gallon drum with our heads resting on pieces of rough firewood, and our hands tied behind our backs. We felt as if our necks were going to snap, but somehow they didn't. Then they started plucking our pubic hair out by the dozens, all the while asking us questions. When that didn't work with us, they placed us in a trench facing each other. This trench was half full of water, and they put a guillotine type head retainer around our necks. The trench was too shallow for us to stand up straight, and too deep to fully squat down, leaving you hanging by your neck when your legs finally gave way. There were ropes floating around in the water which they said were poisonous snakes, and by this time you believed them. When we still stuck to name, rank, and serial number answers, they started pouring water over the top of our head, the burlap sack became soaked, making it almost impossible to breathe. At first, as I was choking and sucking in water, it filled me with so much fear and adrenaline that I bucked four full grown troops off the head board and tried to escape. Several guys quickly subdued me and continued the water torture.

At this point, I think I would have told them anything they wanted to hear, true or not, if they would just let me get my breath.

It amazes me today when members of congress debate whether or not waterboarding is torture. Have no doubt about it, folks. It is an extreme form of torture. When you can't breathe, you'll tell anybody anything just to get them to stop. All of these duly elected public officials should have to go experience it themselves right after they take the oath of office. Then they would have no doubt about it being torture, and thus a very good way to get extremely unreliable information.

They finally stopped the hellish treatment of us, took off our headgear, and bussed us back to the post. Believe it or not, I was glad that I had been caught after it was all over. It taught me a very valuable lesson. Everyone has a breaking point. Everyone! It's just a question of where it is.

The following days came and went and graduation from flight school arrived. In a formal ceremony, we were all appointed warrant officers grade 1, or WO1. The warrant officer ranks had four grades. They are WO1, CW2, CW3 and CW4. The C stood for chief, and the ranks were roughly comparable to, respectively, second lieutenant, first lieutenant, captain and major. Warrant officers generally received the same privileges and pay as their commissioned officer counterparts.

Now with wings on our chests, and officer bars on our uniforms, we were all given a month's leave to visit our families, and to silently ponder where we were headed. I was about to discover that there was no really effective way to adequately prepare yourself to go to Vietnam. I would also soon discover just how much responsibility came with those wings and officer bars.

12.

A Few Days Leave

On the leave home, thinking about where I was going, I tried to drink all the beer in southern Illinois. I didn't get it done but I think I drank at least half of what the Shelton boys had bootlegged into East St. Louis so many years before.

I stayed at my brother's house since I really didn't have a home to go to. My only real home was the army at that point in my life. My mother had remarried five years earlier and moved to a nearby small town. My two brothers and I had encouraged her to marry, since she was lonely after my father's passing and having trouble financially. She married Ed in 1965 and was Ed ever a dandy piece of work and an American original. I say that with fondness.

Ed had been forced to drop out of school when he was in the third grade to help the threshing crews in the wheat fields and to help his father run a saw mill that he owned. In early Illinois there was no law binding a student to a school until they were sixteen years old. You could drop out whenever you wanted or your parents needed.

Even with that glaring educational deficiency, Ed had made a modest success of his life. He had a pension from an oil company while still farming about 120 acres that he had acquired through the years. Ed raised soybeans, corn and wheat, every year, faithfully rotating his crops, and doing virtually all the work by himself with old, dilapidated machinery. Ed also owned and operated a small, homebuilt sawmill some distance behind his house in a woods, where he still raised hogs for market. He was at this time approaching 70, several years older than my mother, who was then just 53.

**Ed in the foreground smoking a
pipe with me in the background.**

Ed also had a colossal temper that he usually reserved for his aging, malfunctioning machinery. Ed was now comically at war with his machinery and had been for several years. His farm equipment of choice was anything that could be repaired with pliers, a crescent wrench, screwdriver and hammer—especially the hammer. Once, I drove up to visit with mom, and as soon as I got out of the car I heard the most awful cursing going on in the side yard and went to investigate. As I went around the house, I saw Ed with a hammer in one hand and a large crescent wrench in the other, as he ominously approached his tractor that apparently wouldn't start. I heard him say to the tractor:

"Why you son of a bitch! You goddamned son of a bitch!" Then he let out a high-pitched WHEW! sound that fell somewhere in the range between the whinny of a horse and a police car siren.

"You're a friggin' riggin' you goddamned dirty son of a bitch!"

This was followed by another high-pitched WHEW!

By then he had cornered the errant tractor, and I watched in amazement as he commenced beating the hell out of it with the hammer and wrench. All the while refraining:

"WHEW! You're a friggin' riggin' WHEW!

When he finally paused to catch his breath, I made my presence known. His face was the complexion of a ripe tomato and I thought sure he was about to stroke out.

I came up behind him and said, "What's the matter Ed? Tractor won't start?

He again bellowed, "WHEW! It's a friggin' riggin', the son of a bitch!"

I said, "Let's take a look at the sediment bulb in the fuel line. It looks to me like it might be clogged." Sure enough that's all that was the matter with it, so we cleaned it out and she fired right up.

I neglected to mention that right before I got to him, he had actually thrown down the hammer and wrench and gone after the tractor with his bare fists. I then suggested that we go inside and see about his hands, that were bruised and bleeding.

I said, "Let's let mom take a look at your hands and take care of them for you."

He thought that was a pretty good idea so we went in the house.

Unlike America, Ed was at war with his machinery, not people. In spite of this war, he was good to my mother and appeared to love her dearly, so we brothers embraced him and got along with him quite well. His sage departing advice to me as I left for Vietnam was memorable.

"By God, uh, you better watch them there commies. By God, uh, they'll kill ye if you don't watch 'em, by God, uh."

His admonition was already in the forefront of my mind. I just couldn't shake it.

PART TWO:
HELLO, VIETNAM

13

A Long Flight Over

On or about September the 30th, 1968, I was taken to Lambert Field in St. Louis, Missouri, by my oldest brother's wife, Pam. We were accompanied by a cousin of mine, Marilyn, and my mother. It was a three-hour trip from my small Illinois hometown by automobile. It was an awkward and solemn occasion for us all.

By this time, America had become a nation of goodbyes. The war had mushroomed into something out of control invading every facet of family life. Train stations, bus depots and airports were filled with men in uniform whispering goodbyes to wives, sweethearts and families. We said our tearful goodbyes at the airport, but I remained upbeat to them, mainly for my mother's sake.

"Don't worry Mom, I'm too damned ornery to get killed and you know it," I said. I might have even thrown in an obligatory, "don't worry this war will be over soon," just to ease her pain.

Mom started laughing through her tears. So did my cousin, Marilyn, and sister in law, Pam. I said my final goodbye, faithfully promising to return to them unharmed and turned and walked toward the Boeing 707. This was back in the days when a passenger walked out on the tarmac and ascended a flight of steps to the entry door of the aircraft. The stairs, on wheels, were then rolled away and the aircraft door was secured. When I got to the top of the stairs, I turned around to wave a final goodbye to Mom and the rest of them, and they were all bawling their eyes out as they limply waved goodbye.

It was as if I were going to face a firing squad immediately on my arrival in Vietnam.

The sight left a lump in the pit of my stomach, tears in my eyes and a resentful taste in my mouth.

How the hell did I get here? How the hell did it come to this?

I flew to San Francisco, California, from St. Louis. From there I was shuttled to Oakland, across the bay, by a large commercial Sikorsky helicopter.

When I boarded, I sat down next to an army private on his way to Vietnam.

I noticed him looking at me with great interest, and he said,

"Sir, boy, am I glad you're on board. I sure don't like flying much, but now I know you can bring this contraption in if something happens to the pilot up there."

He, of course, had noticed the wings on my chest.

I didn't tell him that I wasn't in the least familiar with this aircraft, and that he could probably do as good a job of landing it as me, maybe better. Why burst the guy's bubble. He was already scared enough. So instead I said,

"Don't worry soldier, if anything happens you're in good hands."

He seemed genuinely relieved.

The pilot picked the heavy beast up quite nicely, flew across the bay and made a very smooth touchdown. The private was very happy about the whole thing and couldn't wait to get off before the whirly bird left the ground again.

From there I was taxied to an address in Oakland and met up with two friends of mine from flight school. They were Larry Bodell and Vincent Zappini. I was thrilled to see familiar faces. That night the three of us went back to San Francisco by Metro and hit several downtown nightclubs. I was only twenty years old and the legal drinking age was twenty-one. They seemed to be rather lax about checking IDs and we were in uniform so they all let us in without incident.

All three of us proceeded to get roaring drunk and in the taxi back to Oakland we sang the Fort Polk Boogie. After all, we figured this was our last night in the States. The next morning we were to leave for Anchorage, Alaska, for a brief layover, and from there it was on to Vietnam by way of Tokyo, Japan.

We left early and incredibly hung over the next morning on Flying Tiger Airlines. Flying Tiger was a civilian air transport outfit that did a lot of contractual things with the U.S. military. We were on board what is called a stretch eight. That is a DC 8 that has been altered to have a longer fuselage in order to carry more cargo, or in this case, passengers going to war. There must have been more than two hundred troops aboard.

Vincent (Vinnie), Larry and I were the only officers on board. The rest were all enlisted men, mainly buck privates, and I don't think there was one of them who liked where he was going.

I know the three of us sure as hell didn't.

On the flight from Oakland to Anchorage, Alaska, I thought the captain was asking us to be seated and to secure our seat belts a little too frequently. I mentioned it to Vinnie and Larry and they thought the same. Other than that, the flight was uneventful, except on final approach to Anchorage when the captain came on the intercom and said that they had a little hydraulic problem and they were going to have it looked at in Anchorage.

Well, in my humble opinion, there is no such thing as a "little" hydraulic problem. The pilot controls in the cockpit are run almost entirely by hydraulics and if you lose your hydraulic system you're pretty much screwed. I also knew that aircraft had what's called horizontal backup, in other words, two hydraulic systems in case one failed. But we didn't know how serious the problem was. At least, it explained why he kept telling us to please be seated and buckle up.

When we got off the aircraft we were told to wait in the airport while maintenance looked it over. About an hour later we were told that the hydraulic problem was more serious than first thought and that it would take all night and into the next day to fix it. We were also told that we were to be put up at various hotels in the city, and that arrangements had already been made. We were free to do as we wished as long as we were back at the airport at 0800 hours the next morning.

An Army Major then approached Vinnie, Larry and me and said: "You guys are in charge of these animals. See that they get back here by 0800 hours in the morning. I sure as hell don't envy you, good luck." The Major then walked away, washing his hands of the whole affair as he left. It's called passing the buck and *pulling rank* —two time honored army traditions.

I was elected to be the spokesman of authority, so I called the enlisted men into formation and simply told them, "You guys know what's expected of you. I don't care what you do as long as you're back here and not wanted by the Anchorage Police Department at 0800 hours in the morning."

I then bid them adieu.

Vinnie, Larry and I washed up at the hotel in downtown Anchorage, Alaska. Then we went out to mingle with the locals. None of us had any idea what to expect. Vinnie was from Florida, I believe Larry was from some plain state like Nebraska, though I can't remember for sure, and I was from Illinois, about two hundred miles south of Chicago.

We hit the bars one by one, with our vision and coordination deteriorating with each successive pit stop. The bars were not at all what we expected, even though we had not known quite what to expect. Many of the establishments had worn, closed loop carpet on the bars and the locals were getting drunk and dancing on the bars between people's drinks. Nearly all the dancers were females and when you looked up it was almost impossible to not see up their skirts and dresses. They didn't seem to mind at all, and if they caught you taking a peek they came closer to you and raised their dresses a little higher to insure you had a full view. In the background was a jukebox playing exclusively, hardcore, country and western music. I thought this unusual but homey. It felt and sounded as if we were back in Texas.

Indeed, many of the local guys, sported cowboy hats and boots. They also wore western shirts with snaps instead of buttons and wore classic western string ties around their necks, and big buckled western belts around their waists to hold up their Wrangler blue jeans.

They were really friendly people, and I didn't meet one of them that I didn't like.

Vinnie, Larry and I had an absolute blast with these people, who had an old fashioned respect for men in uniform. They were patriotic folks who treated us with the utmost respect and kindness. I have good memories of the Alaskans.

When the bars closed down and the beer stopped flowing, the three of us staggered out as a result of all the drinks that had been bought in our honor, and we hailed a taxi.

When the cab driver asked the traditional: *where to?* It hit us! None of us could remember the name of the damned hotel and we sure as hell didn't know the address. We cruised around downtown Anchorage looking for something familiar, but nothing did. Everything looks different at night anyway, especially when you're drunk. So, we stopped at three or four hotels, asking if we happened to be booked there and finally stumbled upon it, after racking up quite a cab fee. For the cabby's trouble we gave him a generous tip on top of the fee.

What the hell were we going to need money for anyway? *We were Vietnam bound!*

The next morning I called all the hung-over troops, myself included, back into formation, stood them at parade rest and saw that everyone, miraculously, was present at 0800 hours.

The aircraft, we were told, had been successfully repaired and we were to take off immediately. We boarded for the flight across the Pacific Ocean to Tokyo, Japan. I wondered, as I boarded the plane, what had been wrong with the hydraulic system, and hoped that it truly had been fixed.

We took off and headed west over rocky, jagged, and frozen mountains on our way to the Aleutian archipelago. We had been in the air for about an hour and the captain came over the intercom and said,

"Gentlemen, we are experiencing another hydraulic problem and we are returning to Anchorage as a precaution. We first, however, will be dumping fuel."

Of course, he was going to dump the fuel because we were much too heavy to land safely. We probably would have blown the tires and slid off the runway, or worse. So, here we went again, back to Anchorage. The captain successfully dumped the fuel, got light enough to land the beast, and made a smooth, uneventful, landing back at Anchorage. We disembarked the aircraft and all of us waited for word from maintenance. After a couple of hours, they assured us that the problem had been solved this time and gave the aircraft a clean bill of health once again. I hoped that this time they were right but I wasn't convinced.

We once again all boarded and took off for Tokyo for a second time. The flight was to be several hours long, but that didn't bother me a bit. I knew that the clock had started running on my overseas, one year tour of duty in Vietnam the minute I left the States. Frankly, I didn't give a damn if it took a whole year to get there and we had to turn around and come back. It wouldn't have troubled me in the least. Like the sly old Peter Lisko, I never did relish the idea of people shooting at me every day trying to blow my brains out. What rational man would?

◆ ◆ ◆

When we got out over the Aleutian Islands, they looked beautiful to me from the air. Every so often one of them had a huge airport runway that I could easily see. The ocean waters of the Pacific changed colors from a deep blue to a lighter aqua color as they approached the island shores. As my eyes drifted to the horizon, I was awed by the size of this "peaceful" ocean, and wondered and thought that there were surely many sailors around the world that would beg to differ about the peacefulness of the watery beast.

Then I thought about *my father* and his life. His life was prematurely taken from him one night when I was thirteen years old. I heard him tell Mom that he didn't feel very good, and told her to go ahead to bed. He was going to stay up and read for a while. A couple hours later I heard a commotion downstairs, and went to investigate.

Dad was sitting on the couch unable to get his breath, with the local MD, Dr. Krajec, hovering over him giving him a shot of some sort. Dad was arguing with Doc, as he always did, about what the shot was. Dad had gone to chiropractic school some years before, and in those days, chiropractic and medicine mixed about as well as oil and water.

I remember as a kid that they used to sit down together at our kitchen table with a bottle of whiskey and argue about what the best approach to health care was. It was obvious to anyone observing them, even me, that both men admired and respected one another, but neither one of them would ever admit it. Their relation was about like the characters portrayed by Jack Lemmon and Walter Matthau in *Grumpy Old Men*. This night there was no playful banter. Doc called for an ambulance and Dad was taken to the hospital. I was scared to death.

In the hospital room he continued to fight for his life and they put him in an oxygen tent. That was the state of the art in small hospitals in 1960. My oldest brother took my other 15-year-old brother and me home at 3:00 in the morning to get a couple of hours sleep. When we walked in the next morning, the head nurse said, sympathetically:

"I'm sorry, but your father is gone."

That simple sentence was by far the most powerful sentence that I had ever heard. It annihilated a 13-year old me. Dad had died of a massive coronary just before we got there. As a matter of fact, his jaw started to move as we entered the room and I thought he was coming back to life.

But the doctor in charge said, "No, son. That's just muscle spasms."

I thought, the bastard, *how is he so sure?* But of course, he was right.

My dad was only 50, and I loved him with every fiber of my being. My world was completely shattered. Honestly, I never have completely gotten over it. I've just learned how to live with it. The open wound has healed, but a deep, deep, and painful scar remains, and I suppose it always will.

Dad had been in the Navy from 1925 through 1929, and had sailed the oceans. And that's what I was thinking about over the Aleutians. He had worked in the main gun turret on the battleship U.S.S. Florida when they made a several thousand mile cruise. He had gone to Rome and shook hands with the Pope of the time, whoever that was. He had also been to London and other European ports.

I wondered what he would think about me being on this airplane going to Vietnam as an army officer and helicopter pilot at the tender age of twenty one. I'm sure he would have endorsed my service to my country, but I'm not so sure that he would have endorsed the Vietnam War. I will really never know how he would have felt. I can only guess, but it's a shot in the dark.

I sat on that airplane thinking about Dad and his early life for at least three hours. I said nothing during this time. I was just in silent thought. I was brought back to reality by a scuffle between two troops, and I had to get out of my seat and go break it up.

After that, Vietnam loomed in my head and took center stage once again. Vinnie, Larry and I had no idea what to expect when we got there. We knew we would be assigned a company when we arrived in country. God knows where in Vietnam.

We didn't know if we would be flying in the treacherous mountains, or down in the Delta with its stifling heat. All of us knew that we would have to serve wherever they put us and do as we were commanded to do. One could only hope that you would get a lucky assignment and a fair company commander. We also knew our assignment was going to be the luck of the draw.

14.

Two Nights Out in Tokyo

We flew into Tokyo and the captain said we had been having hydraulic problems all the way across the Pacific, and he was getting damned tired of it. He said he was going to personally see to it that it was properly repaired in Tokyo, or he wasn't going to fly the damned thing. I didn't blame him. I was also getting damned tired of it. So was Vinnie and Larry and all the rest of the troops on board. *Could we get lucky enough to spend a night in Tokyo?*

We landed at Yokahamahemahoma Military Base or some damned thing that sounded like that, just outside of Tokyo. We settled in and dropped our bags and were told we were on our own until 0800 hours the next morning. That was fine with us. Like I said before, we knew the Tour of Duty (TOD) clock started ticking as soon as we left the States.

We were in dress green uniforms, or *class A dress*. They had a black stripe down the lateral aspect of the pant legs indicating we held an officer's rank, along with the WO1 bars and wings on our chest. We had on light beige shirts and a black tie under the green jacket that closed in the front with large brass colored buttons. This officer thing was new to us and we felt important.

The three of us hitched a ride into Tokyo for a night on the town.

Japan was an intriguing place, to say the least, for the three of us. We asked the driver of the military vehicle we were in, where we could go. He told us there were a few bars that the guys stationed there went to, and had Americanized somewhat.

We started with those.

As the beer started to flow once again, we began having a great time, and were temporarily lost from our future and our past. I was enamored with the fact that I was actually in Asia. I was just a kid from a small town in Illinois who had never been out of the United States. Indeed, I hadn't even been to very many of the states themselves. I didn't ask how Vinnie and Larry felt about it, but I suspect that they felt much the same.

After a night on the town, in our Americanized Japan, we hailed a cab and were taken back to the military base at Yokahamahemahoma. All three of us were sedated enough to sleep very soundly. You probably could have done major surgery on me with no additional anesthesia.

0800 hours came very early for us, but we dressed, made the curfew, and were taken to the airstrip only to be told that the aircraft would not be ready until the next day.

We were free until 0800 hours the next morning. *Fine by me. Tick, tock, tick!*

So, it was another night on the town with similar results. *History really can repeat itself.*

When we were awakened the next morning, we were placed on a military bus to take us to the aircraft. I sat in the very back and watched the Japanese, morning, commuter traffic. I couldn't believe how bumper to bumper it was. The locals were driving about twenty miles an hour over the speed limit and so close that they looked like boxcars on a train that were hooked together.

As I said, I was in the very back of the bus and there was a Japanese fellow behind us driving a small truck so close to us I couldn't see his bumper when I looked. A proven master of international hand signals, I started trying to get his attention, by placing my outstretched hands together at the palms, and separating them ever so slightly. This clearly signaled to him that he was only inches from the bus.

He saw me after a short time and kept looking at me curiously. After a couple miles of my hand signals we stopped for another light. He then pulled off behind us, got out of his truck, and started looking the front of it over to see what was wrong with it. Apparently, it didn't occur to him that I was concerned about his closeness. He thought I was trying to tell him something was wrong with the front of his vehicle. *It must have been the language barrier.* As we started rolling again when the light changed to green, he was still looking at his truck, scratching his head and obviously puzzled and perplexed. I guess he missed school the day they did international hand signaling.

When we arrived back at Yokahamahemahoma air strip, we were assured that this time the aircraft had been properly repaired. *Really? I sure the hell hope so.*

I saw that the troops were all there after taking a head count, which also surprised the hell out of me, so we boarded the aircraft for the final flight leg into Vietnam. *I wondered how many of us would not be alive to enjoy the flight home.*

When the captain announced that we were now over South Vietnam, I looked intently from my window seat at the landscape below us. I half expected to see RPGs (rocket propelled grenades) coming toward the aircraft.

The landing proved uneventful. On our long final approach the captain said that the hydraulics had apparently at last, been properly repaired. He then wished us all luck and told us to keep our heads down and cover each other's back. *Great advice from someone going right back to American soil. Thanks for the kind words.*

The aircraft landed and rolled to a stop. We had arrived at the place where history was being written, debated, cursed and praised. We were now going to war.

15

How Far North Will
The Bastards Send Me

Our plane landed in the southern part of South Vietnam near Saigon, at Long Binh Air Base by Bien Hoa. These were the flat lands, home of rice paddies near the delta that drained into the Mekong River, which flowed into the South China Sea. Even though it was the first part of October, it was still stifling hot when we disembarked and headed for a passenger reception area.

I half expected, as I waited for my baggage, rockets and mortars to impact the area, and a war-hardened sergeant to rush up and say, *"Why are you waiting for your baggage? You're not gonna live long enough to need it if you stand here with your thumb up your ass like this! Get your goddamned head down, you idiot."* Nor was it hard to imagine a human wave attack rolling across the runways. A few years before, I had seen a MAD Magazine piece where they took headlines from big newspapers and made parody sketches from them. One of the headlines was *Guerrillas Attack Over Plain of Jars.* The cartoonist had drawn this headline as a bunch of angry gorillas with clubs, running after fleeing humans over a field covered with Mason canning jars. It was hilarious at the time, but now it was hard to find the humor in it.

But no mortars, rockets or human wave attacks greeted us.

Vinnie, Larry and I, were then separated from the enlisted troops, and boarded a bus, which delivered us to a barracks to await our orders for assignment. The first thing I noticed was that the bus had thick, metal, cross hatch wire screens over all of the windows. It was obvious these were there to prevent people from throwing grenades or other homemade bombs called satchel charges into the vehicle. We were now in a war zone.

The next day, we still waited.

Vietnam was divided by the army into four corps from its southern tip to the demilitarized zone (DMZ) at its northern border with North Vietnam. To the extreme south was IV Corp, just to the north and still in the flats was III Corp, further to the North was the mountainous II Corp, and to the extreme north in the mountains was I Corp, commonly known as *Eye Corp*. North Vietnam, a communist country, led by Ho Chi Minh, was the country with whom we were at war. The American mission was supposedly to stop the communist aggression in the south, to prevent all the rest of Southeast Asia from falling to communism if South Vietnam fell. This was McNamara's Domino Theory. *So here we all were in Vietnam. I felt like my young life was the biggest domino of all.*

All three of us received orders. Vinnie and Larry were to report to Assault Helicopter companies somewhere, I believe, in the flatlands of III Corp. I, on the other hand, was to be flown by military transport to Nha Trang, further north on the coast of the South China Sea. I was to wait in Nha Trang for further orders. I said goodbye to Vinnie and Larry and wished them luck and they me. We promised to see each other again *back in the world* when our tours completed. They departed in their own directions and I flew to Nha Trang in a twin-engine Caribou fixed wing aircraft, along with several other soldiers, and in the finest military tradition, *waited some more.*

When I arrived at Nha Trang, I noticed how beautiful the South China Sea was as we made our final approach at the airfield. I thought it was a shame that a guy couldn't safely stroll down the beach and pick up seashells without getting shot. I was housed at a military base in Nha Trang and told that I would receive orders in a day or two. I hoped they would let me stay right there in Nha Trang as pretty as the place was but I knew that probably wasn't in my future.

That evening I sat out by the ramp and watched returning aircraft make their final approaches into the airfield. Most of them, by far, were Hueys, the aircraft that I was qualified to fly. Then all of a sudden I heard a very familiar sound unlike a Huey, and it was the old girl herself, an OH 23 Hiller. From the sound of the engine, I could tell that she was turbocharged. This was a method of increasing the horsepower of an internal combustion engine, by ramming more fuel down its throat. I understood immediately why they would do that, because in the heat of the tropics, the density altitude (DA) tended to get high and make aircraft less efficient flyers.

The DA is given as so many feet above sea level and if the DA is reported as 5,000 feet, then the aircraft thinks it's flying at 5,000 feet above sea level no matter what your actual elevation from sea level is. Since the DA tended to be high a lot in Nam, they would turbocharge the gasoline-powered aircraft quite often, to counteract the high DA by making the engines more powerful.

I watched the pilot fly her in, right over my head, and it took my mind back to my days at Fort Wolters, Texas. It was nice to see another familiar sight.

That night I went to the officer's club and had a couple of beers and was talking to some of the pilots stationed at Nha Trang. One of them asked me if I knew where I was going yet.

"No, man," I replied, "I don't have a clue. I'm waiting here for orders."

He said, "Just hope and pray they don't send your ass somewhere up in II Corp, in the Central Highlands. Some place like Holloway at Pleiku. Holloway's famous for having the distinction of getting mortared and rocketed more than any other place in Nam."

I said, "I wonder why that is?"

"It's because they're close to the tri border of Vietnam, Laos, and Cambodia. That means they're close to the Ho Chi Minh Trail, the major supply route of the North Vietnamese Army to the south. So they're always sending teams out to attack Holloway at night."

"So is Holloway an army post, for aviation companies, or what?"

He said, "Yea it's a pretty large base camp, and it's got several helicopter companies there. They're called Assault Helicopter Companies or AHCs. Usually each company has two slick platoons (troop deployment), and one gunship platoon (combat assault and fire support)."

"Do you know any of the pilots up there?"

"I know five or six guys up there. I feel sorry for the poor bastards. I understand that sometimes several nights in a row they get hit with the gook 122mm rockets. Those poor bastards are out in the trenches half the night with their rifles all the time. And they still have to fly all day the next day. There are no excuses."

Gooks and dinks were slang terms for the Vietnamese adopted for some reason.

I laughed, "Well, maybe I'll get lucky and get assigned with you guys here."

"Well don't get me wrong. It's no country picnic here either, but I'd take it any day over that fucking Holloway, or Kontum, or Dak To."

I went to bed that night fervently hoping I could stay at Nha Trang, near the coast. It was a rich, bustling French-accented city. If Vietnam could be as diverse and peaceful as Nha Trang, this country might be worth a war.

Bright and early the next morning I got orders to join the 119th AHC at none other than Camp Holloway in Pleiku. I saw the guy that I had talked to the night before at the officer's club and told him where I was going.

He shook his head, "You poor bastard you. Keep your fucking head down and good luck."

I got on the waiting C 130 Hercules and headed out.

It was Camp Holloway here I come. I had been told by another pilot just as I left that the 119th did a lot of flying in the Kontum, Dak To area.

Great! Just fucking great! Mark Garrison goes to Pleiku and Camp Holloway. How lucky can one man get? Holloway here I come! I had a feeling the clock was ticking a lot slower now than it had in Anchorage and Tokyo.

16

Hello Camp Holloway

The C 130 Hercules roared down the runway to the east as its four jet- powered propellers wound up to maximum RPM. We swung out over the South China Sea before heading north for a short stop at the coastal city of Qui Nhon. From there we headed west into the mountains of II Corp, Vietnam. We were slated to land at Pleiku Main (Play-Ku), a large air force base that had solid steel plate (SSP) runways. From there we were to be transported by military vehicle to Camp Holloway just a couple of clicks away (click was a slang term meaning 1000 meters). There was a squadron of air force Spad A1Es at Pleiku Main. These were just barely post WW2 piston driven propeller aircraft used for reconnaissance, but could also carry an impressive payload of armament.

After a relatively short flight, we landed at Pleiku Main without incident. The scenery on the way did not escape my attention; it grew more rugged and mountainous as we went.

We first had gained 2,000 feet and went over the An Khe Pass and followed Road 19, as it was called, into Pleiku, the land another 500 feet higher by the time we reached our destination.

As I got off the aircraft, the first thing I noticed was that it was a little cooler and less humid than the flatlands in the Delta. I was thankful for that. It was about time something went right.

A bus awaited those of us going to Camp Holloway. We boarded it and headed out without delay. The bus drivers knew not to delay. Rockets rained on this airport all the time. After a mile or so, we were in downtown Pleiku. The road through town was the facsimile of a badly potholed, paved road in the States that was in crucial need of repair. The businesses and buildings on both sides of the road were rather ramshackle. Most of the businesses had garage-door-like openings in the front and were simply pulled up when they were open or pulled down and locked when the business was closed.

I couldn't believe how many people there were. There were throngs of them. The streets looked as if there was no room for anyone else. People on bicycles were everywhere. It became an obstacle course for the driver, who honked his horn constantly. Many of the bicycles were fitted with a passenger seat on the front of it that was covered with a canopy. Some of these seats were equipped to carry two. There were also motorized vehicles, but these were easily outnumbered by the bicycles.

I asked the driver at that point if it was safe to drive through a Vietnamese city like this virtually unprotected. The driver, who was a buck sergeant, nonchalantly shrugged his shoulders and said,

"Aww, somebody takes a hit now and then," with a prominent southern drawl and tobacco juice dripping from his chin. "Usually it ain't too bad. Problem is, Sir, nobody knows who's who here in town. I mean to tell ya that some of these here folks are commie sympathizers, but they all look and dress the same so you can't tell which ones they are. And they're liable to shoot ya if they take a notion, by god! A feller don't ever wanna get caught down here at night, or they might just skin 'em."

Great, I thought. Here I was unarmed at this point riding through a town with a whole bunch of potential killers. *I feel better, thanks for the buildup, sergeant. Oh well, at least he was truthful.* I remained at the ready. If I was attacked I could throw my duffel bag at them.

The gates of Camp Holloway eventually appeared and looked a little bit like gates of heaven that day. St. Peter wasn't at the gate. The sergeant showed his pass to the heavily armed security guards and we were allowed entry. That also made me feel real good. It was nice to know that I would be living for a year in a place that required several armed-to-the-hilt soldiers to guard the gate.

The sergeant driver, upon request, told me where I could find the 119th. I thanked him for the ride and the comforting information that he had given me, and made my way to the 119th AHC, my new home.

A Spec Four was at the desk of the operations hooch when I walked in dead tired carrying my duffle bag.

"I'm WO1 Garrison reporting for duty, specialist," I said, as I handed him a copy of my orders. He glanced at them and said,

'Sir, we've been expecting you along with a few others. We're sure glad to get you, cause God knows we can use you. Do you want to come with me, Sir? The Major *himself* will want to welcome you to the finest AHC at Holloway." I followed him out of the hooch into another building. The Spec Four then asked me politely to please take a seat once we entered the company commander's hooch, and said he would be right back.

In just a few moments a tall, dark haired major with wings on his chest came from a doorway and greeted me.

"I want to welcome you, Mr. Garrison to the 119th Assault Helicopter Company. Believe me it's the finest bunch of pilots here at Camp Holloway," he said.

"As a matter of fact, you would be hard pressed to find a better bunch anywhere in the world." He then invited me into his office, and we had a friendly, informal chat. He was a very gregarious man who obviously had a lot of respect for the men in his command, and cared about them immensely. The name tag that was sewn on his fatigues said *Larkin*.

It was also apparent that Major Larkin would expect a high level of performance from me and anyone else in his command. Believe me, I felt the pressure immediately.

The major then told me after his welcoming chat, that the specialist would show me to the platoon's first flight of slick pilots, where I was to be assigned. A slick was a slang term meaning a troop deployment and resupply helicopter. Each AHC had two slick platoons or flights, and one gunship platoon. The pilots of the slicks were often called slick drivers, while the gunship pilots were known as gun pilots, gunnies, or Charlie Model Drivers.

The slick aircraft in our company was the UH1H model that was powered by a Lycoming, turbofan jet engine that generated 1,500 horsepower called a T-13. Its rotor blades had a chord (width) of 21 inches and were rather long. They were attached to a hub that fit over the main mast as part of a semi-rigid rotor head system. This meant that they were adequately capable of handling positive G loads, but not negative G loads. This is a way of saying that you didn't dare get the aircraft on its back, or you would probably blade chop the tail boom off, lose your center of gravity(CG) and fall out of the sky like a homesick brickbat. That's generally something you didn't want to do.

The payload of the aircraft (how much weight it could carry) was about 4,000 pounds, which translates into ten to twelve troops including the crew, and a full load of JP 4 jet fuel that weighed 1,600 lbs. The aircraft had a loaded cruise speed of eighty knots, but unloaded it would usually cruise at over 100 knots and still maintain its altitude.

The gunship pilots however flew a UH1C model, commonly known as a Charlie model that was equipped with a Lycoming turbofan jet engine that produced 1100 horsepower called a T-11. It had what is known as a 540 rotor system with a 27-inch chord of the blades, built more for speed and maneuverability. These aircraft took a lot of precision flying just to safely get them off the ground when they were loaded with rockets, ammunition, and a full 1,600 lbs of JP 4 jet fuel, because they were often underpowered. The gun pilots often complained about their lack of power. I might add, I would find out in a couple of months just why they were complaining.

The slick pilots had their hands full also. Getting in and out of tight landing zones with a full load, and a bunch of people shooting at you, took incredible concentration, nerves of steel, and awesome flying ability.

The Spec Four then took me to first flight's hooch, showed me to my quarters, and went his merry way, after saying, "Good luck, Sir." As he said it, I couldn't help but notice that he had an expression on his face that said I was going to need all the luck I could get.

PART THREE:
FLYING THE SLICKS

17

The Checkride and an Orientation to Combat Flying

My first order of business after being introduced to the other pilots, was a checkride with the company instructor pilot (IP). Every aviation company had an IP who gave checkrides to all incoming pilots to verify that they were, indeed, who they said they were.

Our IP for the 119th was a guy named Jet Jackson. He had jet black hair which is why, I believe, he picked up the nickname, Jet. The first thing he did was show me how to strap on a protective ceramic plate that covered the chest and abdomen from the front. This device was called a chicken plate by the pilots, and was designed to stop small arms fire from the enemy. He then handed me a flak vest and told me to put it on over the chicken plate. This vest was to absorb any shrapnel flying around in the cockpit during combat flight. He stressed again and again the importance of always wearing the plate and the vest if I wished to live through my tour of duty.

After I was properly dressed for combat, he had me do several maneuvers in the aircraft, from the simple to the complex, until he decided that I was qualified to safely fly the bird.

Each newcomer pilot to Vietnam was required to fly copilot with more experienced pilots who already knew the ropes. This was essential for several reasons. The experienced guys knew the terrain, the radio protocols, combat flying techniques, and a myriad of other things crucial to mission success.

However, there was a reason which overrode all other reasons. New pilots really didn't know how to fly yet, they just thought they did. In reality new guys like me only knew the very basics of flying.

A novice pilot straight out of flight school faced a very steep learning curve when he got to Vietnam. First of all, new pilots had to learn the art of mountain flight. There were no mountains where we trained in Texas or Alabama. The tire areas on the bluffs in Texas were challenging but they were not mountains. Those challenges were nothing compared to II Corp or I Corp flying in Vietnam. The wind currents in mountains can be difficult, to say the least. You have to understand and be able to anticipate the updrafts and downdrafts indigenous to mountains.

For instance, when you make an approach in a loaded UH1H to a fire base on a mountain ridge, you do it into the wind. What you have to be prepared for is an ensuing downdraft on your approach side of the ridge as the wind whips over the mountain. The pilot had damned sure better be ready for it and be coming in high enough and with enough reserve power to catch the aircraft's descent, or he will become one with the mountain and not in a zen-ful way. That's just one of many things that a mountain flyer has to be aware of. If he's not aware, he and everybody else on the aircraft may well go home through Grave's Registration in body bags.

Another thing that necessitates intensive in-country training from the senior pilots is the necessity of squeezing a chopper into very tight landing zones (LZ) especially with a bunch of enemy troops shooting at you. Sometimes there was only a few feet clearance for the spinning rotor blades before getting into trees, other helicopters, or God knows what.

For instance, dropping a four-man Long Range Reconnaissance Patrol (LRRP Team) into a deep, dark hole in the triple canopy jungle in Nam, when there was barely enough room for one chopper, and barely two- feet clearance of the blades on all sides, was, by no means, an easy feat. Again it was a hard job made even more treacherous when receiving enemy fire.

The North Vietnamese Army (NVA) soldiers were very crafty about it. If they were surreptitiously present on the ground at the LZ, while an insertion of troops was attempted, they would remain hidden until the helicopter was at least half way through its descent into the LZ. These often had top canopies more than 100 feet high, when they caught you half-way down they opened up with small arms fire. The reason they did this, was because they had learned that a fully loaded chopper in a descent in the mountains, often did not have enough reserve power to climb out without getting rid of some weight. In this case, the weight was the LRRP Team, so you had to continue your descent until the team jumped off, then you regained the necessary power to climb out again, all the while taking hits from AK-47s firing on full automatic.

Needless to say, these events could become very hairy, damned quickly.

Then, of course, there were the radios. The aircraft was equipped with three main communication radios. They were the UHF, the VHF, and the FM or Fox Mike, as it was known. The pilot had to learn how to operate these radios with competence, and be able to listen to and understand three conversations at once.

The UHF radio was used as a communication pathway between the slicks to coordinate their activities. The VHF was used between gunships, and the FM was used to talk to ground forces. It was often the case that during a mission someone would be talking on all three of these radios at once. It was imperative for the pilots to be able to decipher what was being said on every one of them. To say this was not an easy task for the novice to learn is to seriously understate the case.

When I first got there, the conversations would merge in my head and become an undecipherable jumble of nonsense. It took time to learn the radios, but it was an absolute necessity that you did. You had to catch and understand all of the traffic or someone might die.

A new guy also had to learn all the names of the various firebases that they would be resupplying. A firebase was an outpost, a lot of times on top of a ridge or summit in II Corp, but not always. Sometimes they were in the dales, or between mountain ranges in scrub lands.

They were called firebases because that's exactly what they were. They were bases that provided artillery fire to support friendly ground troops, or to fire on suspected or known enemy strongholds.

These bases usually had howitzer artillery pieces in four sizes, ranging from 105 mm, 155mm, and 175mm. They also often had what are called 8 inch-mobiles. These were 8-inch diameter artillery tubes mounted on a tank-like vehicle with treads. Mobility was the key to warfare in Vietnam and these booming bitches could rock and roll around the fire base to more easily fire in every direction. The 175mm guns were also usually tracked but were less mobile because they had a long barrel that shot a big shell up to 26 miles. Friction heat was a problem in these field artillery units; the barrels had to be discarded after about 300 fires. The 175's were special project guns.

Incidentally there was also another artillery weapon which took up some air space. She was the USS New Jersey. Because of the mountainous terrain we didn't hear much out of her but it was said of her that she could set 10 miles off the coastline and drop a shell into the mouth of a cave or tunnel system in the middle of the country. The Viet Cong and NVA loved caves and tunnels and when the Jersey spoke, Charlie scattered.

All this talk about artillery brings up another thing that new pilots had to learn in a combat zone. That is this. You didn't dare fly anywhere until you called Artillery Advisory to find out where and when they were firing. You were given the call sign and radio frequencies for the various fire bases, and the prudent pilot would call them and ask for an artillery advisory before entering their area. A radio call would go something like this,

"Tall House Charlie, Tall House Charlie, this is Crocodile 2, ready to enter your area from the south heading 345 degrees, at 3,000 feet absolute, artillery advisory, please, over."

Tall House Charlie (the fire base) would come back with something like,

"Roger that Crocodile 2, firing to coordinates Nancy Papa 27184, about five clicks, max ord 1,500 feet, over."

Then you would courteously reply,

"Roger that, Tall House Charlie, thank you, out."

With that information you knew exactly where they were firing, and what the parabolic curve of the outgoing artillery round was, and thus you knew how to stay clear of it. By 1969, field artillery batteries were almost always equipped with a computer the troops called Freddy FADAC (Field Artillery Directional Accuracy Control). These centers were usually located in big below ground bunkers in the middle of the LZ. When an LZ was overrun by a ground attack the guys in the hole could count on having satchel charges dumped on them.

Field artillery was usually pretty accurate but since the guns themselves still had to be positioned manually, based on a verbal command from the FDC (Fire Direction Center), it was not unheard of for a gun to get off coordinates and a friendly fire accident to occur. Friendly fire deaths were more common than the U.S. Army would like to admit. It was just one more flying hazard for pilots to contend with.

As a pilot, one thing that you definitely didn't want to do is get hit by one of those big exploding bullets coming from a fire base. *It would ruin your whole day, for sure, no doubt about it.*

Yet another thing the new pilot had to learn was how to fall seamlessly into an operation when you had just arrived, and didn't know the idiosyncrasies of the mission. The more seasoned pilots had been through it many times before and it was old hat to them.

But, it was all new to you, the new guy. Sure, you had been trained in flight school about the basics of combat missions, but every unit had developed their own procedures and methods that they employed and you weren't yet familiar with them.

With all of the things that I knew I was expected to learn, and learn quickly, I went to bed that night with a lot on my mind. I was slated to fly my first mission with a man called Cowboy, a slick driver that got his name because of his antics with the aircraft. But, some of the other pilots told me not to worry, that he was a damned good pilot, one of the best in the business.

I thought he better know what he's doing. We'd just had the briefing about tomorrow's mission. Intelligence reports from a LRRP Team indicated that a large number of NVA forces were moving toward an American infantry company of more than two hundred men.

Our job tomorrow was to get them out of harm's way. We would begin shortly after daybreak.

18.

Back to the Wakeup Call

So that's how I got into this mess, folks.

As I sat there in the aircraft, my head was spinning. I really didn't think that I had a shot in hell of living through a year of what I had just been through.

My mind flashed back to the kid with the blown off leg, that we had left at Pleiku's medical pad. I wondered if he was alive or dead. If he was dead I secretly wondered what greater cause he had died for.

I unbuckled myself from the seat, stepped out of the aircraft, and caught up with Cowboy, who was headed back to the first flight hooch.

The slick pilots in the 119th were called Alligators. The gunship pilots, on the other hand, were known as the Crocodiles, or simply the Crocs. I was told when I got there that you had to be a crazy bastard to fly gunships. Right then I was thinking that you had to be a crazy bastard to fly slicks.

We had parked the aircraft in a revetment, a U-shaped structure made from SSP and sandbags, to protect the ship from mortar and rocket shrapnel. There were dozens of helicopters there in row after row, that branched off a main runway at an angle, that looked sort of like a Christmas tree from the air, so that's what it became known as, the Christmas tree.

When I caught up with Cowboy I asked, "That shit that just went on today, does that happen a lot?"

"It happens too often for my taste," Cowboy said. "The problem is a guy never knows when it's going to happen. It always seems to catch you by surprise."

He continued, "You might go a week or two without even knowing they're shootin' at you, then bang, here we go again. Shit like today."

My thoughts: *Goddamn it, a whole week or two without even knowing people are trying to blow your fucking head off. That's really great. I mean, they're shootin at you big time but you just can't see them. Hell! I felt better already.*

When Cowboy and I got back to the company area we found out three aircraft had been damaged by small arms fire and mortar shrapnel, ours included.

In addition, another pilot, a crew chief and two door gunners had been wounded.

At that news, Cowboy exclaimed, "Shit! I was supposed to park that aircraft at the maintenance hangar so that they could patch it up."

"Well, to hell with it," he said.

"If they can't fix it where it sits, I'll move it for them."

Just then Bob Vickrey walked in. Bob was a good friend of mine that I'd gone through flight school with.

"Bob, what the hell are you doing in this God forsaken place, you crazy bastard?" I said, "Don't you know this place is hard on your health?"

Bob looked at me, smiled, and said, "Well I'll be damned. How the hell are you Mark?" It was always good to meet a friend when you were in a combat zone.

"It sure is good to finally run into somebody I know. Are you assigned to the 119th?"

"Yea, I guess I just got lucky," I said. "What about you?"

"Me too. So here I am in the flesh," he said with a shake of the head.

"Were you out there today, Bob?"

"Yep, I flew with a guy they call Baby Huey. That got pretty wild for a while."

"You can say that again," I replied. "I was beginning to think that I wasn't going to live through my first mission."

He said, "I had doubts myself. Damn, I hope every day is not like that."

Bob was a super nice guy and I liked him. He was from a rather prominent family in Dallas, Texas and had enlisted in flight school just like I had when the army was about to draft him.

He was about four years older than me and had been married to a girl that did Chrysler Motor commercials on television, and she was known as the *Dodge Rebellion Girl*. She was a beautiful blonde gal. Bob was divorced from her and was now single.

I asked him what happened one night over several beers and he said,

"Hell, I was a fool, Mark. I'd go downtown in Dallas and get knee-walkin' drunk and call her to come and get me. Then when she'd ask me where I was I'd tell her I was at the corner of *walk and don't walk*, or some crazy shit like that and hang up."

"Did she ever remarry?" I asked.

"Yea, she married again about a year after we divorced."

"Damn, Bob, I think that would bother me, as good looking as she is." We were now talking intensive personal shit.

"Nahhhh, hell, it don't bother me at all. Her layin' there in bed with him and having sex. That son of a bitch. Nahhhh, it don't bother me none. That no good greasy bastard!"

I absolutely belly laughed when he said that and so did he. He had a great sense of humor about life and I like to think I did too. It looked like we were both going to need to generate all the laughter we could to get through what we had facing us for the next year.

Virtually all the pilots in Vietnam were assigned nicknames by the other guys. Maybe it was based on the way you looked, talked, and carried yourself or whatever.

Once the nickname was assigned it was irrevocable, whether you liked it or not. You didn't dare squawk your discontent about it either, unless you wanted to be subjected to relentless and unmerciful razzing about it.

I had just arrived, so they hadn't figured me out enough yet to assign a nickname. But I knew it was bound to come sooner or later.

Some of the nicknames were based on surnames. The slick pilots Clemmons, Samson, and Klemizewski became Clem, Sam and Ski respectively. Cowboy got his because of the way he flew. Lieutenant Burke got the nickname Stoney, because of a rodeo rider character on TV in the early 1960's. Then we had a British-American CO named Harris who had been involuntarily dubbed, "Tea and Crumpets."

There was also Martin Givens, nicknamed high pockets, because he was about six feet and three inches tall, and was all legs and no torso. There was a Croc, nicknamed Elmer Fudd, for reasons that ought to be easy to figure out by now. Then there was another Croc, Richard Gill, who was called Rick, but became Waldo when he grew a walrus-type mustache.

A little later that evening the platoons gathered in their respective hooches for the briefing on the next day's missions. A clear plastic board with grease pencil writing was posted which told you your aircraft number and who you were flying with the next day. The board also stated your destination and mission type. This was to be further verified at the operations hooch in the morning when you dropped by on your way to the Christmas tree, and picked up a mission paper. The written instructions provided the radio frequencies, call signs, etc. of those you would be contacting.

The board said Garrison was to fly with Baby Huey on firebase resupply missions all day.

Good deal! That should be a little less hairy than evacuating a company of soldiers about to be overrun by a few hundred hostile enemy troops.

19.

Learning to Fly in the Mountains

I couldn't sleep so I went to the flightline (Christmas tree) before 0600 hours and beat everyone to the aircraft. I started my preflight check, and was about a third of the way through it, when I heard the aircraft's crew chief coming.

He cheerily said, "Good morning, Sir. It's a rare event for me to get beat to the aircraft in the morning, Sir. Are you new to the 119th?"

I said, looking at his name on his uniform, "Yes, I am, Simms. Yes, I am. That was quite a first flight initiation I got yesterday during that extraction."

Simms laughed and said, "I understand that, Sir. Things tend to get exciting around here pretty often. But if things go as planned, this should be a quieter day. Just resupply the firebase guys, you know."

"Well, Simms, that would suit me just fine."

"Me too," he replied, "I don't like the gooks parting my hair with their AKs much myself."

"Have they come that close to you, Specialist?" Simms was a Spec 5.

"Yes, Sir," he said taking off his olive drab baseball-style military cap. "You see this, Sir?" He pointed to a straight white scar right where he parted his hair.

I said, "You have got to be kidding me?"

"No Sir, that AK round took my helmet right off and creased my scalp right down the part line."

"My God, man, I'm certainly happy that you're alright. How long ago did that happen?"

"About six months ago," he replied, "The worst thing about it is that it itches like crazy. Especially at night, and it keeps me awake."

"Dare I ask where this happened, Specialist?"

He smiled, "Out at one of the firebases we'll be resupplyin' today, Sir. I think it was just a stray round. Nobody ever did figure out where it came from."

I immediately thought about Cowboy mentioning all the people shooting at you all the time that you couldn't even see or hear. It definitely wasn't a very comforting thought.

We had finished the preflight by the time Baby Huey got there. So he, as the aircraft commander, got into the left seat and strapped in as I got in the cockpit's right seat.

In the civilian world, the aircraft commander flies from the right seat in a helicopter and from the left seat in a fixed wing aircraft. In Vietnam combat slick pilots flew command from the left seat, because they were always flying into very tight areas, and they needed all the visibility they could get through the chin bubble and the instrument panel was skewed to the right. This obstructed their view somewhat from the right seat. Gunship pilots, on the other hand, followed the civilian tradition, and flew command from the right seat, because they didn't generally fly into tight LZs.

The crew chief, Simms, got in the back on one side and the door gunner climbed in the other. I was off on another mission.

A Huey has a four-man crew, consisting of the pilot or aircraft commander, the copilot or *Peter Pilot*, as he was known in Vietnam, the crew chief, and the door gunner. The crew chief takes care of the ship, and a good one knows everything about her. It was considered a real blessing to be assigned an aircraft that had a great crew chief, because your life depended on him. The door gunner was just what the term implies.

In a slick, there were two tripod mounted M60 machine guns capable of firing 550 rounds a minute each. This meant that the guns were capable of putting out 1100 rounds a minute, or close to 20 rounds per second. That may seem like a lot of firepower, but as you will see later, these ships were virtually unarmed when compared to a Charlie Model Gunship.

Baby Huey told me to crank the aircraft and take it out of the revetment.

I yelled "CLEAR," to warn anyone nearby, and pulled the start trigger on the collective, after turning on the battery and the fuel. I closely watched the exhaust gas temperature (EGT) to be sure it did not redline, and did not stay in the yellow caution zone for more than the few seconds allowed. If you allow a runaway EGT it can crack the hot end of the jet engine and it inherits a RED X condition in the log book and becomes unflyable at that point; if regulations are followed, that is.

If rockets and mortars are chasing you down the runway, the pilot, if he's got any common sense, will say to hell with the EGT and get the hell off the ground and out of harm's way as fast as he can. If not under fire, the rules are usually followed.

Once EGT stabilized, I wrapped the power on with the throttle on the collective pitch control and it automatically came to the operating RPM of 6,600 (engine) and 326 rotor RPM with the needles joined. I then slowly raised the collective to put pitch in the blades to give the ship lift, and a little aft cyclic so she wouldn't drift forward as I picked her up. I came to a three-foot hover, and gave it more aft cyclic and left pedal to keep the nose centered, and backed out of the revetment. Once the revetment was cleared, I added right pedal to make a right turn and headed out to the runway and ask the tower for clearance to take off. Permission to take off was granted, and we departed to the south.

We picked up a full load of C Rations (canned food) and other things at a supply depot near Holloway, and took off to the east, northeast for our first firebase resupply.

It was about a thirty minute flight and Baby Huey took the aircraft and said:

"Mark, I'll demonstrate the first approach and set her down on the pad at the firebase for us. The winds are shifty up here, and a good way to gauge them is to look for which way the smoke is blowing, from the little fires they seem to have constantly burning on the firebase."

"Judging by what I've seen so far," I replied, "I'm inclined to ask how likely it is to get shot at on our way in and out of these things."

Baby Huey said, "Usually not, but what are you worried about a little thing like that for anyway? You're gonna have your hands full just flying this thing."

I thought, yea, but it seems to me that a guy's hands would be even fuller with hot lead coming through the cockpit.

Huey then said, "Don't worry, if we get shot at we'll call the gunships in to clean things up for us. We always try to call in the Crocs. We know all those guys and they know us. Besides, they're the best there is, and they're always lookin' for something to do." He then laughed before continuing. "Those Croc bastards will put their rockets and miniguns right on the bad guys. Sometimes they're so close to you that you swear they're gonna put a pair right up your ass. But that's what you call good fire support, man."

When we got the firebase in sight, there was smoke from a fire drifting rapidly to the west, so Baby Huey set the aircraft up on an easterly final approach. On long final, he said:

"Now the wind is pretty damned strong up here today as you can tell by how that smoke's flat movin' out, probably twenty knots or better. So we're gonna have to figure out how we're gonna make the approach."

He continued with his explanation, "There's two conventional ways to do it. First of all, you have to be aware of the fact that as that wind whips over the mountain, it's gonna hug our approach side of the mountain most likely, and become a downdraft. So we can either come in low and hot, or high and slow. If we come in low with some airspeed we can use that energy to flare and counteract the downdraft. On the other hand, we could come in higher and slower and try to stay out of the downdraft altogether." He paused to adjust the controls then continued,

"The problem with coming in high is you don't have any airspeed energy to bleed off at the bottom to catch your descent, and you're gonna need a lot of power at the end."

"Now, with this old girl that I've been assigned as my own, 217, there's no problem either way, cause she's got all kinds of power." 217 was the tail number of the aircraft that he had been assigned.

"With that in mind, I'm gonna bring her in high and slow. We'll have plenty of power to stop her at the bottom." He then set up a steep final approach to the pad on the firebase and started our descent while I closely observed him.

We were descending at about a thousand feet per minute with no more than twenty knots of forward airspeed.

I remember thinking at the time that I hoped the damned engine didn't flame out (quit). I wasn't sure we had enough altitude or airspeed to recover and keep from augering into the side of the mountain.

Baby Huey was undeterred.

At the bottom, he pulled power, slowed the descent, and made an exceptionally smooth landing right on the pad. In other words, he nailed the approach. And, by the way, he was right. His aircraft did seem to have a lot of power.

He then said, as the aircraft was being unloaded by ground personnel,

"I tell you, Mark, this old girl's quite a beast. If you can get a load on this thing, I don't care if it's lead, I can take off and land with it."

It was resupply all day to various firebases, broken up only by shutting down the aircraft at noon for a few minutes at Dak To.

Dak To was a large firebase encampment just to the east of Big Mama, a mountain summit so named because it was shaped like a woman's breast. It had an officer's club, a mess hall, an aircraft POL dump (petroleum, oil and lubricants) where you could refuel, and several hundred troops, along with a north/south PSP (perforated steel plate) aircraft runway.

The bad guys (NVA) had a nasty habit of lobbing mortars and rockets into the place frequently. It was just one of the perks of being stationed there. One we Americans didn't much care for. I learned a lot about mountain flying that day with Baby Huey, and got my feet wet by bringing the aircraft in and flying it out of firebases. I was beginning to realize that this is where I would *really* learn to fly.

I hadn't seen a tracer fly by all day to remind me of all the people that may be shooting at me that I couldn't see. *That was fine by me. I needed no visual verification.*

20

Life in the Hooch

We got back to Camp Holloway at about 1800 hours, after logging eight solid hours of flight time. My respect for the UH1H Huey was growing by the day. *She was a real workhorse.*

There was a mess hall at Holloway for the 119th, but hardly any of the guys ever ate there. Dinner was generally several cold beers and canned food from the Post Exchange (PX), which was just a few yards away from our hooch.

The company's pilot quarters (hooches) were ramshackle affairs consisting of a tin roof, and sandbagged walls coming half way up, and screen finishing the wall's top half. The tin roof had numerous tar patches all over it to repair past mortar shrapnel damage. There was no need for glass windows because it was never cool enough to need them. Mortars and rockets would have broken them out sooner or later anyway. Flying glass is almost as dangerous as shrapnel.

In the center of the building was a relatively large lounge area, where the pilots would congregate after the day's missions. This lounge had a refrigerator, a bar, an electric hot plate, and other basic amenities for everyone's general use. The refrigerator was almost always kept chocked full of cold beer from the PX.

On each end of the hooch were front and back doorways that led to hallways which communicated with the central lounge and the outside. On each side of the hallways were small private rooms for each pilot. I guess you could say private, that is. The rooms had only doorways and no doors, but most of the occupants nailed up an army issue green wool blanket for a modicum of privacy.

The pilots respected each other's private space and would generally knock on the wall beside the blanket, and wait for a "come in" from the occupant before entering.

The rooms themselves were no larger than a medium sized prison cell in America. On one wall was a bunk, on another was a small desk for writing letters home, etc., and on another was a small wardrobe, if you could call it that, for uniforms, boots and things. The rooms were separated by thin plywood walls.

Above the beds was a shelf full of state-of-the-art stereo equipment, if the pilot had been in country long enough to acquire it from the PX down the street. Most everyone would eventually buy a seven inch reel to reel tape recorder, a nice turntable like the British made Gerard SL-95, or something similar, and humongous speakers, sometimes four of them. It could get quite loud in the hooch.

Some of the most popular brand names of the recorders were led by Akai, followed by Panasonic, etc. Powerful amplifiers for the systems, such as the Kenwood 240 X, were popular as well, to deliver eardrum bursting music to the evening hour's drunken pilots. Popular brands of speakers were Sansui and Pioneer to name a couple.

I wasn't married and had no family to support at home, save for my brother, Gary, who was an aeronautical/astronautical engineering major at the University of Illinois at Champaign-Urbana. I sent him a little money every month so he could stay in school and not wind up where I was. It was a loan. That left me with extra cash to blow on stereo systems and another hot item, cameras.

The PX saw to it that they had a great selection of state of the art, single lens reflex (SLR) cameras on hand, from Nikons to portrait cameras like the over and under, dual lens Yashica. Indeed, there was a darkroom bunker set up at Holloway where we could develop, enlarge, and print black and white film that we had taken. We couldn't do color film, because we didn't have the precise temperature control needed to properly develop it. While I was in Nam, I wound up buying a nice Canon rangefinder camera and a Pentax Spotmatic SLR with a 1: 1.4 lens.

Most important of all was the canned food at the PX that everybody stocked up on so you could eat at your own time and leisure right in the hooch, instead of hiking to the mess hall at prescribed times and some distance away. You could buy Campbell soups, kippered snacks, tuna, crackers, other canned meats, sardines, Chef Boyardee spaghetti and meatballs and other quick meals. These were always in demand.

You could also buy all the beer and liquor you wanted, and nobody was checking IDs. A case of beer was a couple of bucks and a quart of Seagram's VO was four dollars. A quart of 12-year-old blended Chivas Regal scotch was five dollars.

And a lot of it flowed.

Each evening someone from the operations hooch (op hooch) would come to each of the flights and write the next day's assignments on the grease board. Often this would be accompanied by a briefing on the missions when it was something other than simple resupply.

This board information gave you the aircraft number you were to fly, who you were flying with, and where you were to report.

The copilot, or Peter Pilot, as he was affectionately called, would go to the flightline on the Christmas tree and preflight the aircraft the next morning. This preflight was probably unnecessary in most cases, because the aircraft's crew chief was usually very good about seeing to it that his bird was airworthy. After all, he was flying with us and would have been putting himself at risk if he did a shoddy job. Still, the more eyes the better on a preflight check. It's easy to miss something that the next guy might catch.

So many things can go wrong with a helicopter we made our own definition of a helicopter in Vietnam. It went like this:

hel·i·cop·ter [hel-i-kop-ter,]
noun

> 1. a collection of one hundred thousand complicated parts, flying in loose formation, built by the lowest bidder.

21.

A Hot Insertion

I was to fly with Cowboy again on a hot mid-November day. I had been with the 119th for about six weeks now, and I was starting to get the hang of all the *dos and don'ts* of mountain flying, or so I thought. The mission board said that we were to pick up a nearby LRRP team and take them out and drop them somewhere in the damned triple canopy jungle.

Triple canopy jungle has three major growth levels of trees. The first level reaches a height of about 25 to 30 feet, and the tops form a sort of canopy. The second level is taller, and reaches to about 50 to 60 feet before it canopies. The last and tallest growth of trees may reach, in places, over a hundred feet high, before it forms the top and final canopy.

There was a chase ship at altitude to come after us if possible and if something happened to take us down. A light fire team, consisting of two Crocs flying Charlie Models, was to escort us and give us fire support if needed. The chase ship dove and made a low pass, dropping a smoke grenade on, what I thought was an ungodly small hole in the jungle, marking the area of the LRRP insertion.

Cowboy appeared unfazed by it all. The chase ship climbed back to a couple thousand feet as we made our approach to the smoke marker, a seemingly microscopic insertion point.

◆ ◆ ◆

A lot of times when secrecy was not required, the gunships would prep the LZ with rockets and minigun fire as a precaution. This time, however, we were trying to attract as little attention as possible for the sake of the LRRP team. Remember LRRP's were supposed to see and not be seen, to hear and not be heard.

Cowboy and I made the approach to the area, and came to a hover over a hole in the jungle that I swore didn't have room for half a Huey, let alone a whole one. When we stabilized, Cowboy lowered pitch and started down into the deep, dark hole. It didn't look to me like we had two feet clearance on the blades, and I was as nervous as a whore in church. The door gunner and crew chief were talking earnestly to Cowboy, saying:

"About two feet tail rotor clearance on the left, Sir. Whoa, whoa, you're out of room, Sir!"

Then from the right backside,

"No more room back, Sir. Only about a foot on the right."

In the front, it didn't look to me like we had any room to spare at all. It looked as if the blades would strike the trees at any moment, and we would go down in a fiery ball. I glanced at Cowboy. I had never seen such intense concentration on a man's face in my life. He was staring straight ahead and glancing down through the chin bubble. We were now half way down at an altitude above the jungle floor of about fifty feet. The light faded, getting dimmer and dimmer as we descended.

Then, just when I thought that things couldn't possibly get worse, they did. Things got a lot worse. It became a descent into Hell itself. Without warning, the whole LZ lit up with enemy, automatic bursts of AK47 fire, and it seemed all of Hell escaped its gates. Rounds were hitting the aircraft now, with that all too familiar slapping ping sound. One round came through the Fox Mike Radio that set between Cowboy and I, knocking it out, and then exited through the ceiling plexiglass panel in the cockpit.

Cowboy screamed in the UHF Radio:

"Receiving heavy fire!! Receiving heavy fire!! Nine o'clock! Nine o'clock! Right on LZ perimeter!!!" Both the door gunner and crew chief had already opened up with the tripod-mounted M60s with suppressive fire. Hot brass casings flew all over the aircraft. The LRRPs on board opened up with their M16s and more casings flew, two of them lodging under my shirt collar and descending onto my bare back, burning my flesh, as I flinched forward thinking once again, that this time, I had been shot for sure.

We were still at about 30 feet altitude and it was too high for the LRRPs to jump. As I have previously mentioned, the enemy troops had learned to wait silently and hidden until the aircraft was half way down in the LZ. They knew we would not have the power to pull out until we got rid of some weight, in this case, the LRRPs. If Cowboy had tried to pull out, he would almost certainly have run out of left pedal, lost our directional control, spun the tail rotor into the trees, and crashed to the ground, probably in a ball of flames. The NVA would have barbecued us for dinner that night.

This time, however, the kill-happy NVA had apparently not considered that there were two fully armed Crocodile Gunships quietly lurking above them, having no reservations at all of blowing all their asses away if they misbehaved. And the NVA had, indeed, misbehaved.

Out of the blue, huge explosions from the Croc gunship rockets, clobbered the nine o'clock position. I remembered what Baby Huey had said. The Crocs had, indeed, damned near put a pair of rockets right up our asses.

Cowboy continued the descent and LRRPs jumped, guns blazing. Even with several, gun-toting enemy troops right on the ground before them, they thought it safer on the ground than to remain with us on the helicopter. Suddenly we had the power to escape and began the climb out. As we began our ascent, the explosions were followed by a constant stream of minigun fire at the rate of 80 rounds per second, right on top of the enemy position. Every fifth round was a phosphorous tracer that burned brightly and it looked as if the flow of them was solid. In reality there were four rounds between every tracer that you couldn't see.

As we climbed to the top of the trees, I swear I got a glimpse of Waldo's, walrus mustache as he roared by. He broke left in a steep turn as his wingman's rockets poured out even more punishment to the NVA beneath him while covering his break. The chase ship told the LRRPs to make their way, without being seen, to an alternate landing area about five clicks away for pick up. After all, the question had already been answered about whether there were NVA troops in the area.

As we left the area to return to Holloway, Waldo and his wingman had apparently decided that the bad guys hadn't had enough yet. They were still pounding them unmercifully when we pulled out of sight.

**UH-1C (Charlie Model) gunship
equipped with rockets and miniguns.**

**UH-1H (Slick) driving a ladder extraction. This was done
when a team had to be evacuated quickly and there was
no hole to be found in the dense jungle. These soldiers
were holding on to the ladder in flight.**

22.

Pondering It All

That evening when Cowboy and I got back, he started acting like I had been successfully initiated, and was rapidly becoming one of them. He had been in Vietnam for about eleven months and was due to rotate back to the States in a month. That meant he had only about two more weeks left to fly, since they didn't expect a pilot to fly the final two weeks before he went home. It would have been a shame for a guy to get killed when he was such a *short-timer*.

"Damn, Cowboy, why don't you see if you can quit flying these hot assed missions," I protested. "It would be a damned shame if something happened to you now. Why don't you see if you can do some VIP missions or something? You know, where you fly a few generals around. You know damn good and well they're not going to get close to any combat."

"Nah, I'll stick it out," he said. "If I don't fly it somebody else is gonna have to. That wouldn't be fair to them. I can't wait to get out of here, though. That damn hot LRRP insertion shit got old a long damned time ago."

He then said with just a drip of melancholy, "I really miss my wife. I can't wait to throw my arms around her. This Vietnam thing has been harder on her than me, I think. That is, judging by her letters to me."

"I can't imagine being married and over here," I admitted. "That must really be a bummer, man. At least I don't have a wife at home to worry about me."

I knew right then, that night as I lay in my bunk, that I wanted to be a Crocodile. Not that I didn't respect the Alligator slick pilots.

I had the utmost respect for all of them. I just didn't think I liked going into those hot LZs and feeling so damned helpless. I rubbed burn ointment on my hurting neck and back caused by the hot brass casings earlier in the day.

Yea, there was no doubt about it. I wanted to be able to shoot back.

23.

The Perimeter

We all hated the night attacks at Holloway. Not only were they scary and life threatening, they were a pain in the ass.

A siren blew an intermittent alarm if an attack was expected. If it blew a constant steady alarm, an attack was imminent or had already started. In the fall of 1968, there was always the possibility of a ground attack, and you would sometimes find yourself in a trench on the perimeter of Holloway defending the compound with your rifle in hand and your steel pot (helmet) on.

Another thing you learned very quickly was the difference in sound between an outgoing artillery round and an incoming round. The outgoing had a single syllable BAM sound, whereas the incoming enemy rocket or mortar had a two syllable sound of KA----BOOOMMM!

On the perimeter, every few meters, there was a guard shack occupied by two soldiers. They were usually privates, corporals, spec fours, or sometimes buck sergeants. Their job was to keep a lookout for any enemy activity within eyesight or earshot.

The guard shacks were equipped with two M60 machine guns, along with the two soldier's M16 automatic weapons and a stockpile of hand grenades. The shacks were made of sand bags and wooden or bamboo beams and were on wooden stilts as well. This lifted them up above ground level and gave the occupants a better visual field.

A few meters distant from the perimeter's barbed wire fence, out in, *No Man's Land,* were Claymore mines. These were powerful, anti-personnel land mines that had a directional charge. They were usually rather flat, round, and half buried, with the blast pointed at any insurgents who would crash the party uninvited. There was a wire leading back to the soldiers in the guard shack, with a detonation button on the end of it. NVA sappers or Viet Cong were expert at very silently low crawling through the coils of concertina wire protecting the perimeters of American fortifications, large and small. One of their favorite ploys was to dig up and reverse Claymore mines which were set to blow toward the perimeter when detonated. Knife-in-teeth, these stealthy infiltrators would carefully dig up these mines and reposition them so the killing force was aimed directly at the men who would detonate them. These incursions were usually precursors of a ground attack. When a ground attack began and the guards detonated the Claymore, they would blow themselves away. The wiped out guard post(s) provided a clear opening for a rushing ground attack.

Sappers had patience and nerves of steel. *You have to give them that!* Americans were equally resolved to prevent ground attack penetrations. When the alarms sounded, officers and enlisted men alike, manned their combat gear, grabbed their weapons and reported to the trenches to keep out the infiltrators.

Also on our perimeter, regularly spaced throughout, were the deadly, quad 50 machine guns. These lethal bastards consisted of a steel rack that had four 50 caliber guns attached. The guns mounted on a pivot assembly that the gunner could sweep from side to side, and focus fire on the whole area in front of him. A quad 50 was basically an anti-aircraft and anti-armor gun that was adapted to this use with intent to mow down dozens, even hundreds, of insurgents at a time and neutralize a ground attack of any size. Quads had a slow fire rate, so four of them were used together to defeat that liability.

The army took staying awake at the guard shack very seriously. In days gone by, in previous wars, soldiers manning the perimeter could face a firing squad for falling asleep on guard duty. After all, the army reasoned, there had to be a strong deterrent to a guard's tendency to *let down his guard* on nights when nothing was apparently happening. A sleepy (or sleeping) guard shack could allow a perimeter breach to occur, and the whole compound would be at risk. This laxity has to always be strongly discouraged.

24.

The Night Duty Officer

A military officer that outranked the personnel in the shacks, would be appointed to be the night duty officer. This included the pilots. His job was to make the rounds on the perimeter every so often, unannounced, and see that everything was in order. It wasn't too bad to be assigned this duty, because you got the next day off from flying, and you wouldn't have to dodge AKs and rocket propelled grenades (RPGs). You could sleep in.

The Night Duty Officer stayed in a command bunker in the compound between perimeter inspections and kept a logbook of the night's activities. He had a jeep at his disposal to inspect the perimeter. He was to do that every hour or so. This command bunker was mostly buried and made of sandbags. It was about the size of a prison cell. In the bunker was a makeshift desk, communication radios and a few military, army green, metal wardrobe like containers. These were filled with weapons and ammunition and so forth. These containers were individually known as a Connex.

Sharing the bunker—and night duty—were the ubiquitous rats. *Huge ass rats they were!* They would run from one Connex to the other and hide beneath them.

One night, having been appointed as Night Duty Officer, a large rat ran from under one of these containers, slammed into my boot, reared up on its back legs, and started squealing at me. It *really* pissed me off.

I thought: *"You son of a bitch, I give you the run of the place, and you still don't know your manners.* At that, as the rat scurried underneath one of the Connexes, I drew my weapon; a 45 caliber pistol just like the one Vickrey had had an unpleasant encounter with, and squeezed off two successive rounds.

I missed the rat, but I didn't miss the metal Connex. One of the rounds ricocheted, and barely missed my head. I could tell by the whizzing sound as it brushed by my left ear, at a speed that was only slightly subsonic. I put the pistol back in its holster and sat down to mentally regroup. I decided after serious contemplation that if the unruly rat made another unwelcome appearance on center stage, I would use the bayonet affixed to my M14 Rifle to persuade him to behave.

Another night when I was duty officer, I was making my rounds to the guard shacks in the jeep. Everything was going smoothly as I got out of the jeep at the last shack on line at the perimeter.

As soon as I shut the jeep down, I got out and approached the shack. I climbed the ladder silently, but one of the soldiers in the shack had heard me coming. When I made my presence known, one of them responded with a,

"Good evening, Sir."

The other guard was slumped in a corner and said nothing.

I said, "What's the matter with your buddy?"

The alert soldier said, "I don't know, Sir. He was fine a minute ago."

I walked the few steps to the slumped over soldier, reached down, and shook him by the shoulders, since he didn't appear to have a weapon in his hands.

The last thing you ever want to do is to surprisingly awaken a sleepy soldier with a weapon in his hands. That is, unless you do really want it to be the last thing you ever do.

The soldier awoke with a start, his eyes becoming as large as dinner plates. He leaped to his feet, scared to death. Then he said:

"Yes, Sir, good evening, Sir."

I stared at him for several moments as I weighed my options. Sweat broke out on his brow. He didn't look a day over eighteen years old. I then said,

"What have you got to say for yourself, private?"

"I was just concentrating on the perimeter, Sir, and didn't notice you come in."

Now sweat was rolling down his neck, that was on the chopping block and he knew it.

I stared him down once again, and he started to whimper like a child.

Then it struck me. He was a child that had found himself on the other side of the world, with a gun in his hand, caught asleep on guard duty.

I'm sure he had seen this very scenario in a lot of movies while growing up.

I then turned to the other troop, who was also visibly shaking in his boots and said,

"How long has your buddy been asleep?"

He replied, "I didn't even know he was asleep, Sir."

"Here I come to make my rounds, and you guys damned well know that I'm coming sooner or later, and you're both still stupid enough for one of you to be passed out, slumped over in the goddamned fucking corner." I was pretty aggravated. My ass was also at risk.

I continued, "Give me one goddamned good reason why I shouldn't turn both of you in."

Now sweat was rolling down both of their necks. I had decided at this point that I wasn't going to turn them over to command. Not over to a bunch of bloodthirsty, lifer, gung ho, military officers that would skin them alive. Besides, as afraid of me and what I might do as they seemed to be, I honestly didn't think that they would be stupid or crazy enough to repeat the performance.

I said, "I'm not going to turn you in, because I don't think the punishment fits the crime, fellows."

"But you can be damned sure of one thing. If this happens again, you almost certainly won't get someone as easygoing as I am."

"I'm also not going to say a damned thing about this little Rip Van Winkle episode because I'm putting myself at considerable risk for failure to report a serious infraction to my commanding officer."

"That means that neither one of you guys says anything about it either, understood." They vigorously nodded an affirmative.

The next time I was Night Duty Officer, I made my rounds, and the same two guys happened to be in the same guard shack together again.

When I ascended the ladder this time, they both snapped to attention, saluted me, and said,

"Good evening, Sir. How are you, Sir?" They were both alert and wide awake.

"I'm fine guys, and it looks as if you are also," I replied. "I'm glad to see that there's no Rip Van Winkles out here tonight."

They both said, "No, Sir. Wide awake, Sir."

They both smiled at me at this point. I returned the smile and descended the ladder.

I think I did the right thing.

25.

A Jolt of Reality

A few days later I was talking to Bob Storey, another slick copilot who had only been there a couple weeks longer than me. It was in the evening after a long day of flying for the both of us, mainly resupplying firebases in windy conditions on the mountain tops.

We had just looked at the mission board, and he said, "Dammit! I've got to fly with Marty Givens in the morning on a damned Sniffer mission! I hate those damn things with a passion!"

Sniffer missions were comprised of having a machine in the cargo compartment behind the pilots that would measure ammonia levels in the air. There were generally two guys on board, who operated the ammonia sensing equipment, besides the four man crew.

Since congregations of humans gave off a lot of ammonia as a result of their metabolism, the army figured this would be a good way to find groups of enemy troops. The only drawback was that congregations of monkeys also gave off a lot of ammonia.

It was Standard Operating Procedure for a Sniffer flight to be flown at fifty feet, just above the tops of the trees, at fifty knots airspeed. In other words, it was dangerous as hell.

During the flight, the ammonia machine operators would say "mark!" into the intercom radio and the crew chief or door gunner would throw out a smoke grenade, marking the area.

Immediately a gunship fire team would roll in on the smoke-marked area and blow the absolute crap out of it. I always suspected a lot of monkeys were needlessly massacred.

Well, the dumb bastards, anyway. They should have known better than to go around secreting ammonia with the U.S. Army overhead. They were probably VC monkeys anyway!

The next morning while I was preflighting my ship, Bob was preflighting his, adjacent to me at the Christmas tree.

I wished him good luck and said, "I'll see you tonight, Bob. Be careful."

He replied, "Mark, I've got a feeling I'm gonna need a lot of luck, today, for some reason."

"I just don't have good feelings about this mission, Mark."

I repeated, "Just be careful Bob. We'll have a talk about it over a couple of cold beers when you get back tonight. I'm flying resupply today. We'll be in the area. Good luck."

It was about 0700 hours when we both took off.

After inserting a LRRP Team without incident (about time, I thought), a call came over the UHF radio saying that an Alligator was down.

"Shit!" I thought and hoped they would get whoever it was out unharmed. But, I had a real, real bad feeling about it.

A little later, we got the bad news over the radio. The aircraft had gone down in the trees of the damned jungle and completely burned. It was Marty Givens (High Pockets) and Bob Storey.

They, along with the crew chief, door gunner, and the two man Sniffer crew, had been burned alive. This incident had a deep and profound impact upon me.

I fail to see how someone can completely get over something like this. Indeed, even today, it brings me great sorrow every time I think of it. The only time that I had been that sad in my entire life, was when my father died.

26.

Finishing Up as an Alligator

A few days later, I was flying, and radio traffic indicated that an Alligator aircraft had gone down. We soon discovered that it was Bob Vickrey, my friend from flight school, who was flying as copilot with Baby Huey. The aircraft had gone down in bad guy country as a result of enemy, small arms fire with the engine ablaze. It was a forced landing and the aircraft was heavily damaged when it roughly touched down. Everyone on board, the pilot, copilot, crew chief and door gunner were all shaken up, but no one was seriously hurt. Apparently, it was only due to Baby Huey's flying abilities that they were not all killed. After all, he had taken small arms fire to his left shoulder and a 23 mm exploding round had come through the windshield giving him shrapnel wounds and he still pulled it off.

Standard operating procedure (SOP) in a combat zone like Vietnam, was to disable the radios if there were enemy troops in the area, before you abandoned a downed aircraft, in order to keep the bad guys from confiscating the radios and monitoring aviation radio traffic.

Apparently when Baby Huey made the hard landing in enemy territory, Vickrey was unconscious from a blow to the head. He then carried Vickrey and his crew chief to safety and saw to it that the gunner as well was safely removed. He then successfully gave the aircraft radios disability status by taking an M-60 machine gun from its tripod mount in the back, and giving them all three good bursts.

This just goes to show you how a day in Viet Nam could go to hell in a hurry at a moment's notice.

◆ ◆ ◆

Another incident I was involved in illustrates the danger of radios falling into the possession of the enemy.

A few days later, a LRRP Team was running for their lives; chased by an entire company of NVA soldiers when they called for an emergency evacuation. I was flying with an Alligator slick driver known by the nickname of "Penis."

We were in the immediate area of the coordinates given for pickup by the LRRPs, so we were unanimously elected to go in and get them. I got on the Fox Mike radio and asked them to pop smoke to indicate their position so that we could recover them. There were three smoke grenades detonated in fairly close proximity to one another.

This could only signify one thing. The enemy troops had gotten ahold of some of our radios, had a translator on the ground that understood English, and were trying to lure us into the wrong LZ so they could kill us.

Penis and I looked at one another for a moment, and then he said,

"Tell them to pop green smoke."

So over the radio, I said, "Pop green smoke."

All of a sudden there were two green smokes and a red smoke.

I then took the initiative to say, "Pop yellow smoke."

A red smoke and a yellow smoke appeared. So we went to a small clearing by the yellow smoke and extracted the bedraggled troops. Then we immediately called in the Crocs on the false smoke locations.

Once again the NVA risked their general health and wellbeing on trickery and soon found out they had made a lousy bet. It also reinforced the need to destroy the radios.

The slick missions continued with resupply to firebases, insertion and extraction of troops, larger troop deployments, and night flare ship duty. These were our bread and butter missions. They were routine but never boring.

In the fall of 1968, President Lyndon Baines Johnson stopped the bombing of the Ho Chi Minh Trail due to political pressure. The Ho Chi Minh Trail was the major supply route for the North Vietnamese Army in the south, and was actually routed through the supposedly neutral countries of neighboring Laos and Cambodia.

Until the bombing halt, the U.S. Air Force stationed in Bangkok, Thailand was sending B 52s to the trail at night and hitting it with 500 and 750 pound bombs. These B-52 raids were known as *Arc Lights*. We could lie in our beds in Pleiku at night and hear what we called the *Rumble in the Jungle* on numerous occasions. This disrupted the supply line to the south to our advantage and we soon paid the price at Camp Holloway for a cessation of bombing.

After the cessation, we started getting hit with 122mm rockets and mortars virtually every night, now that the supply line was unimpeded. Needless to say, we didn't like it much.

These constant nighttime attacks necessitated the need for flare ships to be on standby. A flare ship was a UH1H Huey stocked with magnesium flares. When a rocket or mortar attack occurred, pilots on flare duty in the flare hooch would scramble and quickly get airborne. Once aloft, they would throw out the magnesium flares that were about four- feet long, and they would illuminate the ground very well as each flare slowly floated down on its own parachute. This technique sometimes made it possible to spot the enemy rocket and mortar teams in the act. If they did, gunships, either Cobras or Charlie Model Hueys, would take care of business. Sometimes the flare ships would go up and kick out flares before an attack in an attempt to thwart it. It often did.

The slick and gunship pilots on flare duty would sleep in the flare hooch next to their respective aircraft that were ready to *hotstart*. This meant that the rotor blades were untied and everything was ready to go at a moment's notice when the pilots got a call to scramble. Pilots slept fully dressed with their boots on. Their helmets were in the aircraft, plugged in, and all the crew had to do is jump in, don their helmets, turn on the battery switch, fuel switch and hit the start trigger. This put an aircraft in the air almost immediately when needed.

The ground around Pleiku's Holloway was a kind of flat scrub land between the mountain ranges and it was relatively easy to spot rocket and mortar teams at night with the help of the large magnesium flares. Pilots who flew the flare missions at night got the next day off.

PART FOUR:
THE GUNSHIPS

27

A Welcome Invitation

After flying for over two hundred hours as an Alligator copilot, I thought I was ready to make aircraft commander and get my own ship. I had flown about all the different missions several times and was feeling comfortable with them. It was as comfortable as you could get anyway. I didn't think anyone was ever comfortable getting shot at. I certainly understood how careful you had to be as a helicopter pilot in mountain air.

There was a host of ways to get killed in Vietnam other than being shot by enemy troops, that's for sure. One was to get shot by your own troops, called a *friendly fire* casualty. Things get squirrely in combat with hot lead flying everywhere. It's easy to get in the way of about any bullet out there when the whole sky's full of them.

On a hot evening in mid-December, I was feeling sorry for myself about having to fly into those deep, dark holes in the jungle with the whole world shooting at you, and friendly fire, super-hot, brass casings rolling down your neck, when a knock came by my door, next to the olive drab, wool blanket.

"Come in," I said, glad to shake my doldrums.

In came Captain Jeff Weller, commander of the Crocs. Jeff was about five feet-eight and slightly on the plump side. His call sign, Crocodile 6, signified his status as platoon leader. I, of course invited him in. He was friendly, took a seat and got right down to business.

"We've got a slot to fill in the Crocs, Mark. We're short a pilot since Elmer Fudd went home after completing his tour."

Becoming hopeful, I replied, "I hope this means that you're over here to ask me to come to the Crocs."

Weller said, "Not just me, Mark, but the rest of the guys too. As I'm sure you already know, we always take a vote when we've got a slot opened. All the guys are asked who they would like to join us from the Gators if they had their way about it. We had the vote last night, and they voted you in, if you want to join us."

My thoughts returned to the deep, dark holes that I had been flying into, and how I absolutely hated it, just like all the other Alligators did. I gave it careful consideration for two or three seconds before answering. I jumped off the bed I was sitting on, pumped my right fist to the sky, and said:

"I can't believe it! Goddamnit! You're damned right I want to come to the Crocs."

Weller smiled and said, "I figured you'd feel that way, Garrison. I figured you'd feel that way for sure."

28

The Crocodile Initiation

Everybody went through an initiation when they entered the Crocodile gunship platoon of the 119th AHC. There was no way to avoid it.

Captain Jeff Weller told the slick's first flight platoon leader that I was joining them at the Croc hooch, and had made arrangements for a new pilot that had just been assigned to the 119th to take my place.

I had heard my slick platoon leader object.

"Goddamnit, Weller! Here I had him ready to take his AC checkride (aircraft commander) and you go and steal the sumbitch!! You asshole!"

Weller rejoined, "Well, I'll personally see to it that he learns how to give you exemplary fire support when you're flyin' one of those virtually unarmed slick bastard H models into a hole in the jungle—especially when there's about a thousand gooks shootin' at ya."

"Hell, all you got on that thing's two tripod mounted BB guns," he continued, rubbing it in without mercy.

One of the gunship types was known as a *Hog*. It would most often fly the lead in a light fire team of two aircraft. The second aircraft was a *rocket and minigun ship*. This type of aircraft could fly lead or wing and was more versatile.

The Hog had 38, 2.75 inch rockets containing at least, ten pounds of high explosive (HE) in their warheads. These were often mixed with seventeen-pound HE warheads if the pilot had plenty of power to get off the ground with them. The Hog also had a crew chief and door gunner each armed with an M60 machine gun that was hand held. These guns were 7.62mm known in the civilian world as a 308. They could each fire at 550 rounds per minute

The minigun ships, on the other hand, carried fourteen rockets, and two, 7.62mm, six-barrel minigun, machine guns. These are truly awesome weapons. The machine guns were electrically operated from a sighting system in the copilot seat. The aircraft commander (AC) could, however, take control of these guns if he deemed fit. An electronic, piper or bullseye was in the sights and the copilot moved this piper to line up on his target. The sights came down on a mechanical arm from their stowed position when the copilot released them. As he moved the piper, the guns followed.

We generally set these guns to fire at a rate of 2,400 rounds per minute. That meant the ship could put out 80 rounds per second. These guns had a maximum capability of firing 6,000 rounds per minute but that rate was reserved for the faster fixed wing fighter jets. At our fire rate of 2,400 rounds per minute at the speed of 120 knots, a good operator could put a bullet in every square foot on the ground. You don't need any more coverage than that. More would waste ammunition and decrease your available time at a combat station.

Try to imagine what it would sound like if you were to make the single blast of a 308 high powered rifle a continuous sound. Let me tell you, it is a deafening roar when the miniguns kick in. They get hot quickly, so they are set up to fire no more than three second bursts, and then automatically kick off for three seconds, to keep the barrels from melting down.

Each 2.75 inch rocket on board delivered more concussion than the venerable 105mm howitzer artillery piece.

The Cobra, made by Bell Helicopter Company which also makes the UH 1 Huey series, had arrived in the Republic of South Vietnam as well. This was a newer gunship incarnation that carried even more weapon systems than the older Charlie Model. However, the Charlie Model, Huey, gunship platform was still extensively used in the war against the North, and easily outnumbered the available Cobras at the time.

Basically I needed to start over in my training in a gunship, but I was more than happy to do it. I would be covering my slick-driver friends as they courageously went into those small holes in the jungle.

I knew all the Crocs by sight when I got there, but really didn't know them all that well. Pilots tended to socialize with the guys in their own flight in the evenings after missions. It didn't take long for the Crocs to introduce themselves to the new guy.

I was still getting my things in order in my new room in the Croc Hooch, when virtually all of them that could fit, burst into my room guzzling whiskey and beer. They all said in unison:

"Have a drink, FNG Garrison, have a drink. Here's a glass of rotgut whiskey. By God, this'll cure anything ya got, even VD. It'll burn the little bugs right outta ya."

"Have you been down to the Pleiku whorehouses yet, FNG Garrison?"

I could only grimace at the FNG designation but it was true. My fatigues were no longer bright green, I had flown into the face of death many times but I was once again A *Fucking New Guy*.

Their affectionate concern continued to flow as they sloshed their whiskey rotgut in my direction. "Take this rotgut down when you go (to the whorehouse). It's better'n antibiotics. Drink about five good slugs straight from the bottle before you nail one of the whores, and then about five more when you're done. Hell, there won't be anything they could give you that's got a chance in hell of livin'."

It seemed that every one of them had their own bottle of the rotgut, and they all paused and said "Bottoms up," killed the rest, and threw the bottles against the walls, some of them breaking on the floor in my room.

Then one of the Crocs came in with two coolers full of beer and passed it around so they could wash the whiskey off their palates. These empty and half-crushed beer cans also littered my room as they continued to rabble rouse me. My room was approaching maximum entropy in a hurry.

I picked up one of the discarded whiskey bottles that had a little left in it when they weren't paying any attention to me, and tasted it. It was watered down. This was all a goddamned act for my initiation. But the whiskey they were pouring down my throat sure as hell wasn't watered down. It was truly 100-percent rotgut and I was getting bombed fast.

I woke up the next morning with my head throbbing, lying crossways on my bunk, fully dressed and wearing a vomit necktie. Just a moment later, they burst into my room once again with cameras and started snapping pictures.

Someone said, as the cameras clicked and flashed: "We gotta have a nickname for you, Garrison. From the look of the way you keep your room we know what it is. From now on, your name's *PIGPEN*."

The nickname stuck. From that moment on, I was Pigpen and I had been initiated.

Later that day, after I slept off the welcoming committee, I had a checkride with Captain Weller in a Charlie Model.

I felt so bad that I didn't give a damn if I passed it or not. But I passed. Now I was going to learn how to fly a gunship.

29

Learning to Fly the Guns

The first thing I was to understand was that the Charlie Model Huey was underpowered for the job it was expected to do. It had plenty of power as long as you weren't loaded, but if the density altitude (DA) was high, and the ship was loaded to the gills with rockets and ammunition, you often had to run it off like a fixed wing since you didn't have the power to maintain a hover.

This required a lot of precision flying by the pilot just to keep from crashing on takeoff.

I was to fly as copilot again, until I was judged competent in the aircraft and knew all the procedures and protocols indigenous to flying gunship missions. I didn't much care for the idea of basically starting over, but if I wanted to be a gun pilot I didn't have a choice. I understood that. At least, I thought I had learned a lot about flying Hueys and would be better prepared than I was when I got there. After all, I had been flying into fire bases on mountain tops, with the wind whipping around. I had flown into tight LZs with people shooting at me. I had flown numerous sling loads with the cargo sloshing around, back and forth like a weighted pendulum, underneath the aircraft.

I also had picked the aircraft up when it was seriously overloaded, and dove it down the mountain side to gain translational lift as the engine and rotor RPM bled off and the RPM warning siren was blaring in my ears.

I thought with all that combat experience it would be easier to come up to speed flying guns. *That's what I thought. How foolish of me!*

I had known when I got to the Crocs that they were a close knit and proud bunch of guys. That it was considered an honor to be able to join them, was a given.

The exception to the rule was when one of the Crocs went home, was injured, or killed in combat. If, at that time, an FNG came to the 119th, he would sometimes be assigned directly to the Crocs to fill the vacancy. Often, however, the *new* pilot would decide that he just wasn't cut out for gunships and was reassigned to the slicks.

All this is not to take away from the demands and incredible pressure facing the slick drivers every day. These guys were no less than fantastic pilots. As a rule, those that weren't often didn't last very long. Some pilots just did not feel comfortable launching high explosive rockets and releasing thousands of rounds of machine gun fire just feet from friendly troops. I understood this worry.

There was an implicit understanding among the gun pilots that you simply never *rained* your ordinance down on friendly locations. It took a shitload of concentration and ability to see that it didn't happen. This was especially true when giving exceedingly close fire support to *friendlies* about to get the holy hell kicked out of them. You were supposed to be savior and not executioner to these troops each time, every time, all of the time.

◆ ◆ ◆

After the checkride with Weller, to establish the fact that I was, indeed, a chopper pilot of sorts, came my first gun mission. I was to fly with a Croc named Rademacher (Rad-uh-make-er) who had been there in the platoon for several months.

Rademacher, or Rad as he was called for short, was about six feet tall and very thinly built. He chain-smoked unfiltered Pall Malls when on the ground, and in the air for that matter, when he could let his copilot have the controls.

This day we were to escort a slick carrying a LRRP Team for insertion into the jungle. We were to remain in the air at the ready, and silent, unless the slick received hostile enemy fire. On approach into a comparatively large LZ in the light jungle area west of a large firebase called, Soui Doui (Sue-ee-Due-ee), the LZ lit up with AK 47 muzzle flashes.

Muzzle flashes were seen when you were on the angry end of a gun, and you knew there was a piece of hot lead right behind every one of them.

The slick pilot said calmly into the radio:

"Receiving heavy fire, receiving heavy fire, two O'clock, fifty feet."

At that announcement, we came barreling in at close to velocity never exceed (VNE) of 140 knots, or more than 160 mph, and Rad punched off three pairs of seventeen pound HE warhead rockets, and broke sharply right just short of the enemy location.

You never wanted to make a breaking turn right over an enemy location if avoidable, because a gunship, even though the M 60s were blazing, was most vulnerable at that point. The wingman, another Croc, then laid more rockets underneath us to cover our break. We then set up a racetrack-like pattern and continued the assault on the bad guys, as the slick added power and made its escape without inserting the LRRPs. They had been discovered. The LRRPs didn't appear to mind. They were going back to base camp to drink a few cold beers. They would live at least another day before again being loosed in a dark jungle. Their clock, like my own, was ticking. As the slick left, carrying the happy LRRPs, we continued to pound muzzle flashes at the would-be LZ. We made four or five passes and expended all of our minigun ammo and rockets before heading back to Holloway to await another mission, rearm and refuel.

As far as we could tell on the post flight inspection neither Croc aircraft had taken a hit. *That was a miracle after seeing all the tracers coming at us. Life had been good on my first Croc mission.*

30

Getting to Know Croc 4—Waldo

With a scotch on the rocks in one hand, I took the other and knocked on the flimsy wall next to the olive drab blanket that hung over the door. I thought someone had to be in there as loud as the Led Zeppelin music was blaring. There was a short wait before a hand appeared that grabbed the door blanket and moved it aside.

All at once, Croc 4, otherwise known as Waldo, was looming over my meager five feet ten inch, 170 lb frame. He looked like he stood about six feet-four and could easily have weighed a solid 225 lbs. It looked like all bone and muscle to me.

Waldo on the left and Rademacher on the right.

"Hi. I'm Mark Garrison. The one you guys named Pigpen the other morning when I was only half conscious."

Waldo laughed, and said, "Yea, I know who you are. Come on in and make yourself at home." He was friendly. I was quite happy about that.

Waldo was a big and powerfully built fellow who was an ex-college football player from Ohio. He told me that he had to slump down to stay under the maximum height limit for army pilots during his initial flight physical. I believe the army had set the limit at six feet and four inches due to space constraints in the cockpit.

Waldo proved easy for me to get along with and I liked him right off the bat. He appeared to be a gentle giant type of fellow that was highly respected for his flying abilities. Like me, he had started in the slicks, got an invitation to join the Crocs, and transferred to the guns.

It was also implicitly understood that you just didn't fuck with Waldo. As I said, he was a gentle giant, but he wouldn't tolerate a lot of shit either. One guy, sometime later, was to learn this lesson the hard way.

As soon as I took a seat on the edge of his bunk, he said,

"How do you like the Crocs so far, Pigpen?"

"From what little I've seen, I like it a lot."

"Rad told me that you did a good job bringing the Charlie Model in today. He said he can't wait to see how you handle one that's a couple thousand pounds overloaded."

He laughed again.

I shook my head, "Waldo, I don't know. You think all that slick time I got with the Gators will help me?"

He suddenly got serious, "It'll help, that's for sure. But you gotta understand that an overloaded Charlie Model is an unforgiving animal. It's not nearly as forgiving as a slick, *because you just don't have the power!*"

"Pigpen, why did you accept the invitation to the Crocs, anyway? Just didn't like flying slicks?"

"I sure as hell didn't care much for a lot of the tiny LZs that we had to fly into. What about you, Waldo? What made you go to the Crocs?"

Waldo replied, "You got time for a story?"

Waldo pulled his worn, mismatched chair back from the tattered, makeshift desk which had been so generously supplied by the army. He plopped down, lifted his booted feet and sighed.

As he got comfortable, I noticed that he kept his room in surprisingly good order, with the floor swept, furniture dusted, and everything neatly put in its place.

"I flew slicks for two and a half months before I was invited to join the Crocs. Much like you, Mark," he continued, "I got damned tired of being a sitting duck in those goddamned LZs. The mission that broke the camel's back for me though, was one I flew as copilot with T.D. Moon. You know T.D. from the slicks don't you, Pigpen?"

I nodded "Yes I do, I flew with him a few times. I think he's an excellent pilot."

"You're damned right he is. If it wasn't for his cool head and piloting abilities I wouldn't be here tonight talking to you about this." I looked at him curiously, until he continued,

"We were on a night extraction of an FOB LRRP Team, in Laos. By the way, FOB means *Forward Observation Base in Laos and /or Cambodia*. Those places we're not supposed to be, and the President and all the politicians at home continue to deny our presence." A sneer accompanied his words.

I said, "So what happened?"

"Well we were somewhere near the damned Ho Chi Minh Trail in Laos at night, and we went in to get this team in some kind of field full of bamboo stubble. Elmer Fudd and a wingman from the Crocs were covering us with gunships. Anyway, when we got on the ground and the team was retreating toward our aircraft, M-16s blazing, the gooks turned their attention to us and we started taking AK 47 hits all over."

He paused and said, "I could see a couple of them pointing their weapons right at me. Then there were muzzle flashes and rounds hit my seat, the door, the window, and God knows what else. Right after that, there were several huge explosions, close enough to rock the ship and we took rocket shrapnel everywhere. Fudd had seen the bad guy muzzle flashes and put his rockets in the middle of them, and blew their asses away."

He wasn't done yet, as he said, "Then there were so many minigun tracers that it looked like a solid sea of red as they annihilated the gook's position. He blew it all to hell."

"T.D. Moon stayed cool throughout the whole thing, let the troops board, pulled pitch and got the hell out of there, and I was never so happy to get out of a place in my life."

He finished his recount of the events of that night by saying, "On the way back to Holloway that night, I decided if I ever got the chance, I was going to fly guns, so I could shoot back at these bastards. And when I got an invitation, I jumped at it."

"Damn Waldo, you're super lucky to be here."

"I know I am Mark. I don't know how they missed me that night with T. D."

I stayed and talked to Waldo until after midnight. I found out he came from Ohio and had to drop out of college to work for a while, and when the draft board beckoned, he had enlisted for flight school, just like I had done in Illinois. We were just two Midwestern college kids that now found themselves as helicopter pilots in the Republic of South Vietnam, during what was to be some of the heaviest fighting of the war. I felt a deep and immediate bond with him that night.

31

The Lima Charlie Missions

During the winter of 1969, the Crocs would sometimes get what became known as the Lima Charlie Missions. There was a firebase called Soui Doui, a few miles to the southeast, between Camp Holloway and The Mang Yang pass that often requested a gunship team to be on standby at their location, in the event of enemy contact in their area of operation (AO).

A lot of the time, the team would do more sitting and waiting than flying combat, thus the Crocs named it the Lima Charlie Missions, after the military phonetic alphabet for lawn chair. We would actually put lawn chairs in the cargo compartment of the chopper, shut the aircraft down at Soui Doui, get out the lawn chairs, and soak up some sun. We would relax and wait for a mission that sometimes never came. *On those days, life was good and the clock still ticked.*

This is me waiting for a scramble during a Lima Charlie mission at Soui Doui Firebase.

Soui Doui was named after a Montagnard village of the same name, which sat about a click from the firebase itself. Montagnards are a mountainous, tribal people who live in separate villages in the highlands apart from their lowland Vietnamese counterparts. They live in virtually Stone Age societies, with their bamboo and thatch roofed huts on bamboo stilts. They build the huts on stilts several feet high to keep the Bengal tigers from eating them at night.

There's nothing quite like having a few 500-pound hungry tigers roaming around in your backyard ready to eat your ass, to keep you on your toes.

The Montagnards generally did not get along well with the regular Vietnamese population, but, for some reason, they got along just fine with American troops, especially the helicopter pilots.

I strongly suspect that a major reason for their friendliness and cooperation was that we had a habit of bringing things like canned C Rations (military food) and other useful things, which we would give to them, or trade to them for handmade souvenirs and trinkets.

At Soui Doui there was a trail adjacent to where we shut down our aircraft that they were always trafficking back and forth. The men wore nothing but loin clothes, and the women had on nothing but a skimpy bottom without even the thought of a top.

Almost always among them were the ubiquitous, full-grown water buffalo. It was obvious these buffalo hated the Americans. I'm relatively certain that it was because we were always making huge amounts of noise with our jeeps, trucks, flying machines, and machine guns; I don't believe their evolutionary path had prepared them for the noise of war.

With these things in mind, it should be easier to understand and visualize the following incidents. They both occurred after I had made Croc Aircraft Commander but I'm going to throw them in here because they seem to fit.

One day I had just shut the aircraft down, when Paul Banish, who was flying as my copilot, asked me if he might go over to the Montagnard village and take some quick pictures for posterity's sake.

From left to right: WO1 Robert Apgar (Robbie), WO1 Paul Banish (Chipmunk), CPT Jeff Weller, and me.

I said that would be fine as long as he stayed within earshot, and if he heard the jet whine he was to hustle back. He would only be about five minutes away at the most, and I knew that by the time I reached takeoff RPM, he could be back and strapped in.

As I drug out and set up my lawn chair, Paul disappeared down a hill with his camera slung around his neck. The village was reached by descending a hill and then ascending another one to the village proper. Paul had only been gone for a few minutes, when I heard a commotion in the valley between the hills and the commotion appeared to be rapidly approaching my lawn chair's location.

I assumed an alert, upright position, as I closely watched for any unusual activity in the direction of the village.

All of a sudden, Banish's head appeared, then his shoulders, then his chest, and then his flailing arms that were assisting his running speed. His unrestrained camera was violently bobbing up and down on the strap around his neck. His face was crimson, his breathing labored and rapid. Now his legs and feet were visible, but moving so quickly as to be only a blur.

Then the heads of his pursuers came into view, with nostrils snorting and saliva flying. Then the whole bodies came into my sight. There were two full grown, bull, water buffalo in hot pursuit of the kid from Chicago. He realized full well that there were close to two tons of angry meat, equipped with hoofs, horns, and bad intentions, gaining ground behind him.

As the race up the hill continued, with the buffalo still gaining on Banish, I yelled at the top of my lungs:

"Paul, do you see those two small trees close together to your right? Run between them! The buffalo may try to follow you through but they're too big to make it. It'll slow 'em down!!"

Paul heard and followed my advice and the buffalo did follow, crashing into the trees, murdering one, and heavily damaging the other. But it did slow them down, and Banish gained a little breathing room, before the buffalo recovered and resumed the chase. We jumped into the cargo compartment of the chopper, and yelled,

"Come on Banish! You can make it! Run man!! Banish dove into the cargo compartment just ahead of the beasts, and we slammed the doors.

The buffalo proceeded to dance angrily around the chopper for five or ten minutes, snorting and digging their hooves into the ground like bulls at a bullfight. Fortunately, a short time later, the buffalo retreated to their home base.

As Paul had been running up the hill, out of breath and his face crimson, I thought it was amazing how much he looked like a chipmunk being run down by a fully loaded semi.

Paul had his nickname, *Chipmunk*. It stuck.

32.

Crashing a Party of Buffaloes

There's one other incident involving the pissed off buffalo. One day I was commanding a minigun ship, and winging on another Croc, known as Tricky Dick Harbors at Soui Doui.

Harbors was a tall, slender fellow, who always wore his cap with the bill pulled down low in the front, until it rested against the tops of his aviation sunglasses. This gave the appearance of someone observing the outside world through an impenetrable safe haven of some sort.

WO1 Richard Harbors (Tricky Dick)

Harbors had been shot down in enemy territory on more than one occasion, barely escaping with his life, as he ran through rice paddies, with dozens of enemy soldiers in hot pursuit. The poor, unlucky bastard had also had countless mechanical problems, including outright mid-air engine failures, which resulted in more crash landings.

I think this explains why he was rather suspicious and withdrawn. Who wouldn't have been? Harbors had come to the conclusion that if something bad had not already happened, it soon would.

On this day at Soui Doui, the operations jeep raced down and rudely interrupted our Lima Charlie siesta, and said we were to scramble immediately to fight the bad guys who had just engaged a LRRP Team.

We quickly cranked the aircraft to depart to the LRRP location, and I hovered by the side of the dirt strip runway, as I watched Tricky Dick take off to the west. I then fell in behind him and we started to gain speed and altitude. All at once, Harbors started to lose altitude, and made a steep left turn down the hill by the Montagnard village as he continued to descend.

He calmly said into the radio, "Going down. Power failure."

I followed him and watched his touchdown. He put the aircraft into a small clearing covered with native grasses, and *several* grazing water buffalo.

He did a nice job with the landing, under the circumstances, but he did spread the skids (landing gear) and scratched it up a little.

I immediately noticed two things. The first was that there was smoke coming from the engine compartment, and I worried there might be an ensuing fire. The second was that the buffalo had decided that they didn't care much for the intrusion. As a matter of fact, they looked downright enraged as they circled the wounded bird.

On the radio, I said, with some urgency, "Trick, get out of that aircraft! It might burn!"

There was a short silence followed by his transmission,

"Pigpen, do you see any flames, or just smoke?"

"Just smoke right now," I replied.

After a long silence, he said, 'I'm not goin' anywhere unless this thing bursts into flames. Then I still might not go anywhere. Can you see these goddamned crazy buffalo down here? They're flat pissed off. They'll kill our asses if we get out of this thing."

I appreciated his plight but the way he said it was so damned funny that I absolutely cracked up in the cockpit.

After what seemed like a long wait, the Montagnards came and got their animals, and we got Harbors and his aircraft out, that fortunately did not burn. The aircraft was sling loaded out by a larger Sikorsky Sky Crane Helicopter.

So much for the Lima Charlie (lawn chair) missions at Soui Doui.

33

The Mamasans and Papasans

Let me take the liberty of explaining what domestic life was like for the helicopter pilots in Vietnam. What little there was of it.

Every pilot platoon had their own hooch maid, or mamasan. She was usually a middle-aged woman from about thirty five to fifty years old from the camp's neighboring village or city. The mamasan job was highly sought after by the local women, who were interviewed by military security personnel. This reduced the chances of hiring someone who belonged to the Viet Cong, or who were otherwise hostile to U.S. Forces.

These women could earn an exceptional amount of money for themselves and their families, compared to what they could make in their own local economy.

The pilots generally gave her from ten to fifteen dollars apiece a month, and there were always between twelve and sixteen pilots per platoon. That would come to a monthly salary of one hundred and twenty to two hundred and forty dollars a month. This was unheard of in the local economy.

Mamasan's duties consisted of cleaning our rooms, shining our boots, laundering our uniforms, and other household chores. Many of them became quite attached to us, and tried to "mother" us, and watch over us. I, along with some of the other guys, also became attached to them as well.

There were also local Vietnamese men that were hired on post for various duties. These were generally middle-aged men, and their jobs were also sought after for the same monetary reasons. One of the jobs that will always stand out for me, that the papasans did, was "shit burning."

Each morning, seven days a week, on your way to the flightline, you would go past a Vietnamese man, squatted down next to a fifty five gallon drum, filled with human shit, being burned by JP 4 jet fuel. I don't think there's any way, short of death itself, that I will ever forget that smell. Other papasan jobs included cleaning the latrines, office buildings on the post, aircraft hangars, etc.

Speaking of latrines, the pilot rooms had no bathrooms. There was only one latrine building for the whole 119th AHC. All three flights used it. There were six or eight gravity flush toilets, gravity flow sinks and showers.

A large tank of water sat on top of the latrine and fed all the plumbing fixtures.

There was usually water in the tank, but not always. Many times we ran out of water in the middle of a shower, and had to get the soap off as best we could.

The currency given to us to use in Vietnam was called Military Payment Certificates, or MPC. Everything from a nickel to a one hundred dollar bill was represented by a different color paper certificate. Because of the black market in United States of America currency, it was illegal to have or use greenbacks. However, there was also a black market in MPC, so every few months, the military command changed it, and gave the soldiers a couple of days to turn in their old and get the new.

There was also an officer's club a short distance away from the pilot hooches, where meals were served, from breakfast to dinner. The main thing that was frequented by the pilots in the club, however, was the bar, which had a full supply of beer and hard liquor. Combat pilots coming back from hot missions, were a hard drinking bunch, as a rule, and I was one of the elite in this category.

Once, my company commander, a Major, came to the officer's club at night with a bird colonel (one step below general grade). The Major was showing off his first class pilots and the tight ship that he ran. I happened to be snockered at the bar when they came in, the Major steered the colonel to me and said with as much pride as he could muster:

"Colonel, I'd like you to meet a damned good gunship pilot, Warrant Officer Garrison."

It was later verbally relayed to me by the same major when he had called me onto his red carpet and was reading me the riot act about how I had responded to the introduction.

Apparently I said, "How you doing, Sir? Nice to meet you." At which point I raised my beer glass to my lips, downed the rest of it, and then unceremoniously fell backwards off my bar stool.

"I'm going to keep an eye on you, Mr. Garrison," the Major warned.

"Yes Sir, I certainly understand that. I'll do my best not to do an encore of that performance. And for the next several weeks, I didn't have as much as one beer to drink."

34.

Poker nights at the Croc Hooch

When we would get paid at the first of each month, the green, felt-topped, poker table, equipped with chip slots and all the amenities, would come rolling out in the central pilot's lounge area of the Croc Hooch.

For the next several days, there would be poker games every night, until there were big winners and big losers. Bob Vickrey, the guy who had dodged a stunned Baby Huey's radio bullets, had succeeded in coming to the Crocs, and was virtually always a big winner. Vickrey was the best damned poker player that I've ever personally known. He had a face at the table that was almost impossible to read. He might have been bluffing, and then again he might not have been. You never knew until someone called him.

During the course of his yearlong tour, Vickrey purchased several thousand dollars' worth of stereo equipment, cameras, etc. at the PX, and sent several thousand more dollars home.

I don't remember anyone who was a bad loser, or anyone who flaunted their winnings. The games were a tradition and welcome diversion. Too often though, the poker games were interrupted by old Victor Charlie (VC). The sound of incoming rockets and mortars met with a constant blast from a siren meant that you grabbed your rifle, flak vest, and steel pot helmet, and ran to the perimeter trenches to await a possible ground attack.

GUTS N' GUNSHIPS | 135

◆ ◆ ◆

I'll never forget the very first time I ran toward the trench at night and a mortar round landed so close to me that it knocked me off balance. How I wasn't killed is still a mystery to me, but I didn't even take shrapnel from it. As I regained my balance and continued running toward the trench, with tracers streaking over my head, I leaped, in desperation, and was met with a trench full of water. The water was up to my waist as we stayed there most of the night to defend against the ground attack that never came. But, we still had to be at the flightline preflighting our aircraft the next morning. Let me tell you, a long night makes for a really long day.

35.

The Cuisine at the Croc Hooch

I've already stated that the Croc Hooch had rows of rooms on both ends and a company lounge area in the center. There was a refrigerator, hot plates (these were the days before microwaves), silverware, dishes, etc. The refrigerator was usually full of beer with a little room left for soft drinks, but damned little.

There was a kid from Wisconsin that joined the Crocs shortly before we left Pleiku for An Khe. I don't recall his name. His mother used to send hard salami to him in the mail. It was a long tube about two inches in diameter that he would just hang on the wall of the lounge area, for anyone and everyone to enjoy.

We never refrigerated it and nobody ever got sick from it. It would get hard and dried out on the end that we last cut a piece off from, so we would just cut the dried part off and cut a fresh piece. His mother would also send him cheese from Wisconsin which was delicious. We usually refrigerated that. *Needless to say, this kid was popular*.

Also, most all of us had our own private stashes of food that we kept in our rooms that we had purchased at the PX just down the sidewalk a few paces.

Captain Weller fancied he was a chef of sorts, and would brew up some kind of stew or soup now and then. I have to admit that his concoctions were usually pretty good.

I remember one time specifically, when we had gotten back from missions, that he was in the lounge cooking a huge pot of what he called Pepper Stew.

Everyone was complaining horribly about it being so damned hot, but everybody kept going back for more, until it was all gone.

Weller himself marveled about that. Why, if it was too damned hot, did everyone keep coming back with an empty bowl wanting more? He had a good point, and silenced the criticism.

Another pilot, I don't remember his name either, went into Pleiku one day and brought back a sauce that was made and used by the locals called Nuk Bam (Nuke Bomb). It was the foulest smelling foodstuff I have ever had the pleasure of not touching. They told me it was made from fish heads and entrails, and I felt certain that it was, but I was also convinced the ingredients had to go through a lengthy period of decay before use. The Nuk Bam aroma immediately dropped Limburger Cheese to number two on my retch meter. Apparently you can buy a tamed down version of Nuk Bam in the U.S. today.

Then there were the Croc pets, two cats and a dog, which were the recipients of our culinary scraps. No one could think of a good name for the mangy old female dog, so we just called her Bitch. She was a good dog that never bit anyone. She never bit any Americans that is. She hated the Vietnamese people that had jobs at Camp Holloway. She would growl at them and chase them down the sidewalk whenever they happened near.

Here I am petting Bitch right outside the Croc hooch.

A lot of Vietnamese people have been known to eat dogs, and I swear the dogs I saw over there seemed to instinctively know that.

There was also a dog at the Camp Holloway dental clinic that would go absolutely apeshit when it saw a Vietnamese person.

The two cats were twins, grey with black tiger stripes. Their names were not nearly as generic as the dog's name. They were named Flex Mode and Stowed Mode. Let me explain. In a gunship, when the weapon systems of a minigun ship were on safe, or cold, the miniguns retreated to a straight ahead, and slightly upward position, and could not be fired from the cockpit. They were said to be in a Stowed Mode.

When the weapon systems of a minigun ship were on hot, or fire, these same miniguns moved in relation to a pilot's cockpit input, and could be fired. They were said to be in a Flex Mode.

So, somehow, the cats became Stowed Mode and Flex Mode.

One day when a few of us were relaxing in the Croc Lounge, I believe it was Gollogly, nicknamed Golly-Golly, because no one could pronounce his name, was behind the counter trying to close the refrigerator door, and it wouldn't close. I stepped behind the counter and saw that the door's obstruction was, in fact, Stowed Mode's head. Golly-Golly couldn't see the cat because he had his hands full. Every time he tried to close the door, the stunned cat's head was in the way, and his body went spastic as if he were just plugged into an electrical outlet.

I said, "Goddamn Golly-Golly, why are you trying to kill Stowed Mode? He didn't do anything to you." Golly then looked down and saw the cat, as it wobbled out from behind the counter and promptly pissed on the floor. Golly-Golly felt terrible about the incident and apologized profusely. Stowed Mode never was quite the same after that.

A few days later, some of us were once again in the Croc lounge, when we heard the loud retort of a gun, which came from Golly-Golly's room just off the lounge. Seconds later, an ashen colored Golly-Golly appeared in front of us.

He said, "I was just cleaning my weapon. I thought for sure it wasn't loaded. The bullet soared right past my head and out through the roof."

I said, "Come on Golly-Golly. We know how upset you are since you almost murdered Stowed Mode but it's no reason to attempt suicide. Good thing you're such a lousy shot."

Here I am relaxing after another mission.

36.

Getting Acquainted With
an Overloaded Charlie Model

After flying a few missions as a copilot with various Croc aircraft commanders, Captain Jeff Weller decided to check my progress. He did that one day in late December, 1968, by taking me up in an overloaded gunship.

The UH1C, or *Charlie Model*, as she was more affectionately known, had a gross weight of 9,500 pounds. Weller guessed this ship to be at least 1,000 pounds over gross. We had loaded the *Charlie Model* with a few extra 17-pound warhead rockets, a full load of fuel, and some extra M60 ammunition, along with the minigun ammo. The density altitude (DA) was also high at close to 10,000 feet.

I did the preflight checks, and when Weller got to the bird, he told me to go through the startup procedure, fire up the jet, and bring it to flight idle. I did all the preliminaries, threw the battery switch to on, start fuel along with main fuel on, yelled "Clear" to warn everyone around, and pulled the start trigger under the throttle on the collective pitch control.

I also closely watched EGT to be sure it did not exceed red line or stay too long in the yellow, caution zone, flipped off the start fuel, and slowly increased the throttle to the flight idle position. I glanced at engine and transmission oil pressures and temperatures to be sure everything was in the normal green zone, and awaited his instructions.

He then said, "I've had you fly on missions so far to get you started in the guns with ships that were not over grossed, Pigpen."

"But now's the time to do some real flying," he laughed. "I'll take her out of the revetment, and make the first takeoff to demonstrate how the heavy girls act, so pay damned close attention." He continued, "We'll see how you do with her next, so, like I said, pay attention as I talk you through what I'm doing to get her off the ground in one piece."

Captain Weller added power and collective pitch when we were cleared for takeoff and the overloaded chopper groaned and came up slowly to a three-foot hover. However the rotor RPM started to bleed off and she started to settle in to the runway. As it settled, he gave it forward cyclic to lower the nose to pick up some ground speed as she touched down. Now sliding down the runway he gave it more forward cyclic to gain enough speed to reach translational lift and the aircraft grudgingly started to gain altitude and airspeed. Then we both kept a lookout for tall grass and fences for several meters and hoped we didn't have an engine failure. After reaching about 300 feet of altitude, he turned a right crosswind leg to set up a downwind and shoot an approach back to the runway. He said, "Now let's see how she acts on a landing."

He turned final and started our descent toward the runway. When he got to the bottom, he flared the aircraft to lose airspeed, and came to a nice three-foot hover above the strip.

Everything seemed fine for several seconds, but then the RPM started to bleed off once again. He then said, "OK, look, she doesn't have enough power to hold a hover, so I'm gonna let her settle in, and pull pitch just before she touches the runway and I run out of left pedal."

We settled in to the runway.

"Now," he said, "I'll bottom out the collective to get my RPM back, before adding pitch slowly and ground taxiing it forward on the skids."

He then demonstrated the procedure successfully. Afterwards he gave me the controls and said, "Let's see a takeoff and landing just like I just demonstrated, Pigpen."

**Me in the copilot's seat
of a Charlie Model in flight.**

I said, "Roger that, Captain. I'll do my best." As I took the controls, I said, "I have the aircraft, Captain." I was more than a little apprehensive, as I slowly raised the collective. I was accustomed to having extra power when I needed it to get me out of a bind, but I realized that the extra power just wasn't there with a Charlie Model that was loaded to the gills like this old girl was.

Soon, I felt the ship get light on the skids, so I inched the cyclic forward and she began to ground taxi and started to pick up speed. I had only intended to taxi forward for a short distance, but soon I found myself galloping down the runway, like a wild stallion.

We hit translational lift, and the ship lurched violently, onward and upward, only to be followed by a ferocious dive that bounced us off the PSP runway to a height of at least ten feet, and we continued to repeat this diving, bouncing, bucking bronco routine for the next fifty meters.

I glanced at Weller. His hands were ready to pounce on the controls, but they didn't. Apparently, he had more confidence in me than I had in myself at the moment. Somehow, I managed to regain a semblance of control, and establish a relatively normal climb-out.

I guess I got lucky on the landing and didn't have any trouble. After that takeoff, Weller said, "God damn Garrison, I thought we were all dead men for sure!"

"By God, I'll have to give it to you though. You hung right in there til you got the bastard under control." He continued, "We need to do a little work on your overloaded takeoffs, though. That was a little too exciting. Even for a Croc."

I think we must have gone through two full loads of fuel working on takeoffs that day. Once again I learned that I had much to learn.

That evening back in the Croc lounge, Captain Weller felt compelled to rub it in. He told the other, older Crocs, who had already been through their first over-grossed -takeoff nightmare about his galloping, *Hi Ho Silver* adventure with me.

All of them rode me without mercy for hours. I went to bed that night with their jeers ringing in my ears.

37.

Taking a Shower in Agent Orange

The next morning I was scheduled to fly with Waldo. We were to fly to Dak To and contact someone named *Naked 9* on Fox Mike Radio.

The operations man couldn't tell us what the mission was all about. It was just going to be our little surprise.

Waldo and I walked from the Croc Hooch to the Christmas Tree together, engaging in small talk. He said, "Don't let it bother you when they razz you like they did last night. They didn't do any better than you did, taking off an overloaded pig. Everybody has to go through a learning process to handle one of these things."

I said, "Well, it sure deflated my ego yesterday. I thought I knew how to fly, but now I'm not so sure."

Waldo replied, "A loaded Charlie Model is not a slick, that's for sure. And it's not that they're harder to fly than a slick, they're just different."

He continued, "That means everybody has to feel her out for a while, and get used to her, and you're no different than anybody else." By then we had reached the aircraft.

The crew chief had already preflighted the bird, but we did another one just the same. We found the aircraft was flight worthy and strapped ourselves into the cockpit.

Waldo cranked the aircraft, got it up to operating RPM, asked the crew chief and door gunner to clear behind us, picked the aircraft up, and hovered backwards to escape the revetment. He then made a pedal turn and hovered forward toward the runway for takeoff. The ship did not bleed RPM. *I thought, damn, is he smooth on the controls. I could hardly see the cyclic moving.*

When we were clear for takeoff, the ship moved flawlessly down the runway at three feet of altitude, hit translational lift, and climbed out perfectly with no problems. His input on the controls was so minimal and precise that I thought I saw the cyclic move a couple of times, but I couldn't be sure.

Waldo then gave me the aircraft when we were at 2500 feet of altitude and said,

"You've got it, Mark. Remember that the key to flying these heavy duty girls is to make small control adjustments."

I said, "Yeah, I noticed that. I couldn't even see your cyclic moving on takeoff."

"Small control movements insure against washing lift out of the rotor arc," he replied. "It makes the blades more efficient. This is especially important when you do lose rotor RPM and fall through to the runway. It gives you a lot better chance of making a successful takeoff and not rolling it up in a fiery ball."

"That's good to know, Waldo, I appreciate the tip," I replied.

"I never knew that just getting a loaded Charlie off the ground could be such a life and death challenge, and a royal pain in the ass."

Waldo laughed, "I didn't have a clue when I came to the Crocs either. It didn't take me very long to learn though." He then told me to fly to Dak To and make the approach to the south into the prevailing winds.

I flew to the south of Big Momma, the mountain that looked like a breast, made a left bank to the north and came around on a southerly final approach.

On the flight up, I had been concentrating on minimizing my control input, especially to the cyclic.

On final, I started our descent and told myself that I was not going to move the cyclic any more than was absolutely necessary. No more than an inch in any direction, if possible. The aircraft came to a stable three-foot hover, and held its RPM. I taxied to a parking spot on the side of the PSP runway and shut her down.

I glanced at Waldo with a smile on my face.

He smiled back and said, "Good job, Mark. You're getting the hang of it."

The guy sitting next to me, Rick Gill from Ohio, Croc 4, or Waldo, had taught me a very valuable lesson in one flight.

We walked to the Dak To operations hooch and asked where we could find Naked 9.

Just then, a Captain by the name of Brown walked in and said,

"Are you guys from the Crocs?"

We said, "Yes, are you Naked 9?"

"Yes I am, and I'm glad to see you boys made it up here this morning."

"Come with me," he continued, "and I'll tell you about today's mission."

As soon as we were outside and started walking toward the runway, the Captain continued,

"We've been getting hit with intelligence from the LRRPs that there's a concentration of enemy troops massing outside of Kontum. In light of that, the brass wants me to *undress the jungle* over there, so they no longer have a place to hide." He went on, "That C123 Provider aircraft you see at the end of the runway is what I'm going to use today to do that. She's loaded to the gills with an herbicide called Agent Orange. Let me tell you, that this shit will kill any damned thing it touches as long as it's a plant. Don't worry though, there's no danger to humans or animals, just plant life."

Captain Brown then gave us the radio frequencies to contact the C123 pilots, and told us to fly close gun cover for them if they happened to receive fire. He then said that it would be unlikely for any of us to see any hostile small arms fire and that we were there as a deterrent more than anything else.

Waldo and I got back in the Charlie Model, radioed our wingman about what was going on, and fired her up. We then contacted Naked 9 and said we were awaiting instructions.

"Roger that, Crocodile 4. I'll be departing on 18 and flying to coordinates just to the northeast of Kontum. Follow at a comfortable distance, and await word from me, over," Naked 9 answered.

"Roger, Naked 9, wilco (will comply)," Waldo replied.

Naked 9 took off on 18 (to the south on runway 180 degrees) and we fell in behind him. Our destination was only a few clicks away, so after a short while, we received another transmission from Naked 9.

"Croc 4, this is Naked 9, I'm going to make passes over the dump zone on a north/south axis, working from west to east. This load is a concentrated mix, so I'll be letting her go at a couple of hundred feet to get good diffusion and cover more area. Do you copy?"

"Roger, Naked 9," Waldo answered, "we'll pick you up on your first run. If you receive hostile fire, call out the location, over."

Naked 9 made his first pass, dumping a white cloud of Agent Orange over the target area from north to south at two hundred feet. The cloud misted down and blanketed the jungle below us. He then made a steep 180 degree turn and dumped another load from south to north, with our gunships covering him from behind. He did this three times, and was on his last run, when we saw intense muzzle flashes at his 9 o'clock position, and received a frantic radio call,

"Receiving fire! Receiving. Receiving fire, 50 meters at 9 o'clock!!!"

Waldo had seen the muzzle flashes, and had immediately put the Charlie Model in a hellacious dive, and had two pairs of rockets on the way, by the time Naked 9 had got the call off. I had the miniguns out of their holsters, and followed the rockets with intense three second bursts of 80-round- per-second, right on target. It looked like a solid sea of red hitting the enemy location, but in reality, there were four more rounds that you couldn't see between every brightly burning tracer.

Near the end of our first run, we flew through a cloud of airborne Agent Orange that misted our windshield, and came in through the open windows and doors of the aircraft, dampening our flight suits.

Just before the target, Waldo broke left, in a sharp 90-degree turn, and rockets from the wingman impacted below us to cover our break. Our crew chief's and door gunner's handheld M 60's were also firing relentlessly during our turn. The retreating blades of the aircraft sounded like 12 gauge shotguns going off during the turn, and the G forces pushed us down in our seats.

About half way through the turn, we, ourselves, received heavy fire from various nearby locations, as muzzle flashes lit up the jungle below us. At that point, we set up a left hand racetrack pattern and punched it out with the NVA until all the enemy fire was silenced.

We returned to Dak To to refuel and rearm. The Caribou had already returned, but the pilot was still in the aircraft and saw us on final approach. He radioed,

"Croc 4, I want to thank you guys. We were taking AK hits. I don't know how many yet, but as soon as your rockets and miniguns started, it all stopped. My crew said the bad guys turned all their attention to you. I sure as hell wouldn't want your job, over."

"Hey, somebody's gotta do it," Waldo replied. "If you guys ever need any more friendly fire support, give us a call. We're in the Yellow Pages, over."

Naked 9 laughed, "You guys are a bunch of crazy bastards. The best kind of crazy bastards. Take care, Gentlemen, I'm sure glad you guys are there for us when we need you, out."

This incident confirmed that my decision to become a Crocodile in the 119th AHC was a good one. It really felt great to have a hand in getting those guys back to Dak To in one piece. I also realized that I had been copilot to a great aircraft commander that day. His coolness under fire was remarkable. His touch on the controls was outstanding.

I learned a lot that day. And, the most important thing that I learned was that the better I did my job, the more Americans I could get home from that damned war alive.

38

The New Year's Eve Invasion of An Khe

Throughout the month of December, I flew with about all of the Crocodile aircraft commanders, as I continued to learn the ropes of flying the gunships. I considered all of them, to a man, to be quite competent pilots. As a general rule, if you weren't competent in the air, you didn't last very long. You were weeded out by administrative action, pilot error, or both.

Some of the other Croc pilots were James M McDonald (Mac), Robert Apgar (Robbie), Bob Suggs (Dufflebag), Jon Van Leer (Jon-Jon), Jerry Miller (Jer), Paul Banish (Chipmunk), Jack Cloud, Pappy Clark, Hugh Gollogly (Golly-Golly), Sugar Bear, Bob Vickrey, and several others who rotated from the United States.

On one occasion in late December, 1968, Robbie Apgar, Jack Cloud, Waldo and I had flown to An Khe, to support an infantry unit, and was to RON there (remain overnight) to be on standby the next day as well.

An Khe was another Vietnamese city to our east that had a large U.S. Army installation. The base was equipped with numerous artillery pieces, including 105mm, 155mm, and 175mm Howitzers, along with 8 inch mobiles. The perimeter was defended by guard shacks every few meters, manned by two men with M60 machine guns, and Claymore Mines were placed every few feet in No Man's Land. Between the guard shacks, at regular intervals, were teams that manned the dreaded Quad 50 caliber machine guns.

Often, enemy insurgents would attempt to infiltrate the base at night by sneaking through the barbed wire defenses and remain unseen by our soldiers manning the guns. When and if they entered the compound, they would skirt around and place satchel charges (explosives) on helicopters and other equipment. As I said earlier, it surely must have taken nerves of steel to even consider trying to breach a heavily defended perimeter.

There was also an officer's club on base, and that night all of us had gone and drank more than our share. As we left the club at nearly midnight, after flying hot missions all day, we approached a bridge, made of rope and bamboo that was slung over a small creek, about ten feet above the water.

It took good hand eye coordination to make it across the damned thing in broad daylight when you were sober. Believe me it was almost impossible at night when you were drunk on your ass.

We approached the bridge with extreme caution, and were somehow successfully negotiating it, when the whole perimeter lit up with M 60 fire, quad 50, and every artillery piece on the compound chimed in.

The immediate result was that all four of us plunged into the creek certain that we were being overrun by a massive enemy offensive, and that we would be killed within seconds. As the guns continued to blast, we managed to crawl to the creek bank and peek over it to survey the carnage. After wiping away the mud and leeches from our faces we peered over the bank expecting to see a hoard of enemy troops, bayonets fixed, ready to disembowel and dismember us.

But we didn't.

Instead, the guns suddenly stopped, and we heard troops shouting in unison, "Happy New Year! Happy New Year!"

It had been December 31st, 1968 and we had no clue.

I've often wondered what any insurgents on duty that night must have thought.

Probably something like: "Goddamn! I thought we might be seen by someone, but I didn't think the whole fucking place would see us!"

39

The Daily Blur of the War

In Vietnam it didn't make any difference what day of the week, month, or year it was. If the sun came up, you were probably going to fly that day.

For instance, the only reason I distinctly remember flying copilot with Jim McDonald (Mac) on Christmas Day, 1968, is because of a radio transmission we all heard on UHF.

We were flying to the Dak To area that morning, and during a brief stretch of radio silence, someone came over the air and said, in a very deep voice,

"Good morning everyone. This is God, and I just want to wish my Son a happy birthday, out."

Several other people answered with things like,

"Why, thank you Dad. How nice of you to remember."

Our days cascaded together into an eight-day week. There wasn't any break, except for an occasional day off. You flew where ever you were told, performed the mission, and flew back to Camp Holloway, unless you were to remain overnight (RON) somewhere else.

When the day's flying was complete, you parked the aircraft, did a post flight check, tied the blades down, and returned to your room in the Croc Hooch. To get something to eat, you went to the mess hall, officer's club, or simply ate from a can in your room from something you bought at the PX. I usually ate in my room or the lounge area.

Then came the beer and booze to try to forget what you were doing for a living until the next day, when it all started again. You were often roused from your slumber at night, however, by the ubiquitous sound of the screaming siren, indicating it was time to grab your flak vest, rifle, and helmet, and head to the damned trenches which may or may not be full of water.

There was no telling how long you would be in the damned things, watching the perimeter for any threat of attack, until you were allowed to retreat to your bunk, and try to get some sleep before preflighting the next morning.

One of the reasons a thorough preflight check was necessary was because of the sappers (enemy insurgents) who often managed to sneak through the perimeter at night, and booby trap aircraft, among other things. One of the things they were most notorious for, was pulling the pin on a hand grenade and putting a rubber band around the handle to keep it from activating. Next they would remove the fuel cap on a Huey, drop the grenade in the fuel tank, and replace the cap. A couple of hours later the fuel would dissolve the rubber band, letting the handle release, and boom goes the Huey.

It's bad enough if it goes off on the ground, let alone when the Huey is airborne.

To counter this, when we left the aircraft in the evening after a mission, we would put a small pencil line on the fuel cap, extending onto the surrounding metal, and if this line did not line up exactly the next morning, you got the hell away from the aircraft in a hurry, and called the bomb squad.

Before we caught on to what they were doing, a friend of mine and everybody else on board, exploded into a thousand pieces at 2,000 feet. At least they didn't know what hit them.

One thing that was a welcome break from our violent and insane routine were musical groups that would sometimes entertain us at the officer's club at Camp Holloway.

Once during the winter of 1969, a band called *The Surfaris* came to perform. They said they were, indeed, the same group that had recorded the drum sensation, "Wipeout," a few years before, that was on *Billboard's* Top Ten Hits for many months.

I was at a table with some other pilots no more than five feet away from the drummer when they played the song. The performance on drums was excellent, and he got three standing ovations and encore requests. He played it each time, and looked absolutely worn out at the end of it all.

By the end of the night everyone in the place was shitfaced drunk and we paid the poor guy back by pouring his drums full of beer.

The next morning, a few of us went to the club for breakfast before flying. As soon as we entered the club, I noticed the drummer of the night before, sitting in a corner re-skinning his drums. I walked over to apologize for our Neanderthal behavior just hours before, and said:

"Look, man, I'm truly sorry about everybody pouring beer on your drums last night. They got a little carried away."

He looked at me and said, "Oh, hell, don't worry about it. It happens about everywhere I go over here. To tell you the truth, if I had to be over here dodging bullets like you poor bastards have to do every day, I'd probably do a lot worse than pour some guy's drums full of beer."

Another diversion from the day to day blur of the war were the Malayan sun bears.

Next to the officer's club was a large steel cage that housed two adolescent sun bears. These sun bears, indigenous to Southeast Asia, are black with a fawnish face, and weigh more than one hundred pounds. The Camp Holloway bears were captured and rescued as cubs, when the Pathfinders were clearing a trail somewhere in No Man's Land. They accidently got between them and their mother and they had to shoot *Mamasan Bear* when she attacked them. They decided not to leave the cubs in the jungle to die, so they brought them back to the cage, and had fed and raised them since.

Often, when we were walking by the cage on the way to the club, there would be a couple of exceedingly inebriated Pathfinders, wrestling with them in the cage. Admittedly, the bears were not completely grown when I first observed these encounters, but throughout the year, they quickly became fine adult specimens. I guessed their weight at the time to be in excess of one hundred pounds each.

And this was more than one hundred pounds of bear, for God's sake. They had claws, seemingly as long as my fingers, and a set of teeth that any grizzly would have been proud of. In other words, the Pathfinders were regularly getting their asses kicked. The Pathfinders found a way around this, however. They just got the Bears drunker than they (the wrestlers) were before they entered the cage.

An inebriated Malayan Sun Bear in his cage.

Through the bars, they would hand a beer to the bears, who would take it with their front paws, sit on their asses, and down the chute it would go. They would then beg for another, and another, until they were soused. With the playing field now more level, the Pathfinders would still get their asses kicked by the drunken bears, but it took the bears longer to pin them to the mat.

To my knowledge, the bears never injured a Pathfinder, and were always careful to pull their punches.

A lot of soldiers going past the cage would give the cherished bears food and beer. When the bears were drunk, they were hilarious, and, by the way, they were usually drunk. They would stumble around the large cage, falling and rolling into one another, making strange, gurgling sounds as they went. When they eventually stumbled into one another, a world class wrestling match would ensue.

Seemingly, they would merge into a single large ball of fur, and would roll around on the floor of the cage like a huge, hairy, black and brown basketball. Then, when both of them thought the other had had enough, they would sit and face one another, and lick each other's faces with a tongue that looked like it was a foot long.

After recuperation they would again approach the bars of the cage, stand on their back legs, reach through the bars, and beg for beer and morsels of food. More often than not, they would get it.

I have very fond memories of the bears, and would pet them and give them food and drink almost every time I went by the cage. They were there for my whole year-long stay at Camp Holloway, and were a great diversion from the ugliness and violence of the war.

40.

The Mission Statement

Every month, and more often if necessary, Captain Weller would have a meeting of all the Crocs in the lounge area of the Croc Hooch. These meetings were used to air any complaints the pilots had, exchange information on various aircraft, and to bring up any news of interest.

At this meeting, complaints about the war itself were abundant. It was now February of 1969 and the war drug on. Virtually every pilot in the 119th, and probably every other assault helicopter company in Vietnam, knew that the war was ridiculous at this point.

"Why are we even here?" the pilots asked again and again. The war had become a bunch of politically motivated bullshit. I had the same sentiments. It wasn't the army's fault, though. The army had been given a mission statement by the politicians, and was simply trying to do it.

So, we would have a bloody battle over some mountain top, win the fight, and then give it back so we could fight over it again. But this was just a way of engaging the NVA, in an attempt to drain his resources of men and supplies and bring him to his knees. The problem was that the enemy's resources of men seemed limitless. No matter how many we killed they kept pouring across the DMZ. They also kept coming from the supposedly neutral countries of Laos and Cambodia. Remember how neutral Laos was when Waldo went in for the night extraction of the LRRP team with T.D. Moon?

At home on the nightly news programs, like The Huntley-Brinkley Report on NBC, and CBS Evening News with Walter

Cronkite, there was a weekly scoreboard of how many soldiers on each side had been killed in the war. It looked like we were damned near skunking the NVA as the scoreboard showed a million or more enemy killed and more than 40,000 Americans killed or captured to this point in the war.

But this scorecard didn't tell the whole story. The NVA had decades of experience fighting a guerrilla war like this, going all the way back to the Viet Minh. The North had slaughtered the French at Dien Bien Phu in 1954, and driven them out of Vietnam altogether. Then a few years later, here came the Americans to keep South Vietnam and the surrounding countries from *falling like dominoes* to communism.

Of course, even when we left the fighting to the South Vietnamese in 1972 with the *Vietnamization* of the war, and they were defeated in 1975 by the commies from the north, the neighboring countries did not fall like dominoes. The Dulles brothers, and others, in Washington D.C. apparently had covertly influenced Secretary of State McNamara's foreign policy philosophy enough to convince him that all of Southeast Asia would fall to communism if the North Vietnamese Army was successful in conquering South Vietnam. This became known as the "Domino Theory."

Well, McNamara's "Domino Theory" turned out to be bullshit. This "Northern aggression" did not sweep the region. When Vietnam was unified, the NVA went home. In February of 1969, however, we didn't know how it would all turn out. We just knew that we had our hands tied behind our backs because we were forbidden from crossing the DMZ by the politicians and stopping this northern aggression at its source. Yes, airstrikes of the north were allowed, but no ground troops were allowed to cross the DMZ, and this was what was needed if you were ever going to defeat the NVA.

With all this in mind, the conversations in the Croc Hooch often went something like this:

"If we're not here to win, what the hell are we here for?"

"You mean all these guys are dying for fucking nothing!"

This is the disgruntled conversation that was occurring that night in February of 1969. Everyone was pissed off that we were there.

I was just sitting there taking it all in when Captain Weller said,

"You're not saying much, Pigpen, what do you think?"

"Guys, my opinion sure doesn't carry much weight, but I think there's a damned good reason for you and I to continue to fight this war to the very limit of our capabilities."

"Why is that, Pigpen?" someone finally asked.

"Because there are a lot of Americans out there fighting this war. Right now they're out there as we sit here talking. Out there in the fucking jungle, covered with leeches, hoping and praying to see their families again. We know damned good and well that they don't want to be here either. But they are. And what we can do, honorably, is to get as many of those poor bastards home as possible. Get them home alive in one piece!"

There was silence for a while, as everyone pondered what I had said.

Then Waldo spoke up, "You know, guys, he's right. Let's get as many of those guys home alive as we can."

At that, everyone got up, raised their drinks and said, "By God, I'll drink to that."

And that became the mission of the Crocodile gunship platoon of the 119th Assault Helicopter Company. To get as many of our fellow pilots and American ground troops home alive as we possibly could.

We would shy away from nothing. We would always be there on station, giving the North Vietnamese Army all the hell we could give them. They were killing Americans and we were simply going to kick their asses every chance we got. And we were going to do it with overloaded, underpowered Charlie Models. *Goddamnit! You're damned right. That's what we were going to do.*

41

Making Aircraft Commander

It was still February of 1969 when Robbie Apgar and Jeff Weller were sitting in the Croc lounge after missions one day. Weller turned to Robbie and asked, "Robbie, who's our best copilot right now? With Rad going home to the States, we've got an AC slot to fill."

I walked in from the flightline just as Robbie said, "Here's your man, Captain."

Unaware of their conversation I said, "Aw aw, what the hell did I do now?" You get accustomed to army ass-chewing whether deserved or not.

Weller replied, "You're the new AC Pigpen. You wing on Mac tomorrow to Dak To in aircraft 188." I wasn't sure he was serious,

"Roger that, Captain. I was going to take a cruise to the Bahamas with a bunch of naked women, but if you insist, I'll postpone it. They'll be heartbroken, I'm sure."

Weller said, "Fuck the naked women, Pigpen."

"That's what I'd planned to do with them, Captain, goddamnit, and here you come along and mess it all up." I now knew he was serious.

Weller laughed and replied, "Well, I tell you what, Pigpen, as hot as it's been at Dak To lately, you're gonna be too busy picking hot lead outta your ass in the morning to think about naked women."

I said, "Well, Captain, I'd hate to even think that my first flight as an aircraft commander wouldn't be a memorable one."

I went down the hall to the last door on the right and knocked on the wall next to the door blanket.

Mac said, "Yeah, what is it?"

I pushed the blanket aside, and still standing in the hall said, "I'll be flying your wing in the morning, Mac. Weller just appointed me AC."

Mac said, "Well, I wondered who the lucky bastard was gonna be."

He continued, "I haven't checked the mission board yet, do you know which birds we're flying?"

I said, "Yep, I checked just before I came. I'm flying the minigun ship, 188, and it looks like they've got you in the Hog, 564."

"They will probably put us on LRRP coverage. Insertion or extraction, or both," Mac said. "As you already know it's been crawling with NVA up there. We'll probably be busy all day, Mark."

"Yes, I expect we will be, Mac. I'll see you first thing in the morning."

"Congratulations on making AC, Mark."

I thanked Mac and told him goodnight.

That night I had a stomach full of butterflies. There wouldn't be anybody there to turn to now in the aircraft. It was all on my shoulders. And it didn't help any that the goddamned mosquitoes were big enough to have been arrested for breaking and entering.

There was a mosquito net over my bunk, and I swear you could see the net swaying back and forth, as a mosquito dive bombing squadron hit it at about 50 mph going for American blood.

At least the board said my copilot was Jack Cloud. I liked Jack a lot. I also knew he was a very competent pilot. It helped to know that.

Nevertheless, the butterflies and mosquitoes remained. I couldn't sleep. I tossed and turned all night long.

42

First Mission as an Aircraft Commander

The next morning, Mac and I stopped by the operations hooch to pick up contact information and radio frequencies. Apparently, the mission was just what we thought it was, LRRP insertions and possible hot extractions.

You never really knew what was going to happen in a gunship. You might be called to where the shit was flying at a moment's notice. So the mission sheet in the morning was just a rough guide that was subject to change at the drop of a hat.

When we arrived at the Christmas tree, the copilots already had the aircraft preflighted and ready to go, so we strapped ourselves in and fired them up.

I fell in behind Mac at his five o'clock position and 100 meters back, and we climbed to 3,000 feet absolute.

As much as possible, you wanted to fly above the *zap zone* in Vietnam. The *zap zone* was from 50 to 1,500 feet above the jungle, and it was here that you were most vulnerable to small arms fire. As a remedy, you could fly above it or right on the deck, below it. Higher was much safer, but flying just above the trees was much more fun. It was a bona fide adrenaline rush to be right on the trees. This low level flight was called *nap of the earth flying* and we frequently utilized it in combat. We were often *Treetop Flyers*.

Today, however, we climbed higher, and I heard Mac come on the radio,

"Spinner one, Spinner one, this is Crocodile 5, do you read, over?"

Spinner one answered, "Roger, Crocodile 5, go ahead."

"Spinner one, we are about five minutes out, approaching from the south, awaiting your instructions, over."

"Roger, Croc 5, Alligator 4 will be taking off to the south as soon as he gets you in sight. Follow him for insertion, over."

"This is Croc 5, roger."

I said over the Fox Mike radio, "Hey, Mac, Gator 4 is Hawk. I'm gonna give him some shit, just to wake his ass up."

Mac replied, "Go ahead, he probably hasn't had any shit yet this morning."

I got on the UHF radio and said, "Hey Hawk, this is Pigpen, do you read, over."

Hawk, now airborne, answered: "Yea, I read you, Pigpen, go ahead, over."

Hawk was an excellent pilot and treetop flyer, and had a great sense of humor.

"Hawk, listen to me closely. That stick that comes up between your legs is called the cyclic. If you want the whirlybird to go faster, push it forward, and if you want it to stop, pull that stick back. Have you got that, Hawk?"

"I think so, Pigpen. I wondered what that sumbitch was for, over."

"Hawk, you can call that sumbitch a sumbitch if you want, but that sumbitch is your ticket home today, so I don't think I'd piss it off if I were you, over."

"I think the sumbitch is already pissed off, Pigpen. What do I do now? Over."

"Talk nicely to him, Hawk. Promise him a whole case of beer when you get back if he straightens up and flies right, over."

After a short pause, Hawk said, 'Pigpen, by God that worked. I promised the sumbitch a case of beer and he straightened right up. Thanks for the tip."

I replied, "I'm at your service, Hawk. Always happy to help, over."

It was the meaningless banter we often engaged in to keep us sane.

Too soon it was time to get serious. Hawk was now over the insertion LZ for the LRRPs on board, if you could call it that. It was just another small hole in the jungle that didn't look like you could get half a helicopter in, let alone a whole one. Undeterred, the fearless Hawk set up a final approach into the southerly wind, and started his descent to the LZ.

Mac and I followed him in with our fingers on the trigger, in case he received any enemy fire.

As Hawk came to a hover over the LZ, Mac, who had followed him in, made a steep 180 degree turn, and I picked Hawk up while he was in the LZ. Hawk quickly dropped the LRRP team in the LZ, and came straight up, and out of the small hole in the jungle. I then overtook him, and broke 180 degrees and Mac picked him up and covered his climb-out. We then headed back to Dak To. The insertion had gone off without a hitch. I couldn't have been happier.

I got on the radio again and said, "Hawk, this is Pigpen, looks like it was a little tight in there, over."

Hawk replied, "Naaww, hell, we had a good six-inch clearance on all sides, over."

I laughed and said, "Well you know you owe me your life for telling you what that stick between your legs was for, over."

"I don't know what I would have done without you, Pigpen."

There were two more LRRP missions that day. One was another insertion, and the other was an extraction. Both were cold (No enemy contact).

That was just fine with me. When we flew back to Holloway, put the aircraft in their revetments, and shut them down for the day, I felt good about my first day as an aircraft commander. I realized that one of the major reasons that it had gone so well was because I was flying wing on a *damned good* mission leader that knew exactly what he was doing. It was that red headed ex-wrestler from Arizona, named James Madden McDonald.

43.

An Unexpected Night in Pleiku

Bright and early the next morning, two Crocs, who will remain nameless, barged into my room.

"Pigpen, your flight has been canceled this morning, and you are coming with us. It seems that you have not been properly initiated into the Crocodile, gun platoon."

They continued, "And we, my friend, are here to correct that."

Still groggy from sleep, I asked them if I had any choice in the matter.

"No, you sure don't!" they replied.

They grabbed my mattress and rolled me out on the floor.

At that, I said, "Well, I guess you are going to insist. You boys wouldn't lead me astray would you?"

"Now we wouldn't do anything like that, Pigpen."

Sure! I thought what are these devious bastards up to now.

"Damn, I feel better already. I'm sure you're going to take me to the prayer meeting this morning, isn't that right gentlemen?

Sure. "Yes, that's right, Pigpen. *We are* taking you to a prayer meeting all right. By the time *they* get done with you, you'll be praying for mercy."

"Now get dressed Garrison. We're in a hurry, because we've got to pick up a jeep at the motor pool. We've got to go into Pleiku today and stop by the tailor shop. There is a good Hong Kong tailor downtown, and you can really get a damned good suit while you're here. You ought to order one while we're there today, Pigpen."

I said, "You mean my initiation into the Crocs is to get a new suit in Pleiku? That sounds like a piece of cake."

"Well, we've got other plans for you, Garrison, after the stop at the shop."

Officers frequently went into Pleiku by jeep. Parts of town were relatively safe and were patrolled by soldiers from the U.S. Army during daylight hours. One had to be careful, however, because you never knew who the communist sympathizers were. When you were walking down the sidewalk, it was a very strange feeling to wonder whether the person passing you was going to smile at you or shoot you. I never did get used to that feeling during my whole tour. I avoided towns. In any case, however, it was well known that you never wanted to be caught in downtown Pleiku at night, after the military curfew, imposed by the command at Camp Holloway. As an officer, I carried a 45 caliber, 1911 model handgun in a waist holster that was always loaded with one in the chamber.

At this point I'm going to call these two Crocs Jake and Snake, for the sake of simplicity.

I got dressed, and went with them to the motor pool. They checked out a jeep and we were on our way to the main gate to pick up a pass from the guards. It was understood that any soldier who left in a vehicle or on foot was to return to post by 5 PM. If you weren't back by then, you could be in deep shit. *But I wasn't to be gone that long, right?*

We got a pass for the day at the guard shack, and drove toward town, weaving down a half dirt, half paved, potholed road. Of course, it didn't help anything that Jake was driving like a man possessed. I was in the back of the jeep, and Snake was riding shotgun in the front.

As we bounced down the potholed road, I said,

"Jake, Jesus Christ, man, why don't you slow this thing down! If I'm going to die over here I would just as soon do it in the gunship, and not in a damned jeep on the way to a whorehouse."

I had figured out by now, of course, where they were taking me. I had promised myself when I came to Vietnam that I would not under any circumstances visit one of these local establishments. But I learned a valuable lesson after a few months of celibacy. That lesson was that a man gets desperately needy, to the point of being irrational. In other words, good judgment flies out the window and is replaced by carnal lust. I had found out that I was all too human also.

Jake said, "Just sit back and relax, Pigpen, I've got things under control up here."

"I suppose you do have things under control, Jake, if you don't want me to be in the jeep when you get there, because I'm just about to bounce out of this son of a bitch."

Both Jake and Snake thought that my comment was exceedingly funny. I did not think it was so funny. I was taking a beating. I finally got a fingernail hold on a fender that was momentarily delaying my launch into orbit.

When we reached the outskirts of Pleiku, the throng of local Vietnamese civilians on bicycles filled the streets and we slowed down. There was an occasional car or truck that was old, tattered, and beat up, but people on foot or on bicycles were in the clear majority.

Many of the locals wore a black-pajama- like outfit with the conventional straw, pointed, Chinese hat. Both sides of the street were lined with businesses with the slide-down door like entrances I mentioned earlier. Up when open. Down when closed. Many of these business owners displayed their wares on the sidewalks in front of their buildings. The sidewalks were packed with people.

I kept wondering which and how many of them were communist sympathizers, ready to shoot all three of us. To me, it was an extremely uncomfortable feeling. It didn't seem to bother Jake or Snake though. They had been in country almost an entire year and were wrapping up their tours. They were old veterans at this sort of thing.

Eventually we arrived at the tailor shop, and Jake shut the jeep down and we climbed out. This tailor shop actually had a front with a swing-out door and all three of us entered. *How unusual.*

We received a friendly greeting from a Chinese looking fellow who spoke broken English, but was understandable. Both Jake and Snake told the man that they were there to pick up their tailored suits, and handed him a receipt voucher.

The man looked at the vouchers, said he would be right back, and disappeared into the bowels of the store. A short time later, he came back with two suits on hangers, and asked them to try them on. They went into two small dressing rooms, and quickly emerged wearing the suits. I was really impressed at the way the suits fit these guys. I decided right there to order one myself.

The tailor immediately started to measure me. He took all kinds of measurements from head to toe before he was satisfied. This was all new to me. I was just a poor boy from southern Illinois who had only heard of tailored suits in movies and magazines. I certainly had never owned one. The only suit I had at home was a basic black, right off the rack from JC Penney. In other words, my clothier had been *J-C.Penn-A.*

The Chinese guy then told me, when he was finished, that his measurements and specifications would be sent to Hong Kong, and that I was to check with him in about a month. I paid him a deposit of $50, and he gave me a receipt with a number on it. As I recall, the entire cost of the three-piece tailored suit, made from 100% worsted wool, was less than $100.

As we left the tailor shop, Snake spoke with a smirk on his face.

"Now, Pigpen, Jake is going to take you to your initiation site. I'm sure that you'll be thrilled." We got back in the jeep, and bounced down the road. If anything he was driving faster now than he was before, as I held on with every appendage that I could recruit. Then the jeep came to a screeching halt in front of "Mamasans." *Oh, real original name. And not so secure looking either.*

"Are you guys sure that this is safe down here?"

"Relax and don't worry about it, Pigpen. What are you some kind of pussy? Besides it's one hell of a lot more dangerous to fly a goddamned gunship than to screw a whore in Pleiku."

I asked, "Aren't you guys afraid of VD?"

"Hell no, all you have to do is go to the flight surgeon and get a shot of penicillin. You ain't getting out of this, Garrison. You might as well just stop whining around about it and enjoy yourself. Now come on, get out of the jeep and come with us.

I went with them.

There was music playing in Mamasans when the three of us walked in. There were a few locals but the place was mostly filled with soldiers. That made me feel a little better. The music was contemporary American rock 'n roll played on a jukebox in the corner. The place was dimly lit and filled with cigarette smoke. The laughter of the GIs drowned out the silence.

There were several quite beautiful Vietnamese girls in conventional Vietnamese dresses milling around. Their dresses had slits up the side of the legs almost all the way to the waist. As soon as I sat down, a young woman approached me, and asked me if I would enjoy her company.

I told her to please come back after a few beers. She said that she would definitely do that. It didn't take a few beers for Jake and Snake, however. When two girls approached them, they both disappeared into back rooms. When they returned to the table, I had drank a few beers and was still sitting where they had left me.

They both asked me why I was still sitting there, and called the girl who had initially approached me to our table.

Snake told her, "Take Pigpen here back and show him a good time, honey."

I went with the girl to a small room in the back. Softer music was playing, and the atmosphere was relaxed. Needless to say, the beer continued to flow and nature took its course. Afterwards I was asked if I would like a massage for just five more American dollars, payable, of course, in M P C.

I said, "Sure, I'd love a massage."

At this point, I was at least 2-1/2 sheets to the wind, and all I needed to drift off to sleep was a good massage. And that's exactly what I did. When I woke, I looked at my watch and it said 5 PM. I hurriedly dressed and dashed out to the front bar. There was no sign of Jake or Snake. I looked out front and the jeep was gone. Damn, I thought, I've missed the fucking curfew. But why would those guys leave me?

I looked around in the bar and saw that there were no American soldiers. It was filled with local civilians who were curiously looking at me. I went back to the room that I just left and sat on the bed, pondering my next move. I was flat-assed pissed off.

First of all, I knew that if I presented myself at the gate at Holloway, I would immediately be in trouble for missing curfew. I decided I didn't want to do that. Besides, I'd have to walk a mile or so to get there since all of the military people were already back on post. I also knew that there was seldom a bed check in my platoon, and if there was one, the other Crocs would certainly cover for me. I just couldn't figure out why those guys had left me. *Was this their plan?*

It looked to me as if my only other option was to spend the night in Pleiku, and go back to Holloway in the morning when the post opened. But I needed a place to stay. I couldn't stay in the damn bar. They would be closing at about midnight. No, I had to find the girl I was with, and ask her if she could put me up for the night. I realized it was a long shot, but at the time, I thought it was my only shot.

I got off the bed and began my search for the girl. I looked in the bar. I looked in all the back rooms. I looked in all the next-door businesses. I looked in the alleys. I looked in the streets. She was no place to be found.

It was now dark, and I had decided that my only option was to occupy the back alley for the night. I thought about how it would look in the newspapers back home if I were killed by the Vietcong in an alley. I could clearly see the headlines in my mind, *"Warrant Officer Garrison Gunned Down by Sharpshooting Whores in Vietnam Brothel While AWOL, Drunk and Disorderly."*

My mother would be so proud of me.

Nevertheless, I took up residence in the alley behind the bar. Every sound I heard was threatening to me. Frankly I was afraid for my life. Having people shoot at you on an almost daily basis in a helicopter gunship was one thing. Being in an alley at night, when God knows how many people know you're there, many of whom may be Vietcong is another thing. I thought at least I have my 45 pistol.

I checked my left leg pocket on my fatigue pants, and found that I had three extra clips of 45 ammo. Those, along with the one in my weapon, gave me about 30 rounds. I sure as hell hoped that I didn't need them, but at least I knew that I had them.

After I was in the alley sitting in the dark for a couple of hours, the girl that I had been with suddenly and unexpectedly entered the alley from the bar I'd been in. She had been very friendly to me and spoke relatively good English, so I took a chance that she was, indeed, friendly to American forces, and I said hello.

She said, "They tell me you here, what you do here?"

I said, "I missed my damned ride. Can you put me up for tonight?"

She said, "What you mean?"

I said, "You got place for me to stay tonight?"

She said, "You come with me."

I followed her down a labyrinth of alleys for what seemed like forever. The alleys were surfaced with brick, and were wet with water runoff from the adjacent buildings and homes. And damn were they slick. I must've slipped and fallen a dozen times, the last time being right before we got to her place, when I slammed my right knee into the bricks. I had a horrible limp as she opened her back door and motioned me in.

It turned out to be a small apartment in the back of a larger building. She told me that she lived there alone, and the apartment appeared empty except for us. I could occasionally hear other people talking through the walls, but she assured me those were people in adjacent apartments.

I was at this girl's mercy and I knew it. I hoped that she wasn't sympathetic to the north because I really had no other place to go until morning. *That is, if I lived through the night.*

I was struck by how neat and clean her apartment was. I was also impressed with the way she had it decorated. Most of the colors in the room were white and pink, which gave the room a very feminine look and feel.

She had removed her shoes at the door so I had done the same with my boots.

It was getting close to 10 o'clock that night, and I had pretty much sobered up. The girl had gone next door, she said, to talk to a neighbor. All of a sudden she burst through the door and said,

"You must hide, men come to find you. Hurry, hurry, go back to alley behind well and hide. I come get you when they are gone. Hurry! Hurry! Hurry!"

I knew what she was talking about when she said behind the well. I had noticed walking through the alley earlier, that there was a well every few feet in the center of the alley. These were obviously water supplies for the various houses and businesses.

I ran out the back door with my .45 drawn and ready to fire. When I got behind the well, I thought of my boots sitting by the door inside. I thought, dammit, that was real smart Garrison, for God's sake. There is nothing like giving your position away to make things exciting.

I then saw two men enter her apartment. I could see what was going on through a back window from the alley. The men, all of a sudden, started raising their voices, and she was answering them but I didn't know what they were saying.

The men started toward the back door that communicated with the alley. When I saw that, I ran down the alley a short distance and got behind another well. As I reached the other well my bootless right foot slammed into it, and I felt my big toe snap, but I damn sure didn't make a sound.

The men exited the back door of her apartment and looked around in the alley. It's a good thing that I chose to move, or I would've been discovered. Then there was some more shouting between the men and the girl, and the men left, waving their arms.

Son of bitch, that was a little too close for comfort! I couldn't wait for the rooster to crow.

When the men had been gone for some time, the girl came in the alley and called for me softly. I joined her and re-entered her apartment through the back door.

As I came in the back door, I noticed that my boots were gone. I asked her where they were and she said she had hidden them before the two men entered. She then went to a floor cabinet, and pulled my boots out and set them back where they were by the door.

She told me in her broken English that everything appeared to be safe now and that I should try to get some sleep and pointed at her bed. She said that she would keep a watch out for any danger. I told her I did not think I could sleep under the circumstances and would stay up with her. She fell asleep about 3 AM, but I stayed wide-awake.

When the gates to Camp Holloway opened the next morning, I put my boots on and left. The girl was still asleep. Before I left her apartment, I wrote a note to her thanking her for saving my life. I hope that she found someone to translate it for her, because I am truly grateful for what she did. I limped out on the sunlit streets, hopped a ride on an army transport truck, and re-entered the post without incident.

When I got back to the Croc Hooch, the first two guys I saw were none other than Jake and Snake. They jumped up when I entered the lounge and said,

"Garrison, for God sakes where were you? We looked all over for you and couldn't find you anywhere? There were even rumors going around that a soldier had missed curfew and was missing. A sergeant came, ready to do a bed check, but we told him all were accounted for in the Croc Hooch, and he moved on."

"Guys, I just decided to spend the night. It gets a little boring around here at night since you don't have anything to do but dodge mortars and rockets."

"Well, I'll say one thing for you, Pigpen," Snake said. "You sure as hell passed your initiation."

Well, I guess I did. But right then I was more interested in limping back to my room and nursing my wrenched knee and broken toe.

As I left them in the lounge, I said,

"I'll tell you about my relaxing evening in town sometime, when I'm a little more recuperated, guys. I will tell you this right now, though. It's an evening that I don't plan to repeat any time soon."

44.

The Cheo Reo River Runs

Once in a while, we received a mission to fly south to a place called Cheo Reo. It was close to the Vietnamese city of Ban Me Thuot. There was a large training center in that area for The Army of the Republic of Vietnam (ARVN). This was the South Vietnamese army that we were supporting in their war against North Vietnam.

There was a rather large river en route that ran for several miles from north to south. It didn't take the Croc gun teams long to, let's say, use the river as a means to practice precision flying.

By this time most all of us were hardcore adrenaline junkies, and most likely, certifiably insane. I don't care what you say, you can't fly a gunship day in and day out for several months, and remain completely sane. It's just a physical impossibility.

I, for one, was just a small town kid from a place where everyone waved at each other, went to church on Sunday morning and usually minded their manners. There was an established order about things that gave life continuity and direction. About the worst thing any of us did as teenagers was push over outhouses and soap windows on Halloween.

But here we were now, flying incredibly lethal machines, capable of killing hundreds of people in a single pass. And most of these people were trying their level best to kill you. This prospect faced you every day. Granted, not every day was a battle to the death, but you never knew when and where it was going to happen and it happened much too often. Most of us were still in our 20's and many in our early 20's. I was 22 years old when I came back to the States. In other words, we were not far removed from the teenagers back home still soaping windows and pushing over the outhouses. So, like kids, we were always looking for a little fun.

I suppose this is why the army takes young males into service. They are full of testosterone and patriotism, which makes them easy to mold into homicidal lunatics. They are more likely to obey orders without question, no matter what the orders are. Older folks, with the benefit of life experience, are much more difficult to manipulate. They have seen enough of the political bullshit that fuels wars, and are more apt to look upon the whole process with a jaundiced eye. When given a command, they are much more likely to ask why. In short, they have learned to be more rational.

This is true even in the military, and the reason the army and the other branches of the service have middle-aged men and women commanding the kids. The armed services know that if command was left to teenagers, things might not be so rosy. The kids might take it upon themselves to fix things.

They'd really have it fixed alright!

So, in our crazed state, armed to the teeth and ordered into somewhat peaceful territory, what do the kids do? We would dive the aircraft down to the river, reaching velocity never exceed of 140 knots, and pull out right on the deck. Both the lead gun and the wing man right behind him would be just inches above the surface, making our rotor wash churn the water. The object of this game was to see who could stay on the river's surface, and follow its tortuous course without crashing into the trees of the jungle on either bank. The first guy to pull up and pop over the trees was chicken.

Of course, since you were flying right down the river in plain sight of either bank, you were putting yourself at risk of being shot down by AK-47 automatic weapons fire. And, indeed, you would sometimes hear bursts of AK shooting at you and see the tracers, some of them hitting you. If that happened, the crew chief or gunner would mark the area with a smoke grenade, and both aircraft would gain altitude, go back around and do the army's bidding by incinerating the entire area.

We all played these daring and deadly games several times, screaming along behind one another thinking that the other was going to hit the trees in the jungle for sure, but he always seemed to stay the course of the river. I believe my wins averaged about 50 percent during these medieval contests. I will say that when I did lose and have to pop over the trees, I couldn't have lost to better pilots.

When you were flying a gunship in insecure areas, your weapons systems were generally hot. This means that they were ready to fire. In the gunship, there were switches in the center, overhead panel between the pilots that controlled the weapons systems. Before entering the aircraft pattern of any U.S. installation, you made sure that the weapons systems were turned off, which we called *safe mode*. As you left the installation you switched the weapons systems to on or *fire mode*. This was done, of course, for safety reasons. The last thing you wanted to do was accidentally hit the trigger with the rocket selector switch on salvo (all of the rockets go) when you were on final to the Christmas tree at Pleiku. You would have certainly wiped out several helicopters, and your ass would've been in a great big sling.

Once, when we shut the aircraft down for lunch at Cheo Reo, and we had a three-hour layover before we were to do another exercise with ARVIN troops, I bought a beer in town to wash down my C rations. I had made it a policy to never drink and fly, but I knew this beer would be out of my system by the time I cranked the aircraft again.

The beer was called "Bier 33," and was brewed in Vietnam. I noticed that it tasted funny but it was doing its job of washing down my meal, so I continued to drink it. When I finished my C rations, I raised the beer to take a final swallow, and noticed a good half-inch of mystery sediment in the bottom of the bottle. That was the first and last Bier 33 that I ever drank.

45

Somebody Messed With Waldo

I've described before the stereo systems that most all of us bought at the PX during our tour. In the evenings, after flying, the hooches usually sounded like there were several live rock concerts going on at the same time. Nobody said much about it. That was just the way it was.

That is, nobody said much about it until one particular night.

I was in Bob Vickrey's room, the guy that used to be married to the Dodge Rebellion girl. His room was a couple of doors down from Waldo's room. On this night, Waldo's room sounded like he had invited the Led Zeppelin Band in for a private, live concert, but that wasn't unusual. Most of the rooms sounded like they had live concerts going all the time at night anyway. On this night, however, it was getting close to midnight, and I was about to depart Vickrey's room for my own to get some sleep before another day of flying.

Just then the blanket covering Vickrey's door rustled as someone walked by. Then came a loud knock on the wall of Waldo's room, next to his door blanket. We then heard a voice telling Waldo, in no uncertain terms, to turn his stereo down, so others could get some sleep.

By this time, Vickrey and I had stuck our heads out of his room into the hallway to get a better view. We wanted to know who this damned fool was trying to tell Waldo to turn down his stereo. As we looked toward Waldo's room, we saw no one in the hallway. Then we heard muffled, scuffling sounds coming from Waldo's room.

The door blanket suddenly shifted toward the hallway, and an officer and fellow pilot, that Waldo didn't care much for anyway, appeared. The front of his body partially obscured, he seemed to be levitating about a foot off the ground in the hallway, moving slowly backwards. His eyes were quite wide. Then, after a few moments of the levitation mirage, Waldo's clinched fists appeared, holding the officer off the floor by the front of his shirt.

He then told him:

"You mean I'm out there every goddamned day, risking my ass and you tell me I can't even listen to music, you son of a bitch. Get back to your room and shut the hell up!"

The pilot, who didn't like midnight music, went back to his room and, to my knowledge, never asked Waldo to turn his stereo down again. Neither did anybody else.

46

More Agent Orange Baths

As discussed previously, Agent Orange was an herbicide that was used extensively in Vietnam. It was used to kill jungle vegetation to make it more difficult for the North Vietnamese soldiers to hide.

From 1962 to 1971 the United States dumped from 12 to 20 million gallons of this stuff. The main aircraft used for this herbicidal, warfare operation, which was codenamed Operation Ranch Hand, was the Fairchild C-123 Provider.

The C-123 was first developed in 1949, but didn't see its first battle until 1962. One of these Fairchild C-123 Providers, named Patches, is on display in the National Museum of the United States Air Force. Its claim to fame is having taken more than 600 hits from small arms fire in Vietnam.

I think this is reliable testimony that there were a lot of people on the ground that didn't like Agent Orange or a bunch of other chemical shit dumped on them.

Many authorities now think that Agent Orange has caused a myriad of human physical problems through the years. There have been more than 500,000 deaths directly linked to Agent Orange exposure. There have also been more than 500,000 severe birth defects associated with Agent Orange.

In January and February, 1969, the Crocs received several missions to provide gunship cover for these Fairchild C-123 Providers as they spread this herbicide. When these aircraft received small arms fire, the gunships would return fire, or dive through the cloud of Agent Orange to draw the fire away from them and pinpoint the enemy location. I flew several of these missions, first winging on a lead gunship, and later as a gun team lead. I usually winged on Robbie Apgar (Robbie), Jim McDonald (Mac), or Rick Gill (Waldo). Our flight suits would be damp with the stuff on numerous occasions. Some of these missions were around the Pleiku, Kontum, Dak To area, but most of the ones I flew were around An Khe.

An Khe was not much more than a 30- minute flight to Pleiku's east. Pleiku sat on a plain between mountain ranges, and had an elevation above sea level of 2500 feet. To get to An Khe, you flew east, usually following Road 19 to the Mang Yang Pass through the mountains, dropped 500 feet and reached An Khe at an elevation of 2,000 feet on another flat plain. Road 19 was the only major paved road through the highlands, and was extensively used for transport of our troops and supplies.

Going back to the Mang Yang Pass, it was usually foolish and dangerous to fly directly through it, because of enemy small arms fire. To counter this, we usually flew over the mountain range to the south of the pass. Mang Yang had long been utilized by the insurgents back as far as the war with the French. Just to the north of Road 19 as it went through the Mang Yang Pass, were several white grave stones, marking the graves of French soldiers who were massacred at the pass in the early 1950's. The story goes that they were all buried standing up facing France.

I had such a propensity to take hits from small arms fire during these Agent Orange missions, that Robbie Apgar gave me another nickname. He labeled me *Magnet Ass*. Unfortunately, the nickname was accurate. The bad guys did not like this stuff dumped on them.

We were told all along, that Agent Orange would not hurt us. It was stated again and again that it was only lethal to vegetation and did not have any harmful effects to animals. Those statements turned out to be patently false.

I don't know if you can hold the U.S. Army responsible for making those inaccurate statements about Agent Orange, since they were probably only going by what the manufacturers, Monsanto and others, had told them. Other companies, such as Dow chemical, manufactured the stuff and marketed it under various names. After all, the army was given a job to do and they were just trying to do it. They were understandably using everything at their disposal to get this job done. I also cannot assume that Monsanto, Dow, and the other producers, knew that Agent Orange was harmful to humans and animals, because they may well have thought that it was safe at the time.

Agent Orange was extremely effective at doing the job it was designed to do. When you flew over an area that had been doused with it a few weeks before, the previously dosed area looked like a moonscape. There didn't appear to be any plant life left, and it certainly would've been a very poor place for an enemy soldier to try to hide. Because of this usage it most certainly saved a number of American soldier's lives at the time.

As pilots, we didn't think much about the harmful effects of Agent Orange at the time since we had been told that it was not harmful to us. We probably couldn't have done much about it anyway, even if we had known that it was harmful. The U.S. Army had given us orders to perform the mission and we were expected to do it. Period!

The future would hold surprising news for all of us concerning the safety of Agent Orange. I know it certainly took me by complete surprise.

47

Flying Convoy Cover

Another mission gunship pilots often flew was convoy cover. As I have said before, Road 19 was a major supply and troop transport route. Troops and supplies were moved along this road in convoys. It was the most efficient way to move the heavy goods of war but never the safest. Dozens of vehicles hauling food, ammunition and fuel would form up into a single long line. Oncoming traffic would be halted and one by one the heavy trucks would start down the dangerous highways and up the dangerous mountain passes. The trucks hauled critical supplies for U.S. Army installations located along the road, and in the many LZs scattered throughout the Vietnam Highlands.

Favorite targets of the North Vietnamese were the *POL trucks*. These trucks carried petroleum, oil and lubricants. If hit by something like a rocket propelled grenade, these trucks erupted in incredible, fiery explosions. A single truck could carry up to 5,000 gallons of JP-4 jet fuel, and when it went up, it *really* went up, usually resulting in loss of life of the driver and those around it.

On a convoy cover mission, two gunships would fly a circular pattern at about 2,000 feet above the convoy moving along the road below. The helicopter crew continually surveyed the area in hopes of spotting the enemy before they fired. One hit was all it took. Most of the time, this was a rather boring mission for pilots. There was one AM radio station in Vietnam that you could tune in called AFVN that stood for Armed Forces Vietnam. As long as things were moving along smoothly on the ground, you flew in boring circles while you listened to Glen Campbell sing *Galveston*.

However, when things got hot, it was pandemonium. When a POL truck got hit you could usually see where the rocket came from. If you didn't, however, you flew over the suspected site in an attempt to draw enemy fire to pinpoint their location. Once the enemy location was established, the two gunships flying overhead would set up a race track pattern and give the enemy several rockets of their own to play with.

One early February day when I was winging on Waldo, we were flying convoy cover near An Khe, when a POL truck was hit by an RPG (rocket propelled grenade). The resultant explosion was incredible. The poor soldier driving the truck was blown through the front windshield in about a hundred and fifty pieces. The whole convoy came to a halt and soldiers assumed defensive positions. Both Waldo and I saw the origin of the RPG and set up a race track pattern above it. On our first pass we wiped out the rocket location, only to receive enemy fire from a secondary location. That was probably the worst thing that the enemy at the second location could have done if they wanted to live. My crew chief marked the enemy location by throwing a smoke grenade out of the aircraft. We then made a second pass on the secondary location, and they had no further comment on the matter.

That was the thing about Vietnam. You never knew when or where you were going to engage the enemy. There were no conventional front lines as in World War I or World War II. The North Vietnamese usually picked the place and time when they were going to fight. It was difficult for the U.S. Army command to form a coherent strategy. We were always waiting for them to show themselves so we could engage them in battle.

Remember that we could not cross the demilitarized zone with ground troops for political reasons. That kept us from cutting off the head of the snake. Indeed, most of the troops and probably all of the command thought that this was a ridiculous situation. If we were there to win, they reasoned, then why in the hell didn't they let us do it. It was as if they had blindfolded us and tied one of our hands behind our backs. *It just didn't make any sense.*

As pilots, we continued getting more and more disgruntled with the war and wondered why we were even there. I think the only thing that really kept us going as a unit, was the fact that we knew we were still getting Americans home alive that otherwise would not have made it.

So, we just kept plugging. We flew every day in support of our troops, and did the best job that we knew how to do.

But we all wondered, how long could this war go on?

48

Hot Refueling at Dak To

Shortly after the convoy explosion, I was winging on Waldo once again. We had flown three or four short missions already that day, and had flown into Dak To to refuel. We both made an approach into the refueling dump, and had set the aircraft down on pads and rolled the throttle back to flight idle. As the blades spun overhead at the reduced RPM flight idle, the crew chief and gunner got out of the aircraft to refuel it. We had to go right back out on another mission so we did not shut the aircraft down.

When you shut a jet engine down, you have to wait for the hot end of the jet to cool before restarting, or your exhaust gas temperature (EGT) will exceed red line when you restart. That makes the aircraft unflyable until it is examined by certified mechanics. Waldo finished refueling before I did and he had rolled the throttle on to operating RPM. My crew chief was still refueling the aircraft, and I was still at flight idle when there was a huge explosion to my right. I looked as another UH-1H Huey exploded into flames.

Then there was another explosion just outside the fuel dump, and I realized we were under a mortar and rocket attack. As flames from the burning aircraft licked at my window, I wrapped the power on as quickly as I could and yelled at my crew chief and gunner to get back in the aircraft. As the flames got closer and closer, it seemed that it was taking forever for the aircraft to come up to operating RPM.

As I was waiting, I turned again to yell at the crew to get in the aircraft, and was horrified at what I saw. In the chaotic confusion, my crew chief had spilled jet fuel all over himself, and was standing there looking rather dumbfounded.

I screamed, "Hop in the aircraft, man. We've gotta get the fuck outta here!"

The crew chief hopped in.

It was absolute chaos in the refueling dump as aircraft scrambled to take off and get the hell out of there. Then there was another explosion behind me. Whether I had operating RPM or not, *I had no choice— I had to go!* The whole place was on fire. If I stayed where I was we were all going to burn. I pulled collective pitch and hoped for the best. The aircraft grudgingly came off the pad, as the low RPM warning siren screamed in my ears. I nosed her over and pulled more pitch as my RPM bled even more. She crept forward as I lowered pitch and she bounced off the ground two or three times. This at least allowed me to gain a little more RPM. I nosed over further and she bounced again but I was rapidly running out of room to bounce on anything. My RPM was bleeding again and I really didn't even know how we were flying. All of a sudden, I had about 20 knots of airspeed and about 20 inches of altitude, and a serious case of low RPM as the rotor RPM warning continued to blare in my ears. But there was no place to put it down. I wouldn't have even if I could've because there were explosions going on all over now. But I was now over a deep ravine. This gave me the opportunity to lower pitch and flare the aircraft a little in an attempt to gain RPM. I didn't gain all that I needed but it kept me flying. All of a sudden right in front of me a guy appeared standing on the top of a sandbag bunker. I was headed right toward him in a loaded Charlie model gunship. His eyes were huge as he watched us. He acted as if he had no idea what to do. And I don't suppose that he did. He recognized he was just about to be wiped out, not by the weapons of a gunship, but by the gunship itself. Jack Cloud, my copilot, was frantically waving from right to left, imploring the soldier to get out of our way. At the last moment, he leapt into the ravine, narrowly escaping death by gunship, as the aircraft bounced heavily off the sandbag roof of the bunker, collapsing it. And that bunker is probably what saved us, as it allowed me to lower pitch, dive into another ravine, gain some airspeed, and nurse the bird into the air.

I've always wondered what that poor bastard on top of the bunker thought when he saw me bouncing toward him. He saw two lethal six-barrel machine guns, fourteen rockets, two guys with M60 machine guns, one of whom was fuel soaked, and more than five tons of gunship coming right at him. He also saw a pilot trying to fly the overloaded son of a bitch, with a crazed look in his eye, whom he probably thought had suddenly gone batshit crazy, and was intent on killing him.

Wherever he is today, I apologize for his nightmares and wish I could stop them. But I've got my hands full of my own nightmares that I'm still dealing with.

I heard Waldo then say over the radio, "Croc 2, Croc 2 (my official call sign) do you read, over?"

"Roger that, Waldo, I read you."

"Boy! That was close back there, Mark. I didn't know if you had made it out or not."

"I just barely did, Waldo. Did you have any trouble making it out?"

"I was lucky," Waldo replied. "I was almost all the way up to operating RPM when the mortar struck. My crew said that it looked like you were at flight idle still. Is that right?'

"That is an affirmative, Waldo."

"Then how in the hell did you get out of there, Pigpen?'

"Waldo, I don't have a fucking clue. So don't ask me to do it again because I don't think I could do it twice."

Waldo then said, "While you were back there playing with the mortars in the refueling dump, we got a new mission. Come with me; let's go get the bad guys."

"Do you know where they are, Waldo?"

"They have been spotted just to the west," he replied. "We should be able to find them."

It didn't take us long to find the North Vietnamese mortar team. As soon as we got close they opened up with all kinds of AK-47 fire. Waldo broke hard left and I followed. He then set up a gun run and I stayed behind in a wing man's position. I watched as he flew straight into the jaws of intense small arms fire and released three pairs of 17-pound high explosive rockets.

They had made the crucial mistake of giving their exact position away.

He then broke hard right, and made a 180-degree turn as I covered him during the break with three more pairs and several blasts of minigun fire.

Next I broke hard right as Waldo covered me with two more pairs of rockets and several more blasts of machine gun fire.

No one at Dak To ever heard another word from them.

49

It's A Shame About The Chinook

Shortly after the refueling nightmare, I was flying near Kontum, when a call came on the radio from a C-47 Chinook helicopter. The Chinook is a large, long tandem rotor helicopter built by Boeing Aircraft Company. It is used mainly for resupply and troop transport. It also can sling heavy loads.

The Boeing Chinook in flight.

The pilot had said that he was going to make a precautionary landing in a field near Kontum. He said that his transmission oil pressure light was on. I was in the area and decided to investigate.

When I got there, there was a perfectly good Chinook sitting in the middle of a clearing. The crew had been evacuated and there was another gun team on station, protecting the chopper until it could be sling loaded out.

The gun team on station was from the Cougar platoon in Kontum. The fire team was circling overhead protecting the chopper from any NVA that may appear.

John Howard White was leading the Cougar Team, and he had warned those at operations that he was carrying Willie Pete rockets, and may very well set the field on fire if he had to use them.

Willie Pete rockets were white phosphorus rockets, used to basically set fires.

Operations said that they had no one else available and there was no time, and to stay on station and protect the chopper on the ground.

John Howard White was a friend of mine and a quite competent pilot; he again warned them that if he used the rockets he may very well set the chopper on the ground on fire.

Operations repeated that they wanted him to stay on station and use the rockets if necessary.

Sure enough, enemy troops approached the chopper from a tree line on the south, and White and his wingman had to use the white phosphorus ordinance.

As White had warned, the rockets did, indeed, set the field on fire.

Everyone sat and watched as the fire reached the aircraft and completely destroyed it. The only thing that was left of it were the tips of the rotor blades and the two steel masts of the rotor hubs.

I was talking to John a few days later, when he came to camp Holloway and spent the night. I asked John how things were going, and he said under the circumstances pretty well. Then he told me about a mission that he had just flown after the burning chopper debacle.

He said he was on a hot gun run and receiving intense enemy fire, when something broke the plexiglass window in his door. He didn't know what had done it. When the mission was finished and he returned to his base, they shut the aircraft down and got out to do a post flight, and lo and behold, there was a 40 mm grenade lying in the back of the aircraft that had failed to explode.

The crew gingerly disposed of it and counted their lucky stars.

I told John that he was the luckiest bastard in Vietnam. He agreed.

And the war drug on and on. And I, for one, got crazier and crazier. Any purpose or meaning that I ever had given to the war was long gone. Anybody with any sense was saying why didn't they just let us go home if they weren't going to let us win this thing.

No one had an answer.

50

Thornton's Thunder

There was a slick pilot in the 119th known as *Thunder* Thornton. He had gotten his nickname by the quality of his voice, which was thunderous indeed. He was one of those guys whose voice carried two city blocks away when he was whispering. I have no idea what his real first name was.

It seems that Thunder had been having a long-term problem with fungus from the water that we used to take showers. It was a common problem in Vietnam. Thunder was uncircumcised, and the fungus had insinuated itself under his foreskin. Apparently he had tried everything to get rid of it, to no avail.

Finally he went to the company flight surgeon and asked to be circumcised. The flight surgeon advised him that this is not a simple procedure in a grown man, and that he would be in considerable discomfort for some time. Thunder decided to go ahead with the operation anyway.

The day after his operation, Thunder was sunning himself on a lawn chair by the hooch. Evidently he had consumed several drinks because it was difficult to awaken him. He was lying on his back with nothing on but boxer shorts and socks. His butchered penis had escaped the corral, and the bandaged end was in plain sight.

That is when a golden opportunity to use the cameras came into play. Another slick pilot, I won't say who, took several pictures of Thunder's mutilated organ while he slept.

There was a darkroom for the photography buffs at Camp Holloway that many of us used. It was set up quite nicely for a darkroom that was in a combat zone. You could develop just about any kind of black and white film and enlarge it and print it. You couldn't develop color film because the temperature control was too imprecise for that.

Anyway, the guy that took the pictures developed the film, enlarged the pictures as much as he could, and printed them.

We then took the best enlargement and put it in the lounge area of all the platoons in the 119th Assault Helicopter Company.

For effect, we placed it next to several pictures of Playboy centerfolds.

The first time Thunder saw the pictures, you could hear his booming laughter all over the compound. He was a damn good sport about it. He knew he might as well be or he would have caught even more hell in the future.

51

Manual Pest Control

I've mentioned before that we all had mosquito nets over our bunks in the hooches. This was absolutely imperative since the Red Cross and their blood supply wasn't immediately available to us.

Let me say here the Vietnamese mosquitoes were world class specimens. As a matter of fact, in today's environment I'm sure they would have been accused of using anabolic steroids. The same thing can be said of a myriad of other creatures that would fly into the hooch lounge at night uninvited.

You see, we had screens in the rooms of the hooches, but no screens on the doors. That didn't make a whole hell of a lot of sense to me. There was an open side door to the Croc lounge that allowed Flex Mode, Stowed Mode and Bitch to come and go at their pleasure, but it also allowed the critters to do the same. And were there a lot of different critters!

Don't get me wrong. I had been exposed to a whole variety of different summertime life forms in Illinois. Once, as a matter of record, while a student at Southern Illinois University I had found an insect that was so unusual to me that I took it to the entomology department to find out what it was. It had the head, thorax, and front appendages of a Praying Mantis, and the abdomen of a wasp. I gave it to the guy at the department and said,

"Do you have any idea what this is?"

He shook his head in puzzlement. "First of all, if it wasn't moving, and obviously alive, I would have been convinced that you were playing a joke on me, and had combined a wasp and a mantis somehow. But since it's moving and obviously the real McCoy, let's get the book out and catalogue it."

He then murdered the bug with formaldehyde and proceeded to categorize it by mainly looking at its wings through a microscope. He found it in the book, but it had never been reported as far north as Illinois. The farthest north it had ever been seen was Florida. As far as I know, it still sits in the university's entomological display today.

All of that being said, compared to Vietnam, Illinois was like a lifeless, barren moonscape. There were bugs of every conceivable size, shape and color that would fly through the door every night.

One night, that I unfortunately recall, Jim McDonald, Robbie Apgar, myself, and several other Crocs were sitting in the Croc lounge. The combat missions of the day were complete and myself and a couple of other guys were shotgunning Budweiser's, in a race to achieve yeast excrement toxicity. As usual, I was easily leading the competition.

These were the days when a lot of beer cans were still without pull tabs, and you had to open them with a can opener, commonly known as a *church key*, that many soldiers carried with them around their necks along with their dog tags.

To shotgun a beer, you not only opened the top of the can, but also the bottom to see how quickly you could suck it dry. We had done a six pack or so this way, each taking about three seconds to empty, when a gargantuan beetle of some sort flew through the door to join the festivities. Seriously, at first, I thought it was a large hummingbird. That's certainly what it sounded like to me.

Everybody started ducking the creature as it buzzed the room slamming into the walls and then off my noggin. The next gun run it made toward me, the beer I had shotgunned (I had nothing to do with it, I assure you) reached up and snatched him, midflight, bit his head off, and threw his still writhing, headless body on the floor at McDonald's feet.

Witnessing my treatment of the beetle as if it were an hors d'oeuvres, McDonald, Apgar and several others, raced to the side door of the lounge, where the unfortunate beetle had gained entry, and proceeded to deposit their dinner on the ground outside.

Reportedly, at this point, I said,

"What's the matter with you sumbitches? Are you all just a bunch of pussies? How in the hell else are we supposed to control the insect problem in here?"

Then I promptly fell off the stool.

I awakened in the middle of the night and my eyes immediately grew wide, with a foggy memory of an insect entree. By the taste in my mouth, I suspected that it had been more than a dream.

After showering and shaving the next morning, I was walking to the flightline with Mac and I asked him,

"Hey, Mac, what the hell did I do to that huge beetle last night?"

"You sure chewed him up," Mac replied.

I briefly considered the downside of shotgunning Budweiser after that.

52.

An Awesome Fireworks Display

During the closing months of 1968, when I had just become a crocodile, most of us were still in our rooms in the Croc hooch early in the day, when we heard a series of loud successive explosions.

We all ran out to investigate, and found that the main ammunition dump had been hit at Camp Holloway. The North Vietnamese got lucky with a rocket.

The sirens indicating imminent attack immediately started to blare, so we ran back to our rooms and donned our helmets, flak vests and weapons, and headed to the trenches. We stayed there for some time waiting for the attack that never came, but that didn't make it any less stressful. After a couple of hours, we were allowed to return to our company areas, so we all quickly picked up a ringside seat about a half-mile from the action to watch the fireworks display.

It was some kind of a display. I had never seen anything like it. Waldo, Mac, Robbie, Weller, John-John, Vickrey, Sugar Bear, Chipmunk, Tricky Dick, Duffel Bag, Golly-Golly, Jerry Miller, and I along with others from the unit just stood there mesmerized, watching the ammo show.

One explosion would ignite another and another in rapid succession, until we all began to wonder just how much ammunition was in that dump. I had seen some pretty fair fireworks shows at home in Illinois, but this was just over the top. It made the shows that I had seen seem like they set off a single pack of Lady Finger firecrackers.

The explosions went on for hours and hours into the night, as those of us watching got drunker and drunker. After several hours of drinking and watching, I climbed up on top of the bunker that we were supposed to be in, and were not, and appointed myself as a judge of the fireworks display. I told all those assembled that they were to cheer at each explosion, and that the winner would be dependent upon the volume of their cheers. Everyone modified my rating system to one which permitted booing, hissing, and loud hallelujahs. I quickly seconded the motion and the judging began.

The perimeter guards remained on high alert watching for the possibility of a ground attack. Fortunately, the ground attack never came. You always had to stay on guard, however, because you never knew when and if the attack was going to come. And that was one more thing that made Vietnam so stressful. The intelligence about enemy troop movement and their intentions was incomplete at best and nonexistent at worst. After all, this was a guerrilla war and the North Vietnamese were the ones who had the experience in guerilla style. They had helped write the book. The United States war machine was still geared to fighting conventional wars with well-established front lines. *But we were learning.*

Here we were fighting an enemy who had 20 years experience in this war alone, fighting on his own ground. Add to that the fact that we were seriously outnumbered, and had logistical nightmares just to keep our troops supplied with food and ammunition. Our supply lines extended to the other side of the world. The enemy supply lines extended for just a couple of hundred miles at the most. It now seemed the whole Vietnam enterprise was doomed from the Gulf of Tonkin Incident forward. But I guess I'll never know for sure. Somebody, somewhere in our own government, seemed to be making it impossible for us to win. And, the voice of my old baseball coach continued to ring in my ears: *"Boys, if you're going to play....play to win. And if you're not going to play to win, turn in your uniform."*

What a screwed up world we were living in!

53.

The Night Flare Mission

Every so many days the 119th was assigned night flare duty. Since we had been hit with rockets and mortars so often at night at Camp Holloway, the commanding officers decided to keep a slick helicopter loaded with magnesium flares on standby at night. Also on standby, was a light fire team of two Charlie model gunships.

Command reasoned this action would significantly reduce the reaction time to a rocket attack. The pilots and crews assigned to fly these aircraft were to spend the night in the flare hooch. This hooch was only a few yards from the aircraft. Pilots were to sleep in their clothes and boots and be ready to scramble at a moment's notice.

The flare ship and the gunships were preflighted and ready for what is called *a hot start*. That meant they were already flight worthy, the blades were left untied, and all the pilots had to do was strap in, put on their helmets, throw the battery switch on, the fuel selector switch on, and hit the start trigger. We could be airborne in a couple of minutes.

One February night, Waldo and I were assigned flare duty in gunships. We hoped it would be a boring evening but it was not to be.

About midnight, an explosion rocked the base and the sirens blared. We were ordered to scramble immediately.

We dashed out of the flare hooch and ran toward the aircraft. Then there was another explosion close to the end of the runway. Then another that was louder. They were walking 122 mm rockets toward us. That got my attention in a hurry. One of these rockets could blow the hell out of anything it hit. If it happened to hit near a human, it would tear him into pieces. I was tired of running from the bastards the first time I ever heard one go off. As we reached our aircraft and began strapping in, there was another even louder explosion.

Then came a direct rocket hit on a cobra helicopter gunship sitting in front of a maintenance building. We next saw a direct hit on a Chinook even closer to us. Apparently, this Chinook was full of fuel and the resultant explosion was horrific. *It was raining shrapnel!*

Waldo and I were already in our cockpits trying to get the damned aircraft up to operating RPM but it seemed like it was taking forever.

We both helplessly watched as the enemy rockets methodically walked up the runway toward our position. Once again, I felt as if I was in that surreal world that I had experienced in the hot LZs. A strange calm overcame me, as my brain failed to process all of the sensory information it was getting. Then there was another huge, incredibly loud explosion that rocked both ships.

Realizing we had no choice, we added collective pitch and hoped for the best. Both aircraft sluggishly came off the ground and inched forward.

I had about 6200 RPM and I needed 6600. I pushed the beeper switch on the collective with my left thumb to get all the power from the engine that I possibly could.

This beeper allows the pilot to gain a few more RPM in an emergency situation. This was definitely an emergency situation. Glancing at Waldo's aircraft, I realized he was having similar problems.

The rockets now being steered to us, we had no choice but to go. We lurched and bounced down the runway, trying to stay ahead of the rockets and achieve flight RPM. I found myself talking to the damned helicopter as if it were an animate object.

"What the hell's the matter with you, you crazy son of a bitch? Don't you see that you're going to get a rocket up your ass if you don't hurry?"

The helicopter did not seem to listen, the dumb overloaded, underpowered bastard.

But somehow we got the birds in the air. Don't ask me how, because I couldn't give you a rational explanation.

Once we both went through translational lift, the aircraft started to act like it wanted to fly and we started to gain airspeed and altitude. We had just barely evaded the rockets. When we had gained altitude, and the lights of Camp Holloway were below us, Waldo saw a couple flashes indicating the origin of the rockets. We both had to act quickly and he rolled in on a gun run on the position.

I watched as Waldo punched off two pairs of rockets, followed by two bursts of minigun fire, that looked to me like it was right on target. As he broke in a 180-degree turn, I followed his assault with two pairs of my own, but started to receive small arms fire from a nearby secondary location. I quickly lined up with it and punched off yet another pair of rockets, then another, and then another. I then fell into a sort of trance, mesmerized by the flash of rocket motors and bright flashes on the target. My airspeed exceeded VNE as I continued the dive. The final pair of rockets was so loud in the cockpit, that all of a sudden, I realized that I was about to hit the enemy with the helicopter itself. I had become *target fixated.*

Target fixation is a phenomenon where the pilot becomes transfixed on the target and does not realize how close to the target he is, especially at night. The only thing that saved me was the loudness of the explosions in my ears. I pulled out of the gun run right on the deck, probably with less than 20 feet of altitude at close to 200 miles an hour.

I had studied target fixation in flight school but I never thought it would ever happen to me. Well it did, and it damned near cost me my life and the lives of the crew.

We were successful in wiping out the rocket team that was ruining everyone's evening, so we returned to Camp Holloway, shut the aircraft down, and returned to the company area. Almost immediately, a guy from operations came and said that we had not gotten clearance to fire from Dragon Control. It was odd, I thought, and a glance at Waldo told me he did also. This was micromanagement bullshit.

If we needed clearance to fire, why scramble us to wipe out the bad guys in the first place? *Come on guys, things happen fast up there. You've got to shit or get off the pot. It's kill or be killed!*

Since Waldo was the fire team lead, he wound up on the red carpet the next morning in the CO's office getting his ass chewed. Then it came out. Apparently, there may have been a LRRP team chasing the bad guys. *Why in the hell didn't they tell us that in the first place?*

So, instead of getting praise for wiping out the rocket team, we got reprimanded for firing without permission. It really pissed both of us off.

54.

The Fortunate Few

Shortly after the flare mission, I was winging on Jim McDonald (Mac) in a Charlie model equipped with miniguns and rockets. Mac was flying a Hog that had 38 rockets, but no miniguns.

It was a beautiful, sunny day in Southeast Asia and we were dispatched for a hot LRRP extraction north of Dak To. This was *real bad guy land.* On the way up there from Holloway, for some reason or the other, the mission got scrubbed. We turned and headed back to Holloway.

We were on our way back to Camp Holloway, with an almost full load of fuel, and a completely full load of rockets and ammunition. Since we didn't have much to do on the return flight, we were fiddling with the Fox Mike radios and scanning different frequencies.

Remember, the Fox Mike (FM) radio was used for air to ground communication. One of us, I don't remember who, stumbled upon a LRRP team radio transmission. They were desperately calling for help. There were only four of them being pursued by several dozen NVA soldiers who were gaining fast on them. The leader of the team was running and trying to talk into the microphone at the same time. He was panting and difficult to understand.

Mac then asked him the coordinates of his position, and when he gave them we realized we were almost on top of him. The leader of the team on the ground had identified himself as Beta 4.

"Beta 4, we are right in your area at 3,000 feet please pop red smoke, over," Mac said on the FM.

"I can't, they are too close. I will give away our position," Beta 4 replied.

"Beta 4 if you do not pop smoke I cannot help you. I have to know your position before I can fire."

Beta 4 replied: "I can hear your choppers now, and I hope to God you can see us. Here goes the red smoke."

When the LRRP's popped red smoke, we were almost right above them and could easily identify their position. There was a clearing just to their south and we could see North Vietnamese troops crossing it headed north toward the red smoke.

Mac and I knew that we had to get to the bad guys before they got to the LRRPs. It was going to be a race against time. Mac banked the Hog into a steep 90° turn to the right and set up a downwind leg on the clearing. I fell in behind him. After flying a short distance to the west he made a sharp 180° turn to the right and set up a final gun run on the clearing to the east. I fell in behind him to provide cover fire.

As soon as the North Vietnamese troops realized what was happening, every weapon they had, turned and fired on Mac. Mac didn't even flinch as he flew right into a damned wall of lead. He then fired at least four pairs of rockets on his first pass that impacted and exploded right in the middle of the enemy troops. But there were more of them.

As Mac broke hard right to come back around and cover me and my run, I still received heavy fire. There were so many muzzle flashes that it looked like a damned photographic convention. I punched off three pairs of rockets, and my copilot followed that with several blasts of minigun fire. The rockets and machine gun fire was right on target and decimated the enemy.

Mac and I made two more passes to wipe out any further enemy resistance and threat to the team on the ground.

We then called in a slick to extract the LRRP Team. We had done it. We had gotten the team out without a single friendly casualty. We then resumed the trip to Holloway.

My crew chief said we had taken hits, so I intently watched the instruments to make certain everything remained in the green (normal) zone. Fortunately it did.

I still cannot fathom how Mac dodged all the lead thrown at him that day. When you can fly between bullets you are either damned lucky or the epitome of precision flying. *Probably both in Mac's case!*

202 | Mark Garrison

Allow me to break rank and jump ahead a few months. Mac had just gone home and I had only a few weeks left in country. We were having a cookout for the 119th one evening. All of a sudden, I heard someone asking for Mac and Pigpen.

I said, "I'm Pigpen, over here."

A soldier then approached me, and said,

"Are you the Pigpen that's also called Croc 2?" Three other soldiers then walked up behind him.

"Yes I am," I admitted. I suddenly saw four men get teary-eyed and they weren't even close to the smoke emitted from the grill.

"We are Beta 4, Sir," the soldier said with a quiver in his voice. "You and a pilot by the name of Mac saved our asses a few months ago. We wanted to personally thank you and Mac. Is he here?" I told them Mac was now stateside enjoying hearth and home. I recounted for them how much lead flew at us that day.

All four of them, in turn, gave me a heartfelt hug and told me thanks, the tears really welling up in their eyes. They then asked me to give Mac the same hug for them if I ever saw him again. I told them I would. I was almost crying myself by then.

Later, as we enjoyed our feast, I shared the visit with other Crocs. I told them there were men out there in the jungles that they too had saved and that we should all feel proud because our mission statement was working. We were still sending our soldiers home alive.

I was profoundly and deeply touched by this incident. We all had saved a lot of lives but seldom did we get the personal feedback. That one experience alone may have been worth the trip to Vietnam. *Mac and I had gotten four more Americans home alive. Yes, I felt really good about that.* Later, alone in my room, that night in the Croc lounge came vividly to mind. That special night we made it our personal mission to get as many American soldiers home alive as we possibly could.

I also remembered the day after saving Beta 4 when Mac and I had flown to Holloway, I distinctly remember reflecting on the violence of this war and how we were the cannon fodder for the cigar-smoking fat cats. You sure as hell didn't see them or their families out here where the shit was flying. No, that was left to poor men's sons.

I thought then, and still do today, that if the leaders that started wars, or their offspring, had to fly just one hot combat mission, there wouldn't be any such thing as war. I'm sure the bastards would work things out at the table instead.

55

Robbie and Jon-Jon

Robbie Apgar was a fine gunship pilot. So was Jon VanLeer (Jon-Jon). They were both very competent, smooth on the controls, and knew what they were doing. One day, Robbie was flying as aircraft commander with Jon-Jon as his copilot. They were headed a few miles to the south of Pleiku on some sort of *routine* mission. En route, Robbie started to experience difficulty moving the controls, and asked Jon-Jon to take the aircraft and see what he thought. Jon-Jon agreed that something major was wrong, as the controls became more and more difficult to move.

They both diagnosed it as a probable hydraulic problem that was rapidly leading to complete failure, and attempted to put the aircraft into a descent to get it safely on the ground as quickly as possible.

Then they found that the collective pitch control was immovable. The collective has an emergency hydraulic reservoir to be used in just this kind of event, but it also had apparently failed. Robbie had no choice but to roll the power off to decrease rotor RPM, thus decreasing lift, to establish a reasonable descent.

The problem was that Robbie also found out he could not move the pedals to line the aircraft up to run it out to a safe landing, and he had no way to bring the cyclic back to lose ground speed. It was an accident bound to happen, no matter who was at the controls.

Somehow Robbie and Jon-Jon *were able* to slow the aircraft to just a few knots, but it hit the ground at an angle and the chopper rolled over on impact and beat itself to death with the rotor blades striking the ground. Miraculously, pilots and crew were able to get the bird shut down and the entire four-man crew walked away alive.

In all this chaos, Robbie got a *Mayday call* off before impact and almost instantaneously a U.S. Air Force rescue chopper from Pleiku Main appeared and evacuated them to safety. Then a Boeing Chinook came to sling-load the wreckage back to friendly territory.

This aircraft was a brand new Charlie model UH1C Huey that had just arrived in country. Examination of the aircraft revealed that there was a hydraulic fluid line that had somehow come loose, causing a complete hydraulic failure. You simply cannot move the controls of a Huey without the hydraulic system.

Robbie always felt bad about this and has, for some reason, blamed himself for wrecking it. He should not feel at all bad about this, or hold himself responsible. As a matter of fact, in my opinion, he and Jon-Jon did a fantastic job to just get the aircraft on the ground, with the whole crew walking away from it without a scratch. That in itself is an exceptional demonstration of keeping a cool head, fast thinking, and tremendous flying skills.

This also illustrates the exceptional abilities of the pilots of the 119th AHC, both in the slicks and the guns. They were superb pilots who flew under intense pressure on a daily basis with no letup. I've always considered it an incredible honor to have been one of them.

One day, sometime after this incident in the spring or summer of 1969, I can't remember exactly when, I walked into the Croc hooch lounge to see a new guy sitting there talking to some of the other Croc pilots.

He was a personable sort of fellow and held the rank of first lieutenant. His fatigues were new and dark green, giving him away as being new to country.

As I joined in the conversation, I found that he had just been assigned to the Crocs, and was to start flying missions right away with us. Since he was a commissioned officer, it was apparent to me that he was going to be groomed for a command slot in the Croc platoon.

As I sat there talking to him, someone asked me, "Hey Magnet Ass, how many hits did you take today?"

I laughed and said "I don't know, man. I just wanted to get the hell away from the aircraft and I didn't hang around to count."

Then I said, "So what's your name new guy?"

He replied, "Name's Jim Souffley, but they've been calling me *Shoo-fly* since I've been here."

"Shoo-fly," I said. "That's a good nickname. It's sure as hell better than Pigpen or Magnet Ass, which are the two they've given me."

I continued, "So have you taken any hits yet, Shoo-fly?"

He said, "Not in Vietnam, but I took hits at Fort Rucker, Alabama, in flight school."

I couldn't believe what I was hearing.

I said, "What? You took small arms fire in Alabama?"

He replied, "Yea, I landed in a farmer's field during a simulated mission and the farmer apparently didn't like it much. So, I took a couple of hits from a 30.06 in the tail boom before I could get the hell out of there."

At that point, I laughed so hard I almost cried.

When I regained my composure, I said, "All I can say, Shoo-fly, is that if you took hits in flight school you don't have a fucking prayer over here."

Everyone laughed in unison.

Shoo-fly turned out to be a damned good copilot and eventually an aircraft commander. He flew as my copilot several times, and I found him to be a quick learner with a good touch on the controls. I believe, after I left for the States that he became platoon leader. He certainly turned out to be a credit to the Crocs.

56.

The Drunken Food Theft

The war dragged on and on. It seemed everyone required our services. The Alligators and Crocodiles continued to fly. Vietnam was funny that way. All of the days ran together. I often didn't know whether it was Monday or Sunday, because frankly it didn't make any difference. If the sun came up, you were probably going to fly.

The missions seemed to run together also. You might give gun cover to a couple of insertions or extractions one day, and be on a search and destroy mission the next.

A *search and destroy mission* was one where a light fire team was assigned the task of flying at treetop level over a certain area of jungle, to see if you could draw enemy fire. If you received fire, you won an opportunity to eliminate the enemy. I guess it was a little like being sacrificial lamb and executioner. It really was dangerous. You fly low, you get shot at and maybe you get hit. If the bullets don't kill you or a member of the crew, maybe it brings down your aircraft.

This was yet another hazard of Vietnam. There were few places to put the aircraft down safely in an emergency situation. You were almost always above trees or mountains. If that one-in-a-million safe landing spot wasn't in your immediate future, you were going to tear the hell out of your aircraft going down. Fires often followed crashes, as did death and disability. Not to mention death or capture by the enemy. These threats were a constant stress on all combat pilots.

At least it was in the Central Highlands. The guys in the Delta down south had a much easier time of it if they went down. That is not to say they were worry free. There's always a trade-off. It was also easier for the enemy to get a clear shot at you in the Delta of the Mekong River. If you went down, the enemy could be on you before rescue got notified you were down.

One day in late February, I was winging on Robbie Apgar on a search and destroy mission near An Khe. It seemed like everywhere we flew we were receiving enemy fire, punching it out with them, and going back to refuel and rearm at An Khe.

Robbie, you'll remember, was the one that gave me my second nickname of Magnet Ass, because of my propensity to take hits. And, indeed, I took five or six hits on this day, one through the cockpit and the rest through the tail boom.

I believe it was Jerry Miller who was flying as my Croc copilot that day. Jerry was just a really nice guy, and everyone really liked him. He was a quite competent pilot and was being groomed for aircraft commander. As aircraft commander, I had been handling the rocket systems all day and as copilot he had been handling the miniguns.

Since we were to do much the same thing the next day, we were to remain overnight (RON) at An Khe. At dusk we set the aircraft down in revetments and headed to the barracks assigned us. The backseat crews headed to their quarters elsewhere.

Somehow we acquired a couple of cases of beer for the evening. Since Robbie, and his copilot, Chipmunk, were very light drinkers, most of it was left to Jerry and me. That's not to say that Jerry was an irresponsible drinker, because he wasn't. The same thing, however, cannot be said for me in the evenings. I needed an escape hatch at the end of those long grueling days, to maintain some semblance of sanity. At least I thought I did.

After consuming way too many beers, I was not only roaring drunk, but ravenously hungry. Robbie and Chipmunk had long since gone to bed as it neared midnight. Jerry was also hungry so we decided to venture out in search of food. Not only was there no food where we were staying, there was no potable drinking water. Jerry and I had not gone very far down a dirt road when we ran into an apparent storage building just off the road to our left. Jerry had his military issue flashlight with him, so we went to investigate. On the side of the building, was a sign written in military hieroglyphics that indicated there were LRRP Rations and other things inside. I told Jerry we had apparently found the mother lode.

LRRP Rations were a predecessor of today's more famous MREs (Meals Ready to Eat) and required rehydration with water. They were actually pretty tasty when hot water was available. Investigation revealed the door was padlocked, so if we were going to eat we would have to find another means of entry. Examining the building, we saw that the walls were made of corrugated tin nailed to wooden posts. At the very top of the four by eight sheets, was about an 18 inch space between the walls and the tin roof. I convinced Jerry that I thought if he boosted me up I could get in through the opening.

The plan worked and I squeezed an entry. Once inside, I couldn't see a damn thing. It was pitch black. I told Jerry to toss me his military flashlight through the opening. He did throw it and I heard it bouncing around on boxes and coming to rest somewhere in the darkness, but I had no clue where. If it was on when he tossed it, it wasn't on now. I commenced crawling around on my hands and knees in the dark, looking for it. I looked and looked but couldn't find it.

Then I got a bright idea. I reached in my pocket and brought out my trusty zippo lighter. Hopefully there were no explosives in the building. With the light of my Zippo I found some LRRP Rations and started tossing them to Jerry through the top wall opening. When I thought we had enough, it was time for me to make my escape.

I began stacking boxes near a sidewall to form a sort of staircase. When I had finished, I began my ascent. When I got to the top, the whole thing collapsed and I fell on my ass. So I tried it again, and fell on my ass again. This process went on for quite some time. By trial and error, plus better stacking, I finally made it to the top, and went headfirst through the opening.

Then came a discomforting discovery. My hips wouldn't clear the opening and I hung there facing downward. Jerry grabbed my hands and pulled to no avail. I was stuck on the damned corrugated tin. I weighed about 170 pounds at the time, and as I struggled to free myself, I heard the corrugated tin begin to rip away from the wall. However, I was still entrapped and was floundering like a walrus out of water. The flashlight was long gone, and neither of us could see anything.

Finally, the wall collapsed and I went crashing to the ground. Miller was laughing so hard that he couldn't have held the flashlight if he had had it. I got up and staggered back to the injured wall. We replaced the tin as best we could before stumbling back to camp.

When we got back to camp, certain we were in the early stages of starvation, we both suddenly discovered we didn't have any water to rehydrate the LRRP Rations. Not one drop. Jerry then remembered that we had melted water in a beer cooler and used some of that. I on the other hand, also ever resourceful, used lukewarm beer to reconstitute my meal.

I remember waking up in the middle of the night with the worst case of indigestion in the history of the human race. I was so dehydrated from the beer, that I felt like I hadn't had a drink of water for six months. Then I remembered the cooler water. I picked the cooler up and poured the cold water down my throat. It was the most satisfying drink of water that I had ever had.

The next morning I awoke early and immediately wanted a drink of water. I wandered outside, glanced in the cooler to see if there was any water left and froze in my tracks. There, floating in that cooler, were beetles, mosquitoes, flies, centipedes, and a multitude of other carbon based lifeforms. Some were still alive.

I, Mark Vaughn Garrison, aka Croc 2, aka Pigpen and aka Magnet Ass, did a remarkable thing. I, who once bit the head off a hummingbird-sized bug of unknown origin, looked into that cooler and threw up. I couldn't quit retching. I let Jerry do a lot of the flying that day. I was too busy trying not to throw up again. *Oh, it was a long, long day.*

57.

The Bears Revisited

The Malayan sun bears were two of the best beer drinkers I ever knew.

One day when I was walking to the officer's club, I walked by the bears and they stuck their paws through the bars of their cage and begged for whatever I would give them.

I decided to go to the PX and buy some beer just to see how much they would drink.

When I came back with the beer they appeared to know what it was and reached through the bars for it. There were two of them and I gave them each a beer. The bears took the beer, plopped down on their fannies and held the can with their front paws much like a human. They would then rapidly pour it down their throats with their foot long tongues lapping at it. They then would come to me for another one.

I gave the bears seven or eight beers each and after that they were bombed, chasing each other around the cage. Quite a crowd had gathered by then to watch their drunken antics.

Two of the people that showed up were the Pathfinders who had captured them. These two guys got in the cage with them and started wrestling with them. The bears immediately pinned the two soldiers to the mat and gave them a bath with their huge, beer-soaked tongues.

The bears would then chase each other around the cage, stumbling and falling, and then come to the bars and beg for more beer. I didn't have any more, but the Pathfinders did, and the bears got even drunker.

These animals were absolutely hilarious, and a good diversion from the war.

A man needed diversions like that in that God forsaken place. This job of kill or be killed every day, was getting more insane by the second. I began to wonder what it was going to take to reacclimate to American society. What was this war really going to do to us long term? I thought it was a valid question but couldn't come up with an equally valid answer.

Did people actually think that a man could go through this fucking insanity and be unaffected? Did they really expect him to be the same man he was when he left the States?

Or, did they think about us at all? Did they even care?

58.

Rumors of War?

In late February, rumors began circulating about of a massive NVA (also known as Charlie) buildup of troops and supplies. The area of buildup was said to be not far west of Camp Holloway in a place called the Plei Trap Valley.

The U.S. Armed Forces in the Vietnam military chain of command deemed it essential to stop this escalation in its tracks. There was a major supply line to enemy troops in the Ben Het and Dak To areas and it had to be interrupted.

It looked as if we were not going to be able to play with bears for a while. We were already flying every day and dodging rockets and mortars at night the way it was. The Gators and Crocs, along with all the other personnel at Holloway, had become hardened to the nightly bombardments.

It had gotten to the point of hearing the first rocket come in, then everyone listened to see if the next one got louder. If it sounded softer then we would go back to playing poker, listening to music, or whatever we happened to be doing. The softened sound told us they were walking the rockets away from us. Only if the explosions were getting louder, would we take them seriously and duck for cover.

Now, however, it appeared this Plei Trap Valley thing was going to be thrown into the mix to make life even more interesting. We certainly wouldn't have wanted things to get boring.

Apparently, we were not going to be invading Charlie's backyard. We were going to go, uninvited, right into his living room.

Ho Chi Minh was the supreme leader of North Vietnam, who was attempting to unite the country under communist rule. The 66th Regiment was one of the favorite units of Ho and General Vo Nguyen Giap, and was a major player in the enemy infiltration of the Plei Trap Valley.

The 66th was also known as the Tiger Regiment, and had a large component of "Nungs." These were soldiers of Chinese descent who had been in Vietnam for centuries, and were larger and stronger than their North Vietnamese counterparts. They were known for their strength and ferocity as fighters.

Beginning in late February, the Crocs sent at least one gunship team into the Plei Trap every day. For some reason, that team was almost always Waldo and I. We had various copilots, but usually flying with me was Jack Cloud, Jerry Miller, or Paul Banish. Since Waldo was senior to me in the Crocs, I would function as his wingman.

Indeed the Plei Trap *was* crawling with well disciplined and well armed NVA Regulars. It was a standard event to have our aircraft ventilated with AK-47 fire.

The stress on pilots and crews was enormous. We would be at the aircraft doing our preflight between 0630 and 0700 hours, fly several missions a day, and shut the aircraft down at dusk. There was no telling what your day would be like. One day we would be covering insertions and extractions of LRRPs, the next might be search and destroy, and the next, covering slicks on resupply into potentially hot LZs and firebases. *Hot! Hot! Hot! Everything was hot!*

We would work from Dak To, Pleiku, Kontum, or Polei Kleng, to support troops in the valley. Polei Kleng was a special forces camp sitting about a thirty minute flight to the north northwest of Holloway.

One of the big stressors of flying in the Central Highlands was the ruggedness of the terrain, especially in places like the Plei Trap Valley. If you were shot down or had some sort of catastrophic failure, you were most likely going to crash. It was as simple as that.

This was always on a pilot's mind. You tried your best to keep a forced landing area within reach, but, in the Plei Trap, it was seldom possible to do that.

I had a running joke with the other Crocs while I was there. I used to say that if things got too boring for us, we could always crash land in the jungle and fight the Bengal tigers.

I was only half joking. Sadly, the Bengals were no longer the meanest thing in the jungle.

59

A Flying Ball of Fire

The month of March in 1969 had been an absolute hell month for infantry troops and air crews alike. Waldo and I, along with various copilots, had logged several twelve-hour days of hot combat flying. As previously described, we often didn't have the luxury of being able to eat or even shut the aircraft down between sorties. There was simply no time for that. American soldiers were dying.

Now as we sat there listening to the next day's mission briefing, it looked as if tomorrow was to be no exception. Task Force Alpha was to be extracted at first light—if they were still alive at first light. There were about 200 men in task force Alpha, and the briefing officer that night was telling us that there could be as many as five to ten thousand North Vietnamese troops surrounding them. I remember thinking: *Good God! How in the hell are we going to pull this off?* History was to prove that there were more like 2,000-3,000 NVA troops there, but 15-1 or 10-1 odds against, are still a long shot at any track.

After the briefing, I retired to my room and broke out a fresh bottle of scotch and took out pen and paper to write a couple of letters home. The first letter was to my brothers, Gary and Clarence. I had kept them apprised now and then of what I was doing, but I intentionally underplayed the dangerous nature of it all. I did the same thing that night.

The next letter was to my mother, and I reserved my biggest lies for her. I told her not to worry about me, that I was just flying generals around to meetings far away from combat. I went on to say that in the off chance anything would happen to me, for her not to be sad. I was doing what I wanted to do and was happy.

In reality, the last thing I wanted to do was fly into the goddamned Plei Trap again.

If it weren't for the scotch, I wouldn't have slept a wink.

0600 hours came much too early the next morning. I pushed the mosquito net aside and sat up in bed. I glanced around my room and saw my flight helmet sitting next to a half empty bottle of scotch on my desk. I tried to blame why I didn't feel good on the scotch, but I knew it was really because of where I was going. There were two letters there on the desk also. I was glad I had written them before I had drunk the scotch. I had to see that they got to the mail room before I left.

I jumped in some flip flops and headed for the shower in boxers and dog tags. I hoped there would be water even if it would be cold. The showers were fed by tanks on top of the latrine by gravity flow. The water was cold in the mornings because the sun hadn't warmed it up yet, but I felt like a cold shower was just what I needed this morning. I turned on the faucet and what felt like ice water rained down on me unmercifully. I gasped for breath and dropped my bar of soap, and it hit the floor about the same time my crystallized testicles did. I retrieved the soap first and then the testicles. One thing I was going to need for sure today was a big set of balls.

Just then Waldo appeared and jumped in the shower next to me. After he went through the same soap and ball retrieving procedure, we discussed what was likely to happen today.

We would do our best to stay in a racetrack pattern as we covered the slicks going in and out of the landing zone. By a racetrack pattern I mean an oval pattern like you find at Indianapolis Motor Speedway. He would follow the first slick in, giving cover fire if the slick received enemy fire, and once the slick was in, make a sharp 180-degree turn to the left or the right (break) depending on where the enemy fire came from. I would be following at a safe distance and escort the slick out, providing more cover fire. I would then break in the same direction Waldo did and he would, at that point be in a position to cover my break. This oval pattern would continue as long as we were not receiving fire when we broke. If we were, then we would try to find a place to break where we could. We could break short left or short right, long left or long right. You could usually find a place to break where you were receiving minimal enemy fire. This was important because a gunship is most vulnerable during its break.

Waldo and I had worked together as a team on dozens of occasions and that was a strong point. We knew how each other thought and knew what the other one was going to do before he did it most of the time. We both knew we were going to need all the strong points we could muster today.

We walked to the aircraft at the Christmas tree, swinging our helmets in our right hands as we always did, engaged in idle chit chat. We might as well have made small talk. Otherwise, the conversation may have gone something like this:

"Well, Pigpen, what do you think your chances are of living through this fucking extraction today?"

"Well, now that you ask, Waldo, not worth a fuck. What about you?"

"Ditto, Pigpen. Not worth a shit. How do you feel about never seeing your family again?"

"Hell, Waldo, I've lived for 22 years. I've seen my family a lot of times. Besides, the way I figure it's all downhill from here anyway. Everything from hemorrhoids to hearing aids. Too bad I'll miss the nursing home years but that's the breaks. Look on the bright side, Waldo. Have you ever imagined how it would feel going into the jungle at 170 mph, inverted and on fire. Goddamn! That would be one hell of an adrenaline rush."

"By God you're right, Pigpen. I don't want any old hag changing my diapers in an old folks home either."

Then, in unison: "Let's go to the Plei Trap."

That's obviously the conversation we didn't have.

When we got to the aircraft, the crew chiefs had already done preflight, but as was customary, we followed it with another one to see if anything had been missed. Unfortunately, neither of us could find anything to keep us grounded.

I strapped myself into the right seat of a rocket and minigun Charlie Model, and Jack Cloud got in the copilot's seat. I was glad Jack was my copilot today. He was always cool under fire and a good man to have in the cockpit. It wouldn't be long before he was up for aircraft commander in my opinion.

Waldo strapped into his bird and a brand new copilot, who had only flown a few missions *in-country,* buckled up in the left seat. I believe his last name was Martin, although I'm not sure.

As I watched Martin strap into Waldo's aircraft, I couldn't help but feel sorry for him. This mission today was probably going to be an exercise in survival, and he had only been in the air a few times in country. This may very well be a baptism by fire for him, I thought. Whoever put a new guy on a mission like this in the Plei Trap Valley ought to have their ass kicked. That was just downright stupid, I thought, as I prepared to crank the aircraft.

With the preflight done and pre-start procedures complete, I flipped the battery on, the main fuel on, yelled "Clear" and pulled the start trigger. The jet whined and the blades began to slowly turn. I watched the EGT closely to see that it did not go past redline, or stay too long in the yellow zone before it dropped to green. The blades were picking up speed now as I put the throttle at flight idle momentarily. All engine and transmission readings were in the green, normal zone, so I rolled the power on to operating RPM.

I waited for Waldo to back out of his revetment and then followed suit and fell in behind him to taxi to the runway. When we got clearance to take off, I fell in behind him en route to the special forces camp called Polei Kleng. Polei Kleng was just a few miles from where we would be making the Task Force Alpha extraction. There, we would rendezvous with the slick drivers and others for radio frequencies and other info pertinent to the mission.

When everyone was satisfied their ducks were in proper military alignment, we headed out to get the job done. The first slick made an approach into the LZ with Waldo covering. I was behind Waldo, ready to cover his break. All of a sudden the slick called out on the radio,

"Receiving fire. Nine o'clock, 100 feet."

Oh shit, here we go!

At that, Waldo placed a pair of rockets on the enemy location, and broke left.

He came on the radio and said:

"Receiving fire right underneath."

I placed a pair of rockets and a blast of minigun under him and picked up the slick as he headed out of the LZ.

The slick then transmitted: "Receiving fire 3 o'clock 50 feet!"

I placed another pair of rockets at his 3 o'clock and another blast of minigun, and broke hard left. I received fire at my breakpoint and told Waldo, and he put another pair of rockets underneath me and then picked up another slick on its way into the LZ.

This slick also received fire and Waldo put another two pairs of rockets underneath her and broke right this time.

Waldo called to me and said he was receiving heavy fire at break.

I put another pair under him with several blasts of minigun as a follow-up. *The bad guys were everywhere!*

We quickly realized that we simply could not find a safe place to break anywhere. The damned NVA was all over. The American task force was surrounded. Just when I didn't think things could get any worse, they sure as hell did!

On my next pass, I attempted to break right while receiving heavy fire, and all of a sudden, there was a huge explosion that rocked the ship. The aircraft's nose pitched up and to the left as she sliced through the air sideways at 140 knots. I was stunned and my right ear was ringing wildly.

"Jesus H Christ, what the fuck was that?"

I didn't have a clue what had happened, but I knew that I had to try to get the aircraft under control. I gave it forward cyclic, kicked right pedal, lowered collective and made a sharp left turn. I tried to fire a pair of rockets on the enemy position but they wouldn't fire.

Just then, Davis, my crew chief yelled that we were on fire. The rocket motors were burning in the right pod. We had apparently been hit by a Rocket Propelled Grenade (RPG).

Since the firing order was screwed up in the damaged pod, the rockets wouldn't fire. Therefore, I told Jack to hit it with the miniguns. He rained down several bursts of machine gun fire on what looked like a couple of thousand muzzle flashes.

The smell of death was in the air, but a strange calm came over me, once again, as everything seemed to start moving in slow motion. It seemed to happen to the whole crew. Nobody was saying much. We were all too busy just doing our jobs. And mine was to keep this critically wounded bird in the air.

Besides, now I knew that things couldn't get any worse, but they did.

A few seconds later, there was another huge explosion on the left side of the ship.

"God damn, this shit's gettin' old in a hurry, Jack. What the fuck was that?" I asked.

Again the aircraft pitched up, and this time to the right as she slid through the air. I, once again, gained control and now saw that we had taken another RPG hit, this time in the left rocket pod.

Now both pods were on fire, and both my electrical and mechanical jettison systems were shot up and did not work.

These rocket motors were burning right next to warheads and the aircraft's fuel cell. My crew chief and door gunner took the initiative to get half way out of the aircraft and kick the pods until they released.

It is my firm belief that those two men saved our lives that day. If they had not got out on the skids at 140 knots, and kicked those burning pods free, we would have most certainly gone up like a Roman Candle.

But we weren't done yet. As a matter of fact, things got worse again.

Just then several AK-47 rounds came through the aircraft, one of them hitting the copilot's seat and knocking Jack's feet clear up in the air, and leaving through the left door, creating a basketball size opening.

At this point I think I was completely on automatic pilot. I was there, but then again I wasn't. It wasn't so much bravery on my part, although I can't speak for the others. It was just an ability to emotionally divest myself from the goings on around me allowing me to concentrate on nothing but flying the aircraft. It's a good thing I did.

Did I mention that when I was absolutely certain things couldn't get any worse, they did?

Another round came through the cargo bay, de-pinned and activated a red smoke grenade, at the same time knocking it from its cradle and throwing it in Davis's M60 ammo box. We immediately went completely IFR (instrument flight rules) in the cockpit as it filled with red smoke. By this time I was right on the treetops at 100 plus knots and I couldn't see a goddamned thing!

I punched all the left pedal I had and hung my head out the side window in an attempt to see. I felt like I had a huge bullseye painted on my helmet.

In the meantime, the hot smoke grenade had started to cook off bullets in the ammo box, and I screamed at Davis to throw it out. As I glanced back at him after the smoke had cleared a little, I saw a guy take a box weighing more than 100 pounds, with his straight arm between his thumb and index finger and toss it out of the aircraft like a toothpick. I suppose that's what adrenaline will do.

As soon as the cockpit cleared of red smoke and I could see something, I didn't like what I saw. *Things had gotten worse once again.*

We were headed right for the trees on top of a ridgeline. I kicked right pedal and pulled all the pitch I could and at the same time brought the cyclic back as much as possible, and we were able to brush the trees with the belly of the aircraft, and barely skim over the ridge.

I was headed back to Polei Kleng if she would just hold together.

Waldo came over the radio and said,

"I can't believe you're still in the air, Pigpen. I thought you were going down five or six times."

"So did I, Waldo. So did I. But since I'm still airborne can you give me a fly around and see if this thing is still on fire. I've got to try to nurse this thing out of here. If we go down here those bastards will have barbequed Americans for lunch!"

"Roger that, Pigpen!"

Waldo gave me a fly around inspection and said I didn't look too good but I didn't appear to be on fire at the moment. I had about a twenty minute flight to Polei Kleng, if she would just hold together for a few more minutes.

She got us there.

On final approach into Polei Kleng, my rocket pods were gone with the electrical connections flapping in the wind. My miniguns were inoperative, with one pointed at the sky and the other one at the ground. There was a huge, gaping hole in the left door and bullet holes all over the aircraft. Various designs of black carbon tattoos were also evident in numerous places along the sides of the gunship, that had been produced by the caressing flames of combat flight.

As I got to short final approach there was another gunship team starting their aircraft by the side of the runway that were looking at me with great concern. They were going out to take our place for now. As I got close, I gave them the thumbs up. The AC in the lead gunship shook his head, and I couldn't hear him, but you could sure read his lips. He was saying, "Fuck."

I didn't blame him.

At Polei Kleng they patched the aircraft up enough for Jack and I to ferry it back to the more secure location of Holloway. We took off from Polei Kleng and climbed to 4,000 feet absolute to stay completely out of small arms range. I had no sooner leveled off when things got worse again. An electrical fire had broken out in the cockpit.

I said with urgency, "Jack, you've got the aircraft."

The acrid smoke from the electrical fire was filling the cockpit. It was difficult to breath. I had no idea where the fire was, so I started pulling circuit breakers of systems that I didn't absolutely need to keep the aircraft in the air. I pulled three or four and nothing was working. Both Jack and I were having trouble breathing the acrid fumes and we could hardly keep our eyes open, they burned so bad.

But there was one breaker left that I hadn't pulled. I didn't want to pull it either. It was for the electrical fuel pump. This pump was a horizontal backup for the mechanical fuel pump, and I didn't know if the mechanical pump was working. If it wasn't, and I pulled the breaker on the electrical pump, we would lose all fuel pressure and go down in the jungle. However, if I didn't stop the fire, the pilots wouldn't work and we would go down in the jungle.

The smoke and fumes continued to get worse, however, and I realized I had no choice. I grabbed the breaker and pulled. It was hot and appeared stuck.

I pulled it harder, but it still wouldn't budge.

With the fumes still increasing, I pulled it as hard as I could. Now the breaker broke clear away from the panel and came off in my hands.

The fumes started to subside, and I closely watched the fuel pressure gauge.

The fuel pressure stayed in the green zone and the jet continued to purr.

Damn, I thought. It was about time something went right today.

Wondering why the breaker had not blown on its own, I examined it in my hand. It looked as if it had been welded together by heat. I thought, good God, after going through all of that today, and then damned near dying of an electrical fire in the cockpit.

Believe it or not the rest of the flight was uneventful. *Things had finally stopped getting worse!*

Waldo stayed and flew all day, going through three wingmen. How he did it I'll never know. It was as if he had some sort of divine shield over his aircraft. He just kept going back to Polei Kleng and hot rearming and refueling, going back to the extraction LZ, and pounding the hell out of the bad guys.

If the truth were known, I'm sure that Waldo's ability to stay on station all day had more to do with his flying abilities than any kind of divine shield. I'm also sure his heroic, offensive action saved many American lives that day.

The last extraction was after dark and had been successful in getting all of the guys in Task Force Alpha out.

Waldo and I had been talking to the leader on the ground called 24 Charlie all day. At the end of the day, when Waldo was shut down on the runway at Polei Kleng waiting to fly back to Camp Holloway, in the twilight, a figure approached him as he was sitting on the toe of the skid.

The soldier said, "Are you Croc 4, Waldo?"

Waldo replied, "Yes. Are you 24 Charlie?"

The two men then silently embraced one another for a long while. They didn't say anything more. They didn't have to. That morning they didn't even know one another.

That evening they were brothers.

The Alligators and the Crocodiles of the 119th Assault Helicopter Company, along with the other brave members of the 52nd Combat Aviation Battalion had succeeded in furthering their mission.

We had lost seventeen aircraft to hostile fire. Mine was one of them.

Task Force Alpha on the ground had fought with incredible courage, against a force that was perhaps fifteen times larger than their own, and held the bastards off, until American choppers got them all out.

I am so, so proud of all these men. It was an honor to have served with them.

We had done it again. We had gotten 200 more Americans home alive in the face of insurmountable odds.

You're damned right we had done it again!

60.

The Friendly fire Incident

We continued to be called for assistance in the Plei Trap Valley into May of 1969. It seems there were always skirmishes going on there that needed gunship and slick support.

One day in late April, I was now the team leader with Jack Cloud winging on me, when we were called to assist with the extraction of an American force that was about to get their asses kicked.

They had been discovered by a much larger enemy force that was in hot pursuit. We had to get there in a hurry for them to have any chance of living.

We scrambled from Dak To. A specialist 4 from operations had given me the coordinates, frequencies and contact information. The American force had made contact with the enemy just a few miles to the west of Dak To in triple canopy jungle. Information given to me was sketchy at best, but I was led to believe that there was at least a platoon of Americans on the ground. That would mean there were forty to fifty of them. Apparently there was at least a company of two to three hundred NVA soldiers pursuing them.

Slicks had been called and were en route for an extraction, but we had to find them first and stop the NVA. Then we had to get them to a place that the slicks could use for a landing zone.

When I got to the approximate coordinates given to me by operations, I called the leader on the ground on the Fox Mike Radio.

"One Two Echo, One two Echo, this is Crocodile 2, over."

"Roger, Crocodile 2, go ahead, over."

"I am in your vicinity One Two Echo, do you hear me or see me?"

One Two Echo said, "I can hear you, but I cannot see you Crocodile 2."

Then after a short pause. "Wait, *I can see you*. You just flew right overhead."

"Roger that, One Two Echo. Where is the enemy force?"

One Two Echo said, "They are just feet to our west. They're right on us."

I said, "One Two Echo, I will be coming in from north to south. I will tell you to pop yellow smoke so I can identify your exact position. Do you understand me?"

"Roger that, I understand, Croc 2."

I told Jack that we would be making runs from north to south with a right break. I also told him that the enemy was just feet away and we would have to put the rockets and minigun right on the money. He acknowledged.

I turned the aircraft back to the south and set up an extended gun run.

I then called One Two Echo and said,

"One Two Echo, pop yellow smoke, now."

Yellow smoke sifted up through the trees and I had their position isolated.

I said, "Get your heads down, guys. I'm coming in with heavy shit."

The yellow smoke was still sifting through the trees when I put my sights just feet to the west of the friendlies. I knew I had to make this run count. I couldn't fuck it up or the wrong people would die.

Our sights were right on the enemy location, so I let one pair of rockets go, and then another. Then I told my copilot to hit the same area with minigun. I overflew the enemy position, which is something that you never wanted to do if you could help it, but this time I had to give such close fire support that it was necessary. I broke hard right and headed back north.

One Two Echo came on the radio and said, "You're right on 'em, man. You're right on 'em. Keep 'em coming."

At that, I told Jack to put his stuff right where I did and came back around to cover his break.

Jack punched off a couple pair of rockets that were right on the money, then he punched off a third pair, and the one from his

226 | Mark Garrison

right pod spun wildly out of control. I watched as it impacted in the middle of the friendly troops.

Immediately, One Two Echo came back on the radio and said, "Cease fire, cease fire, you're killing friendlies."

What had happened to Jack was what we called a *spinner*. Since we were under intense enemy fire at the time, he could very well have gotten a fin shot off his rocket, causing it to spiral out of control. In no way was it his fault.

We were able to get the Americans to an LZ and extract them.

Waldo was in the air that day leading another fire team in the general area. He heard the, "Cease fire" call on the radio.

He called me on VHF and asked me what had happened.

I told him Jack just had a spinner into friendlies, and would talk to him tonight when we got back to Camp Holloway.

That evening I took a bottle of scotch to Waldo's room in the Croc Hooch.

We sat and discussed how hitting friendly forces with our armament was a constant fear for all of us. I told him that Jack was basically inconsolable since we got back, even though I kept telling him that it wasn't his fault.

Jack kept telling me that I would only know how he felt if and when it happens to me.

I had to agree with him.

Waldo then told me that Major Carrie, our fine company commander, had told him that there were seven friendly troops killed by the errant rocket.

This is just something that happens in a combat theater. Even when the greatest precautions are taken, friendly fire casualties occur. It's happened throughout history in virtually every war that's ever been fought since the invention of gunpowder. When you have hot bullets and shrapnel flying around in the air, sometimes bad shit happens.

It's just as simple as that.

Jack was visibly shaken by the incident. So was every other Croc pilot. I was especially upset for Jack. Jack had been my wing. By God it was an unavoidable accident, and I would take Jack as a wingman any day for the rest of my life. *That was how much I trusted him!*

But there would be no break. We were expected to put it behind us, suck it up, and start flying missions again in the morning. So that's exactly what we did. We all flew missions the next morning like good boys, and filed this episode away in our subconscious mind so that it would be in a position to haunt us later in life. *Could we have done something differently? Was it our fault? Did we do everything that we could do?*

The pressure was enormous and constant on gunship pilots. It was also enormous and constant on the slick pilots as well. In a slick, you were well aware that there were people in your aircraft whose lives depended on you and your abilities. In a gunship, your crew's lives and the lives of friendly troops on the ground, depended on you and your abilities to not only fly the aircraft, but to put your deadly armament in the right place.

One of your seventeen-pound high explosive (HE) rockets had more concussion than a 105mm artillery round. You had to be damned careful to not put one of them up the wrong guy's ass. The miniguns fired at about 80 rounds per second. Just a touch of the trigger with the guns pointed in the wrong place, could mean several friendly casualties before you could even get your hand off the trigger.

We spoke of the possible death of ourselves and our enemies openly, almost nonchalantly, but the death of friendlies by our fire was something never uttered. I guess it was our biggest fear of all.

Speaking of friendly fire reminds me of another incident in Vietnam. I spoke earlier of the chicken plate and flak vest that pilots were supposed to always wear for personal protection against shrapnel and small arms fire. Indeed, it was virtually always with you when you were flying missions.

One day, however, through some sort of fluke, we scrambled for a mission and I didn't have my chicken plate and flak vest with me. I realized that I was without this protective gear about halfway out to a hot LRRP extraction. I kept remembering what Jet Jackson had said, "Always wear these things if you want to live through your tour!" Damn! There wasn't anything I could do about it now, I thought, except to try to prove him wrong.

The mission went off without a hitch, and we got the LRRP team out alive and well. In so doing, however, we had to make several hot gun runs and expend a lot of ammo and rockets on the enemy location, who were bound and determined to interrupt our plans to get everyone out. The crew chief and gunner had their M 60 machine guns going full blast on each of our gun runs.

Now, let me explain something that happens sometimes in just that sort of situation. An M 60 is capable of firing 550 rounds per minute, or about 8 to 10 rounds per second. This makes the gun barrel and the chamber that holds the next round exceedingly hot. Sometimes so hot that you have what is called a *cook off*. In other words, the round in the chamber is so hot that it goes off by itself, without anyone pulling the trigger. As a matter of fact, sometimes you have a run off, where rounds just keep going off until the gunner breaks the ammo belt and robs the gun of any more rounds. Because of this possibility, the crew chief and gunner were always supposed to have their weapons pointed out the open cargo doors, and not toward the cockpit, pilots, or anything else in the aircraft, for reasons that should be obvious.

On this particular day, that important rule was violated, and the gunner had his weapon pointed straight at my back. That's when the gun cooked off a round. Fortunately, I was in an armored, ceramic impregnated seat and it was successful in stopping the round. It hit me so hard, however, that it knocked the breath out of me, and cracked a rib. I had to give the controls to my copilot for a few minutes while I regained my composure and caught my breath.

Then I remembered the flak vest that I had left behind. If I had only had that on, it would almost certainly have cushioned the blow and I would have remained uninjured. To this day, it still amazes me how hard that M 60 hit that seat. It probably only moved it an inch or two, but so fast and with such force that it took my breath away and busted a rib. I never flew without the protective gear again.

61

AAA's and Tanks

Another thing all pilots had to worry about was Aircraft Anti Artillery fire (AAA). In South Vietnam, this usually consisted of 12.7 mm anti-aircraft guns. Every other round was an incendiary tracer, and if you got hit in the fuel cell with one of those you were a goner.

One morning in early April of 1969, Waldo and I were sent once again on a search and destroy mission into the Plei Trap Valley. I recall this morning for two very specific reasons. The first reason was that there was a dense, eerie fog blanketing the valley floor. The second reason was because of what happened that morning.

Waldo was flying a Hog and I was winging on him in a minigun ship that particular day. Nothing much was happening as we were flying east up the valley floor and idle chit chat was going on between the two of us. Just at that moment, Waldo, yelled, "Receiving fire!! Receiving AAA fire from due east at twelve o'clock!!" I immediately saw what looked like supersonic zeppelins coming at us on a collision course.

Waldo instantly reacted by *going salvo* on the AAA location and I followed with everything I had to fire. Apparently we got lucky, because no more commentary exuded from that position.

In the spring of 1969, it was time for Waldo to return to the States. We all felt very happy for him but very sorry for ourselves. He had been an incredible asset to us all in the 119th and would be sorely missed.

Nevertheless, we threw one hell of a party for him and wished him well. A plaque given to him by the officers and men of the

119th that had been appropriately swamped in scotch and beer was presented in customary fashion and he was bid adieu.

With his departure, I, along with a couple of other guys, became the senior aircraft commander of the Crocs in the 119th. Needless to say, a lot of responsibility came along with this new assignment.

A lot of this new responsibility came in the form of supporting a place to our north called Ben Het. It seems that Ben Het, an American military outpost, was almost constantly under some sort of attack by North Vietnamese forces in the spring and summer of 1969. As a consequence of this, the 119th was expected to supply close gunship fire support, troop withdrawal and reinforcement on an elevated priority. They were frequent callers because the fighting went on there night and day.

Ben Het was mainly a Green Beret outpost that was also manned by a particularly ferocious breed of Montagnard fighter who was friendly to the Americans and South Vietnamese fighting forces.

Ben Het sat in a critical position for both the Americans and the North Vietnamese Army, mainly because of its observational capabilities. It afforded a good place to monitor movement on the Ho Chi Minh Trail coming down from the south.

Several critical battles had taken place there over the past several months, but one, in particular, indelibly sticks in my mind.

I was assigned as an aircraft commander and fire team lead with a minigun ship to be my wingman. Our mission was specific. We were to cover heavy metal, fixed winged aircraft into and out of a SSP runway at Ben Het, when they were receiving heavy fire.

When we got there, all hell had broken loose on the ground. The fixed wing supply ships were unable to land on the runway. They were airdropping supplies by sliding them from the back cargo bay. The cargo packs had parachutes attached to slow the descent and speed of the supply drops. As soon as the supplies were dropped, the aircraft made full flap STOL (Short Take-Off and Landing) departures in an attempt to avoid enemy small arms fire, and the supply planes were under constant fire.

For some mystifying reason, the first aircraft that we escorted into the runway, received no observable enemy fire. We broke right and came back around ready to pick up another one with a full load of armament and fuel. *Maybe this won't be so bad after all, I thought.*

Wrong! Just as I was making my 180-degree turn, what appeared to be flaming footballs hurdled past the nose of my aircraft. I immediately glanced down and saw that the AAA fire was apparently coming from a damned T-72 Russian tank.

Tanks! There are no fucking tanks in this war. Especially not Russian tanks. What the hell is going on here?

Knowing that I only had a few seconds to act, I dropped the nose of my aircraft, placed the rocket selector switch on salvo, and hit the trigger. The first two pairs walked their way up to the tank, and the rest of the 16 pairs were apparently direct hits. I watched the soldier manning the turret immediately disintegrate and the tank rolled to a stop. It must be remembered that I had no anti armament ordnance on board, and I consider myself extremely lucky to have stopped it with plain vanilla HE rockets. One of those incendiary rounds striking our aircraft's fuel cell would have lit us up like a napalm bomb. This incident had been much too similar to the previously mentioned AAA encounter with Waldo in the Plei Trap Valley.

Come on! How many of these encounters does one have to suffer before he loses what little bit of sanity that he may have left?

62

A Bunch of Super Pissed Off Bees

After the 119th AHC had moved to An Khe, it was sometime in late July or early August, when a bunch of the pilots had returned somewhat early in the day, due to an aborted mission.

As was customary for most of us, we were all sitting at picnic tables that sat between two rows of barracks that served as our quarters, drinking cold beer.

The barracks were newer and nicer than the ones at Holloway, but they were still sandbag to the chest affairs, with screen windows above that, reaching to a tin roof with about a three to twelve pitch.

After several beers had been consumed, a large population of bees began forming on a branch of a huge tree between the picnic tables in the company area. They were all attaching to each other, until they became a pregnant mass, a couple of feet wide and a foot thick, on the bottom of the branch.

What were we going to do, since we couldn't very well have an active beehive in our midst curtailing our outdoor activities?

I remembered—or thought I remembered—that back home in Illinois, if you disrupt bees while they are in the process of forming a hive, they will often leave and go someplace else. With that in mind, I asked if anybody had a softball or baseball. One of the slick pilots, Dave Parrish, said he had one in his room, went to get it, and threw it to me.

"Watch this, Dave. I am the company savior. I did my share of softball pitching in a fast pitch league back home. I'll hit those bastards dead center with this softball, and you all just watch them leave that tree and go somewhere else."

Then, without further ado, I tossed a perfect strike into the middle of the humongous mass of bees that had been minding their own business.

As it turned out, that was probably the most ill-advised thing that I could have possibly done. I should have listened to that quiet, inner voice that was telling me something else that I knew but must have forgotten. That missing kernel of knowledge was that bees seem to be able to follow the path of disturbed air to find their aggressor attacker. Well, they found me almost instantaneously.

I certainly didn't have a bee suit on. Hell, I didn't even have a shirt on. I was dressed in boots, fatigue pants and dog tags. No protection above the waist. Anyway, the bees that had been minding their own business, decided to make me their business, and that somewhere else that I had said they would go, happened to be all over me.

Several stunned pilots were standing close by, but the bees paid no attention to them. They made a *BEELINE* for me. They immediately imparted their disapproval of my pitching by stinging the holy shit out of me.

I reacted by dashing for a road just outside the barracks, and set a new world record for the one hundred-meter dash, but the bees immediately broke it as they continued to make me the object of their discontent, as I yelled and began to stagger from their assault.

I finally reached the latrine with a few hardcore bees still depositing their stingers around my head and neck, as if they still hadn't finished making their point.

I threw open the door of the latrine and dashed inside. The latrine was built much the same way as our barracks, and fortunately for me, as soon as the bees got inside with me, they headed for the light of the screens and left me alone with my agony, squatted down in the middle of the crapper, fully injected with bee venom.

Just then, Pappy Clark, another gunship pilot, appeared at the latrine door and said,

"Pigpen, them bees are in there with ye."

I said to Pappy, who had gotten his nickname because he was a couple of years older than the rest of us, "No shit, Pappy! No shit!"

Ultimately, my strategy was a success. The bees left and were never heard from again. I was left in considerable pain, however. A couple of other gunship pilots, led by Golly-Golly driving a jeep that he had bushwhacked, raced me to the An Khe Medical MASH unit since he was afraid I might have a fatal reaction to the numerous bee stings.

By then, however, it was about an hour after the bees had donated their stingers for my use, and I was fairly anaesthetized. When we got there, the doctor came out and asked how long ago the stings occurred, and I said an hour ago.

He then scraped away more than a hundred stingers and counted dozens more stings without stingers. Finally the doctor said: "If he was going to react, he would have already reacted. Take him back to your company area and sober his ass up. And, by the way, tell him not to fuck with bees anymore. As large of a dose of bee venom as he got, he may very well react violently the next time."

That warning about future stings was prophetic. I do react violently today from stings and have to carry an Epipen around with me in the warm months. That is, if I can remember the damned thing.

I was so incredibly sore in my head, neck and shoulder area that I couldn't fly for a week. It hurt like hell to turn my head or move my arms and shoulders.

But, it was mission accomplished. The bees were gone and they stayed gone.

We had our company area back.

PART FIVE:
WRAPPING IT ALL UP

63

The R and R

In the summer of 1969, I became eligible to fly to someplace in Southeast Asia for about a week, to lick my wounds and convalesce from nine months of combat flying. There were several destinations that one could choose as long as they happened to be available. Places such as Singapore, Thailand, Hong Kong, Taiwan, Australia, and others. Most of all the married guys went to Hawaii to meet up with their wives. A majority of us wound up in rather more exotic places around the globe. I wound up in Taipei, Taiwan.

I distinctly remember the scene as we were told to board the aircraft. It was an *"on your mark, get set, go,"* sort of thing. As the gun sounded, several land speed records were set by the young males who were chocked full of testosterone as they boarded the aircraft. In any event, the flight to Taiwan was uneventful, although I feel certain that the stewardesses on board were in a much more precarious position than they ever realized.

Taiwan used to be known as the island of Formosa, when Chiang Kai-Shek fled mainland China with Mao Tse Tung in hot pursuit. Since then, it has been known as Nationalist China or Taiwan with Taipei as its capital city.

It's a beautiful island, covered with rough topography, with deep rivers and worn-down, geologically-old, mountain ranges, which are covered with dense forestation.

When I first arrived in Taipei, I was escorted by military vehicle to a place called the Kings Hotel. As soon as I situated myself in my room, I went down to have a drink at the hotel's bar, and was almost immediately approached by a Chinese gentleman who asked me if I would be interested in a female companion for the evening.

I asked what he had in mind and he told me to turn around and take a look. Against the wall behind me was a whole line of women, who had one thing in common. They were all beautiful.

Adopting the old adage of, "When in Rome, do as the Romans do," I took my pick.

Prostitution was technically illegal in Taiwan at the time, so you were asked to sign a contract stating that you were to entertain the young lady for the evening by dinner and dancing and other rather benign activities. These contracts lasted for twenty four hours.

Of course, I was awfully exhausted, and spent most of my time in recumbent positions.

The first time I entered a cab in Taipei, I was absolutely convinced that my mutilated remnants would be pulled from its fiery, twisted, wreckage. I thought flying a gunship in Nam was pretty damned hairy, but it didn't hold a candle to that cab ride.

First of all, the cab itself reminded me of a soda cracker box with wheels, ready to be ground into a deeper level of geological strata at a moment's notice. This was coupled with the obvious fact that the driver had absolutely no idea what traffic lights were even for; let alone how to act upon them. And last, but certainly not least, evidence pointed to the probability that he was at least color blind, and may have been legally blind.

That was the first and last cab ride that I enjoyed in Taipei.

64

In the Soup at Night Over the Mountains

When I returned from R&R in Taipei, the fun and games of Vietnam resumed immediately. I felt as if my number was rapidly coming up, and that one of these days I wouldn't be so lucky. My next mission reinforced these fears.

When you first got to Vietnam, you were designated as an *FNG*. After you were in country for three months, you were just a *New Guy*. When you were there for six months, you were considered *over the hill*. After nine months in country, you were a *short-timer* and the longer you were there on your one year tour the shorter you were.

I was a short-timer, with about a month left in country, when I was sitting in my room and a knock came at the door. I had flown all day and it was approaching sunset. The knock on the door was from a guy in operations who told me there was a LRRP team in trouble west of An Khe, and they needed an emergency extraction. I had been elected to lead the gunship team to cover the mission.

Weather was marginal, and I asked how far out the team was.

The guy from operations said about thirty clicks.

I said, "You know, there's no way in hell that we can make it back before dark. I'd rather not complicate things by having weather sock us in over the fucking mountains. What's the report?"

"If you hurry, Sir, you should be able to beat the weather, according to the report."

I replied, "I sure hope you're right, Specialist. I hope you're right."

A new guy to the Crocs was my copilot that night. I don't remember his name but I'm going to call him Fitch for easier reading. I also don't remember who my wingman was that night. As you will shortly see, I had my hands full with the events occurring in my aircraft, and other trivia about the matter has been lost to time.

We cranked our aircraft and headed to the coordinates given about thirty clicks west of An Khe. I contacted the LRRP team on Fox Mike Radio and the slick that was to do the extraction on UHF Radio.

The LRRP team leader whispered into his mike that he could not pop smoke because a whole platoon or more of NVA were too close and he would give his position away.

I said, "Can you see me in the air?"

He said, "No, but I can hear you."

I said as I headed south, "Am I getting louder or farther away?"

"You're getting farther away."

I turned north and asked, "Am I louder now? Can you see me?"

"Yes, you're getting louder. There you are! You're right over head!" There was hope in his voice now.

"OK, I've got your approximate position. Which direction is the enemy, and how far away?"

He replied, "They are due east of us and only about 30 to 40 feet away."

He was whispering because the enemy was so close he didn't want to give away his position.

"I'm coming back around and setting up a gun run. I want you to pop red smoke as soon as I tell you to. Do you understand?"

"Yes, I've got red smoke. I will pop it at your request. I hope to God you're good with the guns or we're screwed!"

I remained as in-control of the conversation as I could. "As soon as I ask you to pop smoke, you guys get your heads down. Get as low to the ground and behind the biggest trees and rocks you can find. I'm going to come in close with heavy stuff. Do you understand?"

"Yes, Sir, understood."

I continued, "As soon as they see me coming, they'll turn their guns on me. Take my word for it. You use those few seconds to get a few feet farther to the west. Do you copy?"

"Roger that!" He replied.

I flew to the south and told my wingman to pick me up. I told him we would make our runs to the north with a left break until, if and when, I changed things.

He acknowledged.

As I turned north on an extended gun run I said,

"Ok, pop red smoke now!"

I saw the smoke rising from the jungle floor and immediately saw several muzzle flashes just a few feet to their east.

I would have to get closer before I fired anything.

Then tracers zoomed by my aircraft and there was that now familiar slapping ping sound as a bullet hit us. But they had given their exact position away with their muzzle flashes.

Over the Fox Mike Radio to the LRRP team I said,

"Get your heads down now, guys. Get 'em down now!"

I then fired a first pair, then a second pair, then a third pair. All were right on the money. I told Fitch not to fire the miniguns, because I didn't know how good he was with them since he was new. One thing I sure as hell didn't want to do was wipe out the LRRP team with them.

I also told my wingman not to fire unless I called out that I was receiving enemy fire.

I didn't receive any more fire.

We covered the slick in and out of a makeshift LZ without further incident.

To the slick, that is.

As I covered him out I received a sprinkling of small-arm objections to my presence.

I told my wingman that I was going to make one last run to rid the area of NVA and for him to cover the slick home. I said I would catch up shortly when I finished cleaning up the LZ.

As soon as I made my final run to clean up the LZ, I turned east and headed back to An Khe. It was now getting dark and I could see the lights on the slick and my wingman in the distance to the east.

Then all of a sudden, everything disappeared. The clouds had dropped and I was IFR (Instrument flight rules) or CSC (Can't see crap).

I called my wingman and asked if he still had visibility.

He said that he did have, and so does the slick.

I advised, "Fly as fast as you can to get home, because I'm socked in right behind you. I'm going to have to call An Khe approach and ask for a GCA (Ground Controlled Approach) if I don't break out of this soup soon."

My wingman said, "Good luck, Pigpen. Be careful, man."

"Yea, no problem. This is just what I need. A little instrument flying over the mountains at night, in the fucking soup in goddamned Vietnam with just a few weeks left."

I then said to my Peter Pilot Fitch, "Look at the sectional (MAP), Fitch. Tell me what the highest peak is out here while I get ahold of An Khe approach."

There was no response. I glanced at him. He was staring straight ahead with his mouth open. His hands were clenched together like a knotted rope. He was terrified and in a panic.

I can't say I blamed him much. The chances of us hurling into a mountainside somewhere were pretty high at this point.

"Fitch, goddamnit! Snap out of it. I need your help watching the engine instruments while I try to keep this damned helicopter from getting upside down. The radio, roll in 217.4!"

He then kind of came around and tuned the radio to approach control.

I said, "An Khe approach, this is Crocodile 242, over."

"Crocodile 242, this is An Khe approach. Go ahead, over."

"Roger, An Khe approach, I am about twenty five clicks to your west in the soup and request GCA please, over."

"Crocodile 242, you sure picked a nice night to fly. Squawk 6900 on your transponder, please, over."

"Roger, An Khe, squawking 6900 now."

A transponder is an avionics device in an aircraft that allows you to be identified on a radar screen. The man at An Khe approach control was looking at his radar screen and when I squawked my transponder my dot of light on his screen started blinking brightly to identify me. Hopefully he would know how to weave me between the mountains and into An Khe.

An Khe approach said, "Ok, I have you on my screen, Crocodile 242. Climb and maintain 4,800 feet and turn right to a heading of 135 degrees."

"Roger, An Khe approach, climbing to 4,800 feet and turning right to 135 degrees, over."

"Crocodile 242, report when reaching 4,800 feet."

When I did so I reported back: "I have just leveled off at 4,800 feet, An Khe."

"Roger, Crocodile 242, descend and maintain 4,200 feet and turn left to a heading of 080 degrees."

"Descending to 4,200 feet and turning to 080 degrees, over."

"Crocodile 242, report when reaching 4,200 feet, over."

I was really nervous about descending out here in these mountains. I sure as hell didn't want to run into a big pile of rocks in these clouds. Besides, I hadn't flown instruments very much since flight school. It's something I didn't relish doing in a combat zone in the real world.

"An Khe approach, leveled off at 4,200 feet heading 080 degrees, altimeter setting please."

"Roger, Crocodile 242, descend and maintain 3200 feet and turn right to a heading of 100 degrees, over, altimeter setting 2942."

"Roger An Khe, turning right to a heading of 100 degrees and descending to 3,200 feet. Will report when reaching."

"Roger, Crocodile 242, over."

"Crocodile 242, descend and maintain 2600 feet and turn left to a heading of 090 degrees, over."

Damn we're getting low, I thought. I hope this guy knows what the hell he's doing.

"Roger, An Khe approach, turning left to a heading of 090 degrees and descending to 2,600 feet, will report when reaching."

"An Khe, Crocodile 242, I have leveled off at 2,600 feet."

Time had again come to a crawl but not as it happened in previous combat missions. It was like I was locked in a dark closet and there was a thick, humid fog inside. I was vaguely aware of another presence in the closet with me. But that person was paralyzed by fear that had rendered him almost motionless. The only light was from the gauges on my control panel. Occasionally, I could see the rotating tail beacon bounce on the nearby clouds, only to be absorbed and dissolved in the pea soup. The drone of the engine noise was muffled but constant and I felt sure that if I would extend my hand in any direction I would touch a mountain and that mountain would explode, taking me with it into oblivion.

"Crocodile 242, turn left to a heading of 360 degrees and descend and maintain 2,400 feet, over."

"Roger, An Khe, turning left to a heading of 360 degrees and descending to 2,400 feet."

"Crocodile 242, you are now on extended final approach at An Khe, please descend to 2,200 feet and maintain 360 degrees."

The elevation above sea level at An Khe was 2,000 feet and here this guy was telling me to descend to 2,200 feet in the soup when I couldn't see a damned thing but my instruments in the cockpit. I didn't like this scenario one little bit. But I was in his hands and there was nothing I could do but exactly what he said to do. I wasn't going to fly by the seat of my pants - that much I remembered from flight school.

"Roger An Khe, descending to 2,200 feet and maintaining 360 degrees."

"Crocodile 242 continue to descend until you have runway in sight."

I sure hoped we were on extended final and still not over the mountains. You couldn't prove it by me though. I still couldn't see a damned thing. I was getting more and more nervous about this whole affair.

"Roger that An Khe, I'm slowing this thing down to 60 knots. Altimeter setting please."

"Roger, Crocodile 242, altimeter setting 2942, over."

"Roger 2942."

"What is the ceiling at An Khe, over?"

"Crocodile 242, it's right at minimums, no more than 50 feet."

"Oh great, I'm at 2100 indicated and your elevation is 2,000 feet and I still can't see a damned thing."

I continued to descend with no visibility so I slowed the aircraft to about fifty knots. Finally, right on the deck at about twenty feet we broke out of the clouds and I honked the cyclic back to bleed off my fifty knots of airspeed and I came to a hover right over the runway.

The crew in the back let out a loud cheer. I looked at Fitch and he was starting to get some blood back in his face. I, of course, was extremely relieved. I was incredibly appreciative of the fact that I had gotten a sergeant in air traffic control that knew what he was doing with a ground controlled approach. Believe me, I knew that our lives were in his hands.

As I sat there at a hover, I got on the radio again and said, "Sergeant, where are you in relation to me on the runway right now?"

"Sir, I'm in this small green building at about your four o'clock position."

"Thank you sergeant, now step outside so I can come over there with the whole crew and we can all personally kiss your ass. As far as I'm concerned, we owe you our lives, Sergeant."

"I was just doing my job, Sir. But thank you for the compliment."

"Sergeant, I am forever in your debt. May the Gods smile upon you."

"Thank you very much, Sir."

Suddenly, I remembered another night. A night when four members of a LRRP team came looking for two pilots they knew only as Mac and Croc 2. Damn! Maybe the old wives tale is true. You know.... "What goes around, comes around."

If you're out there somewhere, Sergeant, and you saved Crocodile 242's ass in the late summer of 1969 at An Khe, with a GCA, I would love to hear from you.

65.

Another Windy City

A few days after I had pissed off the bees, and they had exacted their retaliation, a Specialist Four from operations came to me and asked me how I was feeling.

"Why do you ask?" I said suspiciously.

"Well, Sir, I have a non-combat mission for you that will be a piece of cake. That is, if you feel up to it."

"Now what could be a non-combat, piece of cake mission in Vietnam, Specialist?"

"Sir, all you have to do is ferry one of our gunships to Qui Nhon. It needs some mechanical repair that we're not equipped to do here at An Khe."

"What kind of mechanical repair does it need, Specialist?" A pilot is naturally suspicious about ferrying a helicopter in need of mechanical repair, anywhere.

"I don't know the specifics, Sir. They just said that the problem did not make the aircraft unsafe to fly."

"You're a Specialist, and you don't know the specifics? That's an odd combination, isn't it?"

"Yes, Sir, I suppose it is. I'm just a gopher and a flunky around here though, and I seldom know the method behind the madness in this place."

I laughed, "Don't feel alone, Specialist. I don't think there's been one time that I haven't asked myself what the hell I was doing as I was voluntarily strapping myself into a chopper in this God forsaken place."

He returned the laugh, "I don't even pretend to understand how you pilots do what you do every day, Sir."

"Well, we have something in common, Specialist, because neither do I."

"Would I get to take another pilot along on this *safe, voluntary mission*? This is a two pilot aircraft, you know."

"Yes, Sir, Mr. Cloud has expressed an interest in going with you. If that's all right?"

"Of course, why wouldn't it be? Jack Cloud's a good man. So when would we leave with this bird? And, by the way, which one is it?"

"It's 188, Sir. It's in a revetment in front of the maintenance hangar."

He continued, "You'll be expected to sign for it when you go get it. You can leave right away and spend the night at Qui Nhon, and they should have it ready for you to return with it tomorrow afternoon."

"Sign for it! That's just like the military. What the hell do they think I'm going to do with it? Steal the broken son of a bitch?"

"It's just protocol, Sir. It's merely a formality."

"Ok then. Why don't you swing by Mr. Cloud's quarters and tell him I'll meet him at the aircraft in an hour."

"Will do, Sir."

"There are just a couple of things I'd like to clear up before I leave. First and foremost, is the weather. What about that tropical storm sitting off the coast in the South China Sea?"

"The weather report says that storm is supposed to peter out today and not be a problem, Sir."

"Well, now, I've certainly heard that song before. I hope the weather man's right."

I continued, "The other thing, what's the nature of the mechanical problem on 188? I'm going to check the aircraft log to see what they're doing with it, and if I'm not comfortable with flying it, the deal's off."

"Fair enough, Sir. I'll tell operations that unless we hear differently from you in the next hour or so, that you will be ferrying the aircraft to Qui Nhon right away."

"Good enough, Specialist. I hope this really does prove to be a piece of cake."

Jack Cloud was more than happy to go with me. He needed a break from the day to day combat flying just like I did. Although the bees had already given me three or four days off, I was in no hurry to get back in combat. I felt like this little trip to Qui Nhon was a very welcome diversion. I had taken aircraft there to the maintenance hangar before, and it was only about an hour flight to the east from An Khe.

You flew over the An Khe Pass and dropped down the mountain range 2,000 feet to just above sea level and continued east to the beautiful South China Sea. This is where I had spent the night when I first came into country, right after I had received the good news about Camp Holloway the day before in Nha Trang. Oh well, I'd lived through my stay at Holloway and now I was spending my last few weeks at An Khe.

When we reached the aircraft, I checked the log and found that it was due for a rotor blade change. Rotor blades didn't last long in the tropics. They supposedly had a 1,000-hour flying life, but here you were lucky to get 200-300 hours out of them. I inspected the blades and they looked worn, but certainly serviceable, so I decided to go ahead and fly it.

I watched as Jack did the startup procedure and cranked the aircraft. He came up to 6600 engine RPM with rotor RPM needle joined and in the normal green zone, yelled clear, and picked the bird up to a hover and backed it out of the maintenance revetment. We hovered toward the runway, got clearance to take off, and departed. We left the pattern and headed east toward the An Khe Pass. Highway 19, which went through Pleiku, also went through An Khe and the An Khe Pass. We followed the road and reached the Pass after a few minutes.

I felt like kidding Jack a little, so I said,

"What's the matter with you Jack? You're flyin' this son of a bitch like an old woman. This is a goddamned gunship for Christ sake. Kick this bastard in the ass will ya? By God, let me see some real flying!"

Jack took the bait and plunged the aircraft off the side of the mountain toward sea level to the east.

"By God, that's more like it Jack. I thought for sure I was gonna have to drop you at the old folks home there for a while."

Next I said, "Jack, do you see that river down there at the base of the mountain? There's usually a few rice farmers and their fucking mean-ass water buffalo there. Let's see if they're there and we'll buzz their ass. You know how the buffalo hate it and go apeshit."

The buffalo and rice farmers were there as Jack hit velocity never exceed and pulled out right on the river. Our rotor wash was on the water, and the retreating rotor blade sounded like a shotgun going off again and again.

Much to my amusement, we buzzed right over the buffalo's heads, and they bolted, dragging the farmers through the water, as they were trying to restrain their beasts of burden.

A few minutes later, standing before us was a giant statue of the Buddha, in the middle of a clearing. Jack buzzed the statue so we could get a good look. It looked as if it were made of gold, but was probably bronze or brass or something like that.

Qui Nhon was now in our sights, and we swung out over the South China Sea and made our approach to the west. I had called ahead and told them we were coming, so the ground crew personnel met us and directed us to a parking spot.

We shut the aircraft down and went with another Spec 4 in a jeep to our quarters for the night. But Jack and I were thirsty, so we went directly from quarters to the bar at the officer's club.

Talk at the officer's club that night was all about the damned tropical storm that had just been upgraded to a frigging typhoon. I told Jack that the Spec 4 at operations had said that the weather report predicted it would lose strength and fade away like Douglas MacArthur.

So much for the fucking weatherman!

I asked a captain sitting next to us when the typhoon was supposed to hit shore. I didn't notice until after I asked him that he was extremely liquored up.

He slurred back at us, "Goddamned fucking typhoon! Goddamned fucking Vietnam! Fuck all these cocksuckers, the sons of bitches." Then he took another big slug of whiskey.

He never did answer my question. I also got the idea that he wasn't in a very good mood. But, to be fair, at least he didn't fall off his bar stool.

So I asked another warrant officer with wings on his chest. I figured he would know because he was probably slated to fly if the weather permitted.

"I guess it's to make an initial appearance about mid-afternoon tomorrow. Winds are going to hit shore at about 100 knots supposedly," said the warrant officer.

"Now isn't that just ducky! Jack and I are supposed to ferry a Charlie Model back to An Khe tomorrow. I hope the boys at maintenance are on the ball and get her done early. It would just be a damned shame if we had to spend another day or two here in Qui Nhon, a secure area like this on the beautiful South China Sea."

The warrant officer laughed softly and said, "If I were you I wouldn't be in any hurry to get back to where the war's going on either."

"Well, I guess we'll just have to wait until tomorrow to see what happens."

The next morning Jack and I had some breakfast at the officer's club, then dropped by the maintenance hangar to check on the progress they were making with the gunship number 188. I couldn't believe it, but they already had the rotor blades on and were in the process of blade tracking when we got there.

Tracking the blades is a process whereby someone holds a pole with a piece of chalk on the end of it, and slowly raises it to the spinning blades from underneath, until contact is made, leaving a chalk mark on both blades. This chalk mark on each blade is then compared and adjustments are made until the marks are as close to identical as possible. Blades that are not tracking properly will create one hell of a vibration in the aircraft in flight.

The chief maintenance officer saw us standing there and called to us,

"Are you Warrant Officers Garrison and Cloud?"

"Yes, we are."

"Your company called and said they're in dire need of this aircraft today. We're finishing it up now, so come and sign these release papers and take off before this damned storm hits."

"Why do they need it so badly today?" I asked. "If I get caught in these winds, it's going to be one hell of a ride for Jack and me."

"You know the damned military," he replied. "They've got to do it their way no matter what."

"Yea, we know all too well, goddamnit!"

By the time we got the papers signed and were strapped into the aircraft, the jet had cooled enough for a quick start. I rolled the power on as I looked out over the South China Sea only to see an angry black sky rapidly approaching. I took off and left the traffic pattern, and had just started my climb out to the west when the winds hit. Still on the Qui Nhon radio frequency, I heard them ground all traffic.

I should have said to hell with An Khe operations. I should never have listened to the bastards. I knew now that if I wrecked this thing, it was entirely all my fault for taking off in the first place against my better judgment.

I called Qui Nhon approach and said I was going to try to bring the bird back and set her down. They basically said "good luck."

As I brought 188 in on final, the tower was reporting 40 knot winds with gusts to 60 knots. I brought her down to about a ten foot hover and my airspeed indicator was showing 40 to 50 knots with gusts to 60, and I was sitting still over the runway.

The wind was tossing us around like a ping pong ball on the sea, and I saw I had very little chance of safely setting it down.

I called the tower and asked for the weather at An Khe.

They reported the winds at An Khe were still calm and that if I hustled, I might just get there before the winds did. I bid them adieu and headed for the An Khe Pass.

For the first few miles toward the pass, let me tell you, it was one exciting ride. It was as if we were on a roller coaster, and someone would suddenly pull the tracks away, and we would drop like a rock, then shoot up again.

What was I doing flying in a goddamned typhoon in Vietnam? That's what I get for getting cocky and thinking I could beat the storm. I had no right to put Jack at risk.

I should have just told An Khe operations to go to hell and spent another day or two at Qui Nhon. It was too late now.

By the time we got to An Khe, the winds had subsided some and they were reporting them at 30 knots, gusting to 40. I told Jack that I was going to take her in, and that if I rolled her up in a ball, I would take full credit for it. *I had signed for the aircraft, after all.* I told him that the winds were only going to get worse, so I was going to set her down the first approach.

"Hang on," I warned.

I brought the aircraft in on final approach and was sitting at a three foot hover with no ground speed and my airspeed indicator registered 40 knots. I kept my nose into the wind and hovered sideways, until I reached a place to set her down, slowly reduced pitch and touched down. I pushed the cyclic stick forward to a large degree to tilt the rotor plane down into the wind and rolled off power and hit the rotor brake. The blades began to quickly slow as the wind buffeted the aircraft. When the blades stopped, Jack, who had already jumped out of the aircraft, grabbed them and tied them down.

I got out of the aircraft and Jack and I walked back to the company area bowing against a stiff headwind.

"Well, Jack, wouldn't you know it. It turned out to not be a milk run or a piece of cake after all."

"Yeah, it got pretty exciting there toward the end."

"Jack, for Christ's sake, if I were you I don't believe I'd fly with me anymore. I take so many small arms hits that they've named me magnet ass. You were with me when we got shot to shit in the Plei Trap and barely made it back to Polei Kleng. Then we had an electrical fire in the damned cockpit that almost got us killed. You've got to be thinking that I'm hazardous to your health."

"That's the breaks, Pigpen. But remember you've got me home every time so far. In spite of all that bad luck shit."

I looked at Jack intently. He had paid me a high compliment. It was not mandy-pandy bull shit from some office-chair warrior. It was a sincere compliment from a fellow pilot who lived on the brink just as I did.

"Well, have it your way, Jack. But the crazy shit that happens when you and I are together in the cockpit is absolutely unbelievable."

"Well, maybe one of us will write a book about it someday."

"Maybe, Jack," I said with a smile, "but first we've got to live through this damned war."

66

The Banana Boat Incident

We were in the An Khe Officer's Club after flying all day sometime in August 1969, when a Major Johnston approached me and asked me how long I had been in country.

I told him that I had been in country for going on eleven months and was scheduled to return to the States the first part of October.

He said, "Mr. Garrison, do you mind if I sit down?"

"Not at all, Sir. By all means have a seat." He seated himself and began to explain that this was his second tour in Vietnam, and that he had only been in country this time for a couple of weeks. He said he had been assigned a company to command, somewhere in I Corp.

I Corp was the northernmost section of South Vietnam that bordered the Demilitarized Zone and North Vietnam.

The major wanted to see what I knew about where the fighting was occurring and how the war had evolved since he had been here back in 1965. I'm sure he had read all the intelligence reports, but acted as if he just wanted to get a day-to-day pilot's opinion on how the war was progressing.

I said, "Major Johnston, may I speak frankly?"

"Yes, you may. I want you to tell me your honest feelings."

"Alright, Sir, I certainly will." I then went into salvo mode.

"This war is the biggest bunch of bullshit that I can imagine."

"How do you mean that, Mr. Garrison?"

"Well Sir," I continued without reservation, "The NVA comes down the Ho Chi Minh Trail in Laos and Cambodia with all their supplies, comes across the border into Vietnam and engages us in combat, always at his discretion. Then they run back across the border into the supposedly neutral countries of Laos and Cambodia and we can't go after them. The same thing happens with the DMZ. They can come across any time they damn well please and we can't go across with a ground force to cut the head off the serpent once and for all. So, the war trudges on, Sir."

"They tell me, Sir, that back home in the U.S. there's a body count of those killed on both sides of the war. It says we've killed a couple million of them and they've killed forty some thousand of us. It's being treated like a goddamned basketball game. But they'll keep coming, and coming. We've won every battle, Sir, and we're losing the war."

"What do you think the U.S. Army's role in this is?" Major Johnston then asked.

"Hell, Major, it's not the U.S. Army's fault. It's the goddamned politicians that have us blindfolded with our hands tied behind our backs."

"Thank you for being forthright with me, Mr. Garrison. I have to say that I agree with much of what you have said."

Major Johnston also had wings on his chest, with a star and wreath above them, meaning he was a Senior Master Aviator. That meant that he had at least 5,000 hours logged in the air and was probably rated in many different army aircraft. He then asked me how the flying was going and I told him of my recent tussle with the winds on the skirts of a typhoon.

The major then told me of an incident that happened on his first tour in Vietnam in 1965. He said he was flying one day in the Central Highlands, sling loading a water blivet up to a mountaintop firebase. He was flying a UH-21, commonly known as a banana boat because the fuselage was shaped like a banana. It had a tandem rotor system, with one main rotor sitting directly behind the other one spinning in the opposite direction to cancel the torque, so there was no need for a tail rotor.

The UH-21 Banana Boat.

The water blivet weighed about 4,000 pounds and was attached to the chopper underneath by a cable, called a sling. When helicopters carried cargo in this fashion, it was said they carried a *sling load.*

The major said as he approached the firebase, his engine quit, and he slammed down the collective and punched off the water blivet, releasing it. Although he was in mountainous terrain, a field miraculously opened up in front of his eyes, and he flared the aircraft and made a perfect forced landing into the field. He was relishing his amazing life-saving feat, when he heard a terrible noise up the mountain. He and his copilot and crew all looked up to see the water blivet hurtling down the mountain, directly toward them. Major Johnston said there wasn't a damned thing they could do, as they watched the water blivet careen down the mountain, and slam into the middle of the UH-21, completely destroying it.

So much for a wonderful forced landing, but at least no one was hurt.

They should name and teach those rules in flight school. Especially the one that says when you think things are as bad as they can possibly get, don't be surprised if they get worse anyway.

67

The Beginning of the End

Finally, finally, the end of September, 1969, rolled around on my calendar, on which I had been faithfully marking off the days, one by one. As I have previously mentioned, the last two weeks of a pilot's tour in country did not include flying duties. I flew a couple of times during this period when I was needed, but generally I laid on top of the flat roof of the company latrine in swimming trunks, soaking up the tanning sun, and listening to Dusty Springfield sing "Son of a Preacher Man."

The Charlie Model gunship with tail number 242, that had been assigned to me as my principle aircraft, had now been given to another up and coming aircraft commander. It's a huge understatement to just say that I had become very attached to this aircraft. I had flown more than five hundred missions, a few of which I have described in this book. Although I flew every ship in the 119th gunship platoon, many of them, if not most, had been in my beloved 242.

She had always brought us home. Sometimes on fire, sometimes full of bullet holes, and a couple of times so badly wounded that she barely held together. But she did. The pilots out there who are reading this will understand esoterically. I grew to love her like a family member.

It was thus with great concern, that I watched from the roof of the latrine as the new commander brought her in short of the runway, and settled into very tall grass and weeds. He was, however, able to hop her, in short bursts, out of the thicket and onto the runway with no apparent damage. I breathed a big sigh of relief. I take my hat off to him for being able to get himself out of that jam. Flying a loaded gun ship is not easy.

When it came time for me to leave the unit, everyone threw a little party for me, and gave me the customary plaque which said, "From the Officers and Men of the 119th AHC, with appreciation." I still have that plaque today hanging on the wall of my private den. It hangs next to the medal for the Distinguished Flying Cross, the Vietnamese Campaign Medal with four Bronze Stars, 25 air medals, among various and sundry other awards. Whether the war was right or wrong, I remain proud that I served my country when she called. My greatest honors, however, do not fit in case or frame. They are the faces and memories of soldiers that I helped get home to America alive. Many of them I never even saw. I pray they came home and had loving families and have spent many happy years with them as I have been privileged to do.

When the time came for me to leave, one of my fellow pilots ferried me in a Huey to Pleiku Main Airport, where I boarded a fixed wing, turboprop and flew to Cam Ranh Bay. Here, we readied ourselves for departure from Vietnam via a Flying Tiger Airlines DC8, by way of Tokyo, and then on to Seattle Tacoma International.

68.

The Flight Home

As soon as the aircraft took off and departed Vietnamese airspace, I told myself that I would never complain about anything again. I felt extremely lucky to have been on the flight home. I thought about all the close calls I had had flying missions, and knew that I could well have been killed in combat. I was also extremely proud to have had a hand in getting a lot of Americans home alive who would not have made it without the helicopter pilots.

Of course, I'm human, and I have failed miserably about the "not complaining" promise that I made to myself. But when things have gotten tough in life, I remember how things were then, and it helps to put things in perspective.

I thought about Vince and Larry that I had flown to Vietnam with, as the only other two officers on board the flight. I thought about all the other guys I had known in flight school, and every other pilot that I had befriended along the way. I deeply hoped that they had all made it through their tours safely. But I didn't know. I would have to wait and somehow discover their fates when I got back to the States.

It was a long and tiring flight home, all the way to the other side of the world. We made a short stop in Tokyo for fuel, and then continued on to Seattle Tacoma International. When we touched down in the States, there were loud cheers from everybody on board. We were home. When I had left home, I was a green, inexperienced college kid. Now, I was wondering how I was going to reacclimate to civilian life. After all the death and violence, things didn't make much sense anymore. I had left as a naive kid, and came back as a battle-hardened veteran trying to drink away the memories.

The aircraft taxied to the tarmac. In those days a ladder was brought to the aircraft, and you walked down it, across the tarmac, and into the terminal. From there I was catching a short hop to Los Angeles to visit my Aunt Myrtle (my father's sister) before catching my connection to St. Louis, where my family members would be waiting to take me home for thirty days leave. Then I was to report to good old Fort Wolters for instructor pilot training. This time I would be an instructor. I planned to be every bit as tough as Toth was with me, to give my students every chance of making it home alive, as I had done.

I entered the Seattle Tacoma Terminal along with the other soldiers, and we were met by a rather large group of war protesters, carrying placards that said things like, "MOTHERFUCKING BABY KILLERS, WAR CRIMINALS and FASCIST PIGS."

Then their spit hit my face.

EPILOGUE

I will never forget, when I was in Los Angeles visiting my aunt, on my second day back in the States, before I left for St. Louis to meet the rest of my family.

We were watching the news together when it was announced that my unit at An Khe had been hit by enemy forces. The report said that all of the aircraft in the company had been destroyed, but the report was sketchy about casualties. I know now, in retrospect, that I was suffering from survivor's guilt, and I became frantic, wanting to fly right back to Nam and help my comrades.

Of course, I was helpless to do anything and it was a hellish feeling of impotence. I couldn't believe 242 wasn't there anymore, or any of the other aircraft that I had flown for that matter. What really bothered me, however, was that I didn't know what had happened to all my friends. I later found out that no pilots were killed, though some were seriously injured and evacuated to a hospital in Japan.

When we came back from leave, Waldo and I both found ourselves stationed as OH23D Hiller instructor pilots at Fort Wolters, Texas. Our old friendship resumed as if it had never been interrupted. The same thing occurred with Jim McDonald and Robbie Apgar. As a matter of fact, Robbie and I were roommates in a house in downtown Mineral Wells when we were instructor pilots after Vietnam. As mentioned before, Mac, Robbie and I have been in contact through the years. We even got together for a reunion in 1985, in Palm Springs, California, and since my oldest brother, Clarence, retired to Phoenix, I have also visited Mac on a couple of additional occasions.

When Waldo and I parted company, however, we lost track of one another for several years. Both of us had heard through other sources that we had both died.

I knew that Jack Cloud had apparently been in the construction business in the Houston, Texas area. Jack and I had a couple of nice, lengthy phone calls in the eighties and early nineties. I heard later, through other sources, that he had passed away from a cardiac condition sometime in the early 2000's. I have never been able to absolutely verify that, and I desperately

262 | Mark Garrison

hope that I am wrong. I cared deeply for Jack Cloud and considered him a great pilot and a great friend. Nothing would please me more than to get another phone call from him, telling me that I had received erroneous information and that he too is alive and well.

When I was able to access information about some of my friends, the findings were tragic to say the least. Larry and Vince, whom I had flown over to Vietnam with, were both killed there. Larry was killed by small arms fire in January of 1969, and Vince was shot down in a gun ship, went inverted, and drowned in a river before he could be rescued, not long before finishing his tour. I found more than a dozen other friends who had been killed in Vietnam. To find the name of another friend and learn that face, that smile, that laugh had been forever silenced, was one of the most difficult things I've ever had to do in my entire life.

Nonetheless, going on with my life, as one must, I finished my bachelor's degree, went four more years to Palmer Chiropractic School in Davenport, Iowa, and became a licensed chiropractic physician in the state of Illinois.

Later, I bought my own airplane with my older brother, Gary, and continued to fly off and on through the years. I also became current again in helicopters, and took my wife, children, and immediate family up for several flights so that they could get an idea of what flying a chopper was all about. Eventually, I had to quit flying and cease medical practice altogether due to complications from massive Agent Orange exposure in Vietnam. The complications have been, and still are, life-threatening.

One day out of the blue, in about 2005, I received a phone call from a doctor that I had seen in a large VA Medical facility in the Midwest. He stated to me that he had just seen a patient, who had told him that he used to fly with a guy in Vietnam from southern Illinois and gave the doctor my name.

Since the doctor had been unable to give this patient my name, or any other medical information without my permission, due to the then new Health Information Portability and Privacy Acts (HIPPA) regarding medical information, he asked me if I would like for him to share my contact information with him.

"My God, man!" I told him. "Of course! Do it as soon as possible! I would love to talk to anyone that I flew with over there!"

I had recently been in contact with Jim McDonald (Mac), who still lives in Arizona, and Robbie Apgar, who lives in southern California, so I knew it couldn't have been either of them.

We set up a rendezvous point in a reception area in the same VA medical facility and agreed upon a time. Time had ravished our bodies but as soon as we saw one another, recognition occurred. *It was Waldo! Two lost brothers had been reunited!*

To paraphrase Mark Twain, *The reports of our deaths had been greatly exaggerated.*

Needless to say, it was one of the most emotional reunions that I have ever experienced. We had lived within two-and a-half-hours of one another for several years and didn't even know it.

Rick had briefly left the army. He met a woman named Pat, and they both earned college degrees, got married and had a family. They both then re-entered the service and Pat retired as a full colonel in charge of nursing at a large medical facility and Rick retired as a battalion commander after serving in Iraq during Desert Storm.

Strangely enough, after all the combat hours in Vietnam as a pilot in command under horrendous conditions, Rick was riding in the back seat of a helicopter when the young, inexperienced pilot lost power, blew the forced landing and almost killed everyone on board. Rick was thrown out of the aircraft, breaking several bones and suffering many internal injuries, and went through a lengthy and painful rehabilitation. This incident forced his early medical discharge as a lieutenant colonel. I assure you that this was the army's loss.

Since then, we have re-established a close friendship. We visited the Vietnam Memorial (The Wall) together in Washington, D.C., along with our wives, and have visited each other on several occasions. We look forward to many more good times together without a bunch of people shooting at us.

By the way, I mentioned that I had come back as a battle hardened veteran trying to drink away the memories. Of course, that only made things worse. It only took me twenty years to learn that. I guess I'm just a quick study. Anyway, I don't drink anymore and haven't for several years.

My wife, Lynn, and I have been married for forty two years. We have four children: Andrea, Gary, Megan, and Andrew.

And, oh by the way, things finally did get better.

About the Author

Mark V. Garrison was honorably discharged from the U.S. Army on December 31st, 1970. He went on to receive a bachelor's degree from Southern Illinois University in 1973. Garrison then completed four more years of study at the oldest and largest chiropractic school in the world, Palmer College of Chiropractic in Davenport, Iowa, where he received a doctorate in 1977. Dr. Garrison then practiced in Illinois for 30 years before retiring in 2006.

Dr. Garrison and his wife of 42 years, Lynn, have four children and five grandchildren. His hobbies include flying, painting, drawing, playing his guitars, and writing. He is now starting his second book about things he encountered in medical practice.